Love♡Hard

Love ♡ Hard

International Bestselling Author
MONICA JAMES

Copyrighted Material
LOVE HARD

This book is a work of fiction. Names, characters, places, and incidents are the product of the author's imagination, or are used fictitiously. Any resemblance to actual events, locales, or persons living or dead, is coincidental. Any trademarks, service marks, product names or named features are assumed to be the property of their respective owners and are used only for reference.

Copyright © 2024 by Monica James

All rights reserved. No part of this work may be reproduced, scanned or distributed in any printed or electronic form without the express, written consent of the author.

Cover Models: Monica James & Switzerland
Photographer: Michelle Lancaster
Editing: Editing 4 Indies

Interior Design and Formatting by

E.M. Tippetts Book Designs

Follow me on:
authormonicajames.com

Other Books By
MONICA JAMES

THE I SURRENDER SERIES
I Surrender
Surrender to Me
Surrendered
White

SOMETHING LIKE NORMAL SERIES
Something like Normal
Something like Redemption
Something like Love

A HARD LOVE ROMANCE
Dirty Dix
Wicked Dix
The Hunt

MEMORIES FROM YESTERDAY DUET
Forgetting You, Forgetting Me
Forgetting You, Remembering Me

SINS OF THE HEART DUET
Absinthe of the Heart
Defiance of the Heart

ALL THE PRETTY THINGS TRILOGY
Bad Saint
Fallen Saint
Forever My Saint
The Devil's Crown-Part One (Spin-Off)
The Devil's Crown-Part Two (Spin-Off)

THE MONSTERS WITHIN DUET
Bullseye
Blowback

DELIVER US FROM EVIL TRILOGY
Thy Kingdom Come
Into Temptation
Deliver Us From Evil

IN LOVE AND WAR
North of the Stars
Fall of the Stars

REVENGE IS SWEET SERIES
Crybaby

HEART MEMORY TRANSFER DUET
Heart Sick
Love Sick

STANDALONE
Mr. Write
Chase the Butterflies
Beyond the Roses
Someone Else's Shadow
Love Hard

This book is dedicated to the broken hearted—we survived another day.

Preface

This memoir is a work of creative nonfiction.

While all persons and the situations the author writes about are inspired, in part, by real people and events, no names are used to protect the innocent… and the guilty.

Certain events have been fictionalized. The conversations are not a word-for-word retelling because a lot of gin was consumed. This is how the author remembers things…she thinks.

The author is a lover, not a fighter, so don't come at her. She knows she has made some really stupid decisions throughout her life—you'll soon see.

She thanks you for not looking at her with judgy eyes.

This is not a story of the author's life. But rather, it's a story about life.

Happy reading, and Godspeed…

Love♡Hard
TRACKLIST

"The Lovecats" by The Cure

"Miss You Love" by Silverchair

"Lover of Mine" by 5 Seconds of Summer

"Love Gun" by KISS

"Only Love Can Hurt Like This" by Paloma Faith

"Bad Boy for Love" by Rose Tattoo

"Only Love" by Meg Mac

"Love Buzz" by Nirvana

"Love Her Madly" by The Doors

"Love at First Feel" by AC/DC

"Tainted Love" by Soft Cell

"Love On the Brain" by Rihanna

"Love" by Lana Del Rey

"My Love" by Florence + The Machine

"Lovestruck Lobotomy" by VOILÀ

"Love is Embarrassing" by Olivia Rodrigo

"Burning Love" by Elvis

"Falling in Love" by Cigarettes After Sex

"I Believe in a Thing Called Love" by The Darkness

"Not About Love" by Fiona Apple

"Lovely" by Billie Eilish

"I Fell in Love with the Devil" by Avril Lavigne

"Lover, You Should've Come Over" by Jeff Buckley

Hidden Track: "Back To Black" by Amy Winehouse

One

"The Lovecats"
The Cure

"Are you high?"

"Is that a trick question?" I ask my best friend BUNNY while sipping my mojito.

"How could you submit this? I mean, it's about…cats." BUNNY peers at me above the rims of her sapphire-rimmed glasses, clearly unhappy with my topic choice as she reads my latest online article.

I raise my hand to get the attention of the hot bartender with a Mohawk because one mojito is never enough. "I love cats!" I scream to be heard over Miley Cyrus singing about heartbreak and flowers, a song which I relate to all too well.

I suddenly need another mojito *and* three shots of tequila.

ANGEL smiles, the forever peacekeeper. I've been friends with her since I was twelve. She knows me. And knows when not to push. "Everyone loves cats. I think the article is great."

But BUNNY isn't buying it as she arches a blonde brow.

I commence humming the tune to "The Lovecats" by The Cure, but this shit doesn't fly with my friend.

"Even though I am fucking biased, you are the most talented writer in the entire world—"

Wait for it...

"But...what the fuck is this?" BUNNY's screen flashes before me as she flips her cell so I can see the little floofy ball whose face I just want to squish.

"That is Merlin, the rag doll whose favorite band is Queen. He is renown in my apartment block for—"

"I don't give a shit, Z." She slides her phone away in fear it'll detonate and spew my boring drivel all over her. "This is bullshit."

Thankfully, the bartender arrives, saving me from the wrath of BUNNY.

"Another mojito?" he asks with a flirty wink.

ANGEL not so subtly nudges me in the ribs, but I ignore her because I am not interested. It's not because MOHAWK isn't attractive. On the contrary—he's hot.

Young. Tattooed. With muscle in all the right places, but I am done... D-O-N-E with men.

I won't allow another man to destroy my life. You live, and you learn, and I've learned that good men are like unicorns. Everyone talks about them, but no one actually sees them.

Thirty-odd years on this planet have taught me many things, but the one lesson I seem to never learn from is that love will break your heart—over and over again.

"Yes, and three shots of tequila. Please."

MOHAWK nods and thankfully reads between the lines as he silently goes to fill my order.

"Why?" BUNNY asks, begging me to explain, but I don't want to discuss this.

Now.

Love♡Hard

Or ever.

I wish there was a simple answer, but the truth is, there isn't. However, if I were to summarize, I guess it all comes down to me being a hopeless romantic who seems to fall for the wrong men.

My history with men is so tragic that I don't need fiction—real life is dramatic enough.

With that thought in mind, I gulp down the rest of my mojito, and when MOHAWK places the shots of tequila in front of me, I throw them down consecutively.

BUNNY pays for my drinks, shaking her head because she knows all my secrets.

Even though she presses, she knows why I haven't been able to write anything remotely heartfelt over the past few months. That's the reason I opt to write about cats instead of relationships and love. When it comes to this topic that seems to rule the world, I am a complete fraud.

Now, anything to do with romance makes me want to projectile vomit—Regan MacNeil style.

On cue, my shots threaten to come back up.

But I thump a fist against my chest because I can't go back to work with tequila-soaked Louboutin pumps.

"You know what you should be writing about," BUNNY says, slipping her glasses atop her blonde hair. "Love. And heartbreak because that's what people want to read about. Oh, wait a second…that's what you *used* to write about before—"

"Where are we going for H's birthday?" I ask, interrupting her because I don't want to hear it.

I've heard it numerous times, but it doesn't change the fact that I am broken.

Sitting in front of my laptop and writing about love was my outlet.

It started in seventh grade when I wrote an essay on *Romeo and Juliet*. I was the only one in my class who went against the norm and argued that this wasn't a love story; it was about two kids who knew one another for a few days, and due to lack of communication, they ended it when all could have been resolved if they weren't so damn impulsive and so fucking emo.

I failed the paper and was told to rewrite it, which I did. I was at the top of my class when I wrote what my teacher wanted to read, and that was when I learned that we shouldn't let the truth get in the way of a good story.

I lived and breathed literature and knew early on that I wanted to make it my career.

When I submitted a short piece to the *New York Times* and won a competition they were running, everything changed from then.

Writing about love was my life, but now, love can go back where it came from because love don't live here anymore.

My cell rings, and when I see my boss calling, I instantly regret the shots of tequila.

"Hey…yo, yo, yo, what's up?" I close my eyes and shake my head because trying to remain elusive that my lunch break has consisted of no actual lunch being consumed has just been shot to hell.

"Get your ass down here. Now," BOSSMAN says before hanging up.

"Fuck," I curse, tossing my phone into my leather bag. "I've been summoned by the spawn of Satan."

BUNNY pauses mid-sip of her passionfruit mojito. "Hopefully, he can spank some sense into you."

I ignore her quip because I know she is serious, which is why I love her.

"I've read your journals. Write about that. Write about *him*. That's what people want to read about. Not fucking cats. I know he broke—"

"Nice talk. If I wasn't minutes away from being fired, we would have a serious talk about boundaries."

I don't want to have this talk—again.

It always ends the same way—tears and gin. Gin and tears.

I kiss ANGEL on the forehead, and she giggles. "Looks like you have another admirer."

When I follow her line of sight, I see she refers to a businessman looking down at my shoes. I don't get it, but my entire dating life, men and women have had a thing for my feet.

If everyone had a superpower, that would be mine.

I have three pickup lines I hear…constantly.

I like your shoes.

I give really good foot rubs.

And my all-time favorite because who said romance is dead.

Nice shoes. Wanna fuck?

But right now, I need to use these feet to run the fourteen blocks back to work.

I quickly make my way through the grungy bar, which has been our haven for as long as I can remember. Not your typical retreat for successful boss women like "us," but there is nothing normal about us; a fact we're proud of.

The moment I step outside, the heavens open and dump a month's worth of rain. Most would wait for the rain to stop or catch a cab. But I am not most, and I like the rain.

Everything seems so much clearer after a rainstorm.

I hightail it through Manhattan, the concrete jungle that I call home. You either love it or hate it. It's survival of the fittest, and I am a fucking Amazonian when it comes to living in this city. Eat or be eaten is the motto I've lived by and the motto which follows my soaked ass into the elevator as I take it to the fifty-sixth floor.

The moment the doors open and I see O, the receptionist, she shakes her head and tosses me a packet of tissues over her marbled counter.

"I need these for all the tears I'm about to shed when he fires my ass?" I tease with a smile.

"Just ask if he's been working out, and all will be forgiven."

BOSSMAN's ex left him for a European god, so we usually blow smoke up his ass, stroking his ego by saying *he* is the hottie with an exceptional ass and not the sex god his ex left him for.

I burst into inappropriate laughter as the stuffy suits waiting in reception look down their noses at me. I shrug it off because another thing I learned early on was never to judge a book by its cover—literally.

O informs BOSSMAN I am here, and I make my way into his high-rise office, looking like a soaked Chihuahua in killer heels.

BOSSMAN sits in his leather seat, long fingers steepled over his mouth as I enter. He doesn't look twice when he sees my appearance because honestly, I've entered his office looking worse.

"Hey, BOSSMAN," I quip, slumping very ungracefully into the seat in front of him.

BOSSMAN is in his mid-forties, in fit shape, and fucking hot with dirty blond hair and piercing green eyes. But he's also a pain in my ass, so any hotness cancels out when he rides my ass—and not in a good way.

"I read your latest piece."

I nod, gathering sections of my hair and wringing it out onto the pristine white carpet. Droplets of water somersaulting onto the floor bounce between BOSSMAN and me.

But my uncouth antics don't deter him.

"I thought we agreed you would show me your submissions before publication?"

"Did we?" I ask, hoping he drops this.

"Cut the crap, Z. I have tried to be patient. But you are a romance writer, and there is nothing romantic about a cat who can sing Freddie fucking Mercury."

"I beg to differ. I mean, did you listen to—"

"Enough." BOSSMAN shakes his head, not at all humored by my theatrics today, and I know why.

I am or *was* his most successful writer. His online magazine, *Love Me, Love You Not,* has won endless awards thanks to my witty, honest columns.

He started with three writers, but now, he has over a hundred because being a writer at *Love Me, Love You Not* means you "made it."

The reason we are so successful is because we just don't give a fuck. We write about things that people want to read about, but just don't have the balls to say. We write about the things people usually need to google when the lights are off in fear they'll go to hell.

We are the holy sex bible.

So alas, when I submitted my piece about cats, it was the wrong type of pussy.

"I know the divorce has been hard on you, but…it's been…months."

The D-word—I much prefer another D-word, but thanks to my creative constipation, I can't write about anything relating to *D*'s or any other initial in the alphabet.

"Maybe my time has come? Maybe I've just run out of words?" I offer because it's very probable.

I used to write about love, and considering we are now strangers, it seems plausible that my writer's block is here to stay. I have come to terms with it. Whenever I try to write about love, all I want to do is dance to Fiona Apple in my underwear and drink cheap wine.

But BOSSMAN shakes his head and when he holds up a piece of paper, I curse the day I ran into BUNNY when she was taking photos of PUNK.

"Where did you get that?" I ask, pausing from wringing out my hair because I recognize my handwriting.

BOSSMAN smiles. "Your best friend scanned and emailed some of your journal entries. I printed out my favorite entries."

"I'm going to kill her," I mumble under my breath, envisioning ways to make her demise appear like an accident.

"You should be thanking her. These"—he stabs his finger at the page—"are what you should be writing about. I knew your pieces were based on personal experiences, but Z, these are fucking great. *This* is what our readers need."

"Ramblings of a neurotic lunatic?" I offer with a shrug.

"Stop doing that. Stop using your humor to hide behind."

His words hit hard because I learned from the best.

"I want you to write a memoir."

I look at him like he just spoke to me in Swahili.

"A memoir about love…or, more specifically, a memoir about your first love, and the ones that have followed."

I open but soon close my mouth because surely BOSSMAN has gone mad.

"Who the *fuck* would want to read about *that*?" I question when I can swallow past the lump of "what the fuck" caught in my throat.

"Everyone," he replies, his fingers tapping on the keys on his laptop before he flips it around so I can see the folder that consists of my entries…and just my entries. "You have enough material here to write thousands of entries. I mean, I didn't even know what a rusty trombone was until I read—"

"Oh, sweet Jesus."

This is not happening.

Yes, I've kept journals my entire life, but they are private. Rarely have I written about my life because it is PRIVATE.

I may have used some experiences as inspiration, but a memoir? BOSSMAN may as well have asked me to stand naked in the middle of Times Square and brand me with a big, red letter A.

"This is a bad idea. Like a very bad, bad idea. Okay, the cat idea wasn't my best work. But there is a couple in Queens who collect spoons and—"

"This isn't negotiable. I want the first piece sent to me in two days. Then we can discuss your future here."

"You dickhole," I curse, and BOSSMAN bursts into laughter.

"Where can I find that reference?" He spins his laptop around to read over my journals.

"In this case, you're an asshole," I reply, standing abruptly because this conversation is done.

"Now we're talking. Assholes sell."

I salute him with my middle finger as I blow him a kiss.

"I love you, Z, but if you don't present me with a piece I can publish, you're fired. I know this is hard love, but I think you need it since you're clearly going through something."

"And you're clearly still an asshole. I hate you."

"No, you don't." BOSSMAN smirks. "This will be your best work yet. I just know it will be. Think of this as therapy."

"Gin is a lot cheaper."

"Two days."

I turn to leave but look over my shoulder, giving him a once-over. "I was going to ask if you've done something new with your hair. But nope, you still just look like an asshole."

I slam the door shut behind me, BOSSMAN's laughter following me.

I don't bother to visit my desk because apparently all I need are my journals, which I should have kept hidden under lock and key.

The walk to my apartment is a blur because I knew this day would come. You can only outrun your past for so long until your best friend sends your private musings to your boss.

My apartment complex isn't the nicest place to rent, but I lived in nicer and my bastard ex took half. So this suits me just fine because it's mine.

The moment I take the stairs, the aromas of what everyone is cooking fills the stairwell, and I do what I usually do—I envision what is going on behind closed doors. My creative brain, of course, conjures up all sorts of lewd behaviors because it's nice to think I'm not the only weirdo trying to survive this thing they call life.

I shoulder open my apartment door because the cold weather has stiffened the wood. Pun usually would be intended, but now, I feel nothing.

I know why that is, and it's all my fault.

Opening my freezer, I reach for the bottle of vodka and take a long sip.

This is bullshit.

Haven't I paid my penance?

I made peace with the fact that a happily ever after was never on the cards for me. I had my fun. I chased what I wanted, and it left me divorced, broke, and wishing I never went back to something that was always going to end in tears.

When a knock sounds on my door, I know who it is. "Go away."

"I'm sorry," BUNNY says through the door. "But what kind of friend watches their friend throw their life away?"

"The best kind," I retort, kicking off my shoes.

"I read what you wrote, Z. I couldn't stop. I wish you had told me."

"And I wish you would mind your own business. I'm fine."

"You are not fine! I didn't know what you were thinking for the past few months. But your journals finally allowed me to see you and him, and—"

"Stop talking about him!"

"No!"

We're arguing through the door, and I don't care that my neighbors can hear us. There is no way I'm letting her in. I can't stand to see the look of compassion on her face because I don't deserve it.

I went into this willingly. I knew he would break my heart, yet I went back to him—time and time again.

When you love someone wholeheartedly, but they don't love you back, it destroys you. It eats away at you until nothing is left but pain. And to deal with that pain, you build a wall, a wall so high that you can't see over it to appreciate the sunrise. Your world is then shrouded in darkness, and soon, you learn to be one with the shadows. You learn to accept what it's like to live with a piece of your heart missing.

Either we accept the fact or we surrender to the pain. For me, I accepted it, but I've never forgotten my first heartbreak because I relive it every time *he* disappears.

Love♡Hard

The villain in this story is me, and I hate myself for it. I hate that I knew better, yet I didn't learn my lesson until I was totally destroyed.

"I love you. No matter what you say or do, I'll never stop. I'll love you even when you don't love yourself," BUNNY says, and fuck her, my lower lip begins to tremble, but I don't allow the tears to fall.

I don't love myself. I haven't in a very long time.

"Your story is one people need to hear. They need to know that they're not alone."

"Why?" I ask, my hoarse voice betraying my emotion.

"Because your story is mine. It's everyone's. You just have the balls to write about it. You can't write your story because you're afraid of what happens when you write the end. But it's not the end…it's just the beginning."

I don't reply because I don't know what to say. Words escape me. They have since the moment he re-entered my world and shook things up beyond repair.

When she doesn't say anything else, I know she's gone, leaving me to stew over what she just said.

Opening a window, I sit on the ledge, the only place that has provided me any comfort for a long time. I look into the vast skyline, knowing I am merely a cosmic kiss in the universe. But what if BUNNY is right?

What if my story could help others? What if I could show others that they are not alone when it comes to feelings of love?

Tears I've not allowed myself to cry slide down my cheeks. I've cried enough tears. But the moment I switched off, yes, the heartache subsided, but it was like I switched off to everything else in the world. Hence, the writer's block.

To write, you need to feel. And I haven't been doing any of that.

I was happy to live this way because it stopped the pain…but I now realize it was merely a Band-Aid.

With a bottle of vodka in hand, I look over the ledge and realize how easy it would be to make the pain go away. Just one simple step and I can live in the darkness forever.

The universe curses my name when a song comes on the radio, a song which I can only ever associate with *him*.

When "Crazy Crazy Nights" by KISS plays randomly on Spotify from my phone, I don't know if it's a blessing or a curse. But it's the slap to the face I needed because something happens, something which hasn't happened in a very long time.

I want to write…

I don't know what I want to write or if it'll be any good, but I kick my legs over the window ledge and race into my bedroom, drop to my knees, and throw open the lid of the red velvet blanket box. It's in here that my deepest, darkest secrets are kept.

I run my fingers over the tattered journals that have been my savior for as long as I can remember. I never felt alone because I had these. I never left home without a book and pen in hand because some entries are simply quotes I read while riding the subway or parts of conversations I overheard.

These journals make up parts of me. They *are* me.

Do I really want the world to see the most intimate parts of me when I, myself, don't even want to see what's behind door number one?

Pushing aside the newer journals, I hunt for the red-and-white exercise book—my first journal.

You always remember your firsts…and that gives me an idea.

Coming to stand, I quickly take off my wet clothes and sit cross-legged at the foot of the bed in only my underwear as I wait for my laptop to power up.

Spotify waits for me, and I hesitate because once I put on this playlist, I know there's no going back. But I wasn't raised a quitter, and that gives me an idea.

BOSSMAN wants a memoir, but I don't want to skim around the edges and give my readers a best-of. To understand me, they need to know it all so they can understand why their beloved narrator made the decisions she did when she knew better.

Love♡Hard

The flashing cursor blinks at me, awaiting command. This is the one thing I am in control of, the one thing I can take back as mine after being powerless against this invisible thing called "love" for so long.

But once I start, I know I won't stop.

Do I really want to go there? Do I really want my readers to know I'm not the hero in this story?

I close my eyes and allow my playlist to decide. Music has played such a huge part in my life, so why not now?

And when "I Hate Myself for Loving You" sounds over my speakers, it appears the love gods have spoken.

There's no turning back now…

Two

"Miss You Love"
Silverchair

How many of you remember your first love?

I do, and that's pretty monumental because I don't remember a lot. I don't remember losing my first tooth, meeting my first best friend, or the first time I got drunk.

But falling in love for the first time...I remember that.

I remember the giddy feeling and all the clichés that go with meeting "the one." I was eighteen. A young, impressionable woman who viewed the world through rose-tinted glasses. But when I met him, my world became him...

What a fucking idiot I was.

This is not a love story.

This is a life story.

The good.

The bad.

The fucking heartache.

It's all here.

By the end of it, some of you may hate me. Hell, I hated me at times while writing this. But to hate, you have to know love...well, you can try.

Let me introduce myself. You may call me Z, your narrator, so buckle up. This is going to be a bumpy ride.

Love.

What is it?

What is it about love that has driven many throughout the ages to the point of insanity?

How can one single emotion have the ability to transform rational-thinking humans into infatuated, neurotic, lovestruck fools? Whether you're the heartbreaker or the brokenhearted, we all know how it feels to fall in love.

But that's the thing about your first love—we all have a love story. A story that usually shapes you into who you become because the thing about falling in love is that it's usually brutal, grueling, and often, at times, it ends—period.

Love is truly a battlefield...

Love is fucking scary, and anyone who tells you otherwise is lying.

When you love someone with your entire heart, you leave yourself open to being destroyed...and that's what I did and still do even though I know better.

But it doesn't make a difference.

Love doesn't make sense. It doesn't have a conscience. It doesn't care who it hurts. Honestly, the more it hurts, the happier love seems. It takes what it wants, consequences be damned.

So why do we bother? Why are we seeking out love when we know it has the power to destroy us beyond repair?

Because that's the best kind of love. To lose yourself and just let go is...freedom. But that doesn't mean it doesn't fucking suck.

I want to make one thing clear, however...I chose love...it just didn't choose me.

It is so hard letting the one you love go. But I had to do this to save myself because I knew from the moment I met him that he would be the death of me.

Love is awkward at times. And honestly, I have no idea why it takes hold and doesn't let go. We can all wave goodbye to our sanity because love seems to take over, leaving us helpless in the aftermath. When I find my person, I've come to learn that I am loyal and stubborn.

Great traits to have, right?

Wrong.

When it comes to love, these characteristics can cause you to bend where you wouldn't normally. You make excuses and exceptions for those you "love" because you want to believe that the love you give is reciprocated.

I shake my head daily at some decisions I've made.

Many will try to help the brokenhearted with positive affirmations—bless.

It's their loss...

You can do better...

Or my all-time favorite—there are plenty of fish in the sea.

That may be the case, but the fish in my tiny pond was hard enough to find with his light eyes, dark hair, tattoos, and piercings. Imagine if I were to dive into the depths of the seas. I would surely drown.

It's not that easy finding your someone, which is why I think we put up with their shit because better the devil you know and all that.

And if they have a killer dick game, then we're screwed...

But before I bleed my heart out all over the page, let's go back to the first time I ever felt love—true, unguarded love.

It was being a daughter to a man whom I love with every inch of my heart.

My father—the man who kept the monsters away. I can say I honestly know what love is because the day my dad died, I wanted to die with him. Everything lost its color. And it will always remain that way.

When you lose someone you love that much, it doesn't get easier; you just learn to deal with the pain.

But that's a story for another day.

I was born to two immigrant parents who moved halfway across the world to better their lives. They met at that precise moment, at that precise corner store because that's how life works. It yells SURPRISE when you least expect it and then leaves you to deal with the aftermath like the sadistic little bitch that it is while watching on happily at the chaos it created.

My mom disliked my father. That's what she tells me, anyway. But it's hard to dislike my father, and I'm not saying that because I'm his daughter.

He was the kind of man who smiled through the storm and told me to appreciate the darkness because we cannot grow in the light if we don't have the dark to balance its shine.

And he always smelled good.

She didn't stand a chance.

Eventually, she gave in to his persistent advances, and they went out on a date—with my grandma and uncle in tow, of course.

Before long, it was true love. Marriage came, as did my sister and me.

I was always different from her.

I don't like labels, but I was the one who rebelled, a trait I inherited from my dad because he was in the Navy...need I say more?

But when he settled down with my mom, he dedicated his life to his family. He worked eighteen-hour days, sleeping on the road and barely being home so he could provide for us.

My mom stayed at home, looking after us, which was a full-time job.

Although my parents didn't see one another often, they made it work because their love was that solid—it was a love I grew up with, a love which I thought everyone shared.

So when I became a teen, I believed that was the love destined for me. I was going to find my Prince Charming, and we would live happily ever after.

How wrong was I.

I went to an all-girls Catholic school. Again, thanks to my dad working his ass off to provide for his family. So meeting boys was hard. But honestly, it didn't bother me as much as it did my friends.

All my friends talked about what most teenage girls do—boys, boys, and boys. I thought something was wrong with me because I was more interested in checking out the latest book from the library or listening to obscure music with band names I could never pronounce.

But looking back now, I realize I was just finding myself, and boys were never a part of that, and for that, I pat my fourteen-year-old self on the back.

If only that had continued for the rest of my years, I wouldn't be here…

All my friends had boyfriends, but I didn't. I was short, plump, and awkward, so talking to boys was not something I felt comfortable with. But when I did, they bored me with their squeaky voices and peach fuzz.

I thought they didn't like me because I wasn't pretty enough. Or cool enough. That I wasn't enough—period. But I soon realized they didn't like me because I outsmarted them. I didn't hang on to their every word detailing the latest video games, and I didn't fawn over their latest skateboard kickflip like my friends did.

I only liked watching them skate to see them fall.

I was the girl who dyed her hair pink, played bass guitar, and wore black—all the time. I soon realized my friends weren't friends at all and drifted to another circle who were labeled the "freaks." This was my world. A world where I belonged.

There was no talk about boys. Only poetry and music.

I thought we would be friends forever, but sometimes, forever is cut short. But regardless, like all relationships we form throughout our lives, I learned a lot from those six girls. Two of the girls, C and K, flipped off all teenage girl stereotypes when they became lovers.

And this, this was my first glimpse into what teenage love was like.

I never saw a problem with them making out or holding hands. It wasn't forced. They weren't hurting anyone. But it seems being comfortable in one's skin is a problem for others who don't agree with their choices.

They were ridiculed and ostracized for being "different," which just made their love grow stronger. Through hate, they found love, and it was beautiful to watch.

Both C and K were creatively talented, which was reflected in their love. K would sing C songs she had written for her. While C would sketch artwork for K because she was her muse.

As I think about it now, their love was the truest form of love I ever witnessed when in high school. All the other "normal" relationships were just bullshit. For girls to gossip with their friends about, afraid of being the last one who gave a blow job in their circle of friends.

I hated it, which is why I decided I would never be that "girl." I would rather hold on to my V-card and dignity because I wanted more.

I wanted the love I read about in my Jane Austen novels because that's the love I grew up with. That's the love I deserved.

And that's the love I found when I met S.

He wore ripped jeans, played guitar, and had dirty-blond hair longer than mine. The moment I saw him, I felt it...that thing I read about in books. That thing that has hormones taking over my good sense.

My friends and I went to an all-ages gig where some bands played. It was a hot, sunny day. I was wearing my cherry Doc Martins and favorite black dress. Some of my friends were dressed as fairies. Others donning the latest band tees, jean shorts, and Chucks.

We were just there to have fun and be among our people.

I was talking to my best friend at the time, E, but soon forgot everything when S started singing. He was grungy. And cool. And had the bluest eyes I had ever seen.

His aloof attitude had all the girls swooning, but that didn't matter to him because I knew he was destined for great things from the moment I saw him.

His voice was like the spawn of the devil and an angel, and I needed him like yesterday.

Once they finished their set, he coolly walked off that stage, and I knew if I didn't speak to him, I would regret it for the rest of my life.

My friends saw my starry-eyed look and all but shoved me toward him when he emerged into the crowd. Girls asked for pictures and autographs—he was the hometown hero, which surprised me because he was considered a misfit by most of the popular girls and jocks.

But he had something, something magnetic. He was older. I thought that might be it, but when we made eye contact, I knew it was just him.

He smiled.

I smiled...then I ran away.

Total chickenshit move and not my finest moment, but I was sixteen and in "love."

We throw that word around so freely.

"I love tacos!"

"I love the color red!"

Love is precious. But it also hurts...something I came to learn.

I left that day without speaking to S, and I felt regret for the first time in my life.

I was free-spirited and wild. I still am. But I regretted not finding the courage to talk to S, which went against everything I believed in because I did what I wanted, when I wanted, and no one would stop me—much to the distaste of my mother, who I fought with incessantly.

Her strict Catholic background had her praying for my soul many Sundays in church. But my father told me to embrace who I was because there was only one me, and he was right.

So that's why I made it my mission to find S and make him fall in love with me. Note to reader: don't do this—like ever. You cannot and should not make anyone fall in love with you.

My "love" soon turned into an obsession, and I started doodling our initials in love hearts and envisioning our life together on the road as he toured the world with his band.

S and Z kissing in a tree...

Looking back, I see that what I felt for S was infatuation. Love doesn't and shouldn't have any labels. But that's the only word I can use to describe how I felt.

I felt I would die without him, which, I know, is absurd. But to a sixteen-year-old, it made perfect sense. He was the first thing I thought of when I woke and my last thought when going to sleep.

My friends were supportive of my crush because that's what it was. I thought it was love, and at the time, I believed in my heart of hearts we would marry and be together forever.

But there is no such thing as forever.

However, forever came when E told me S was coming to her cousin's birthday party.

I. Died.

I don't remember what I wore, but I know it would have been black. I do remember I had on my Chucks because when I finally stood in front of S, I remember how tall he was. My Chucks squeaked when I stood on my tippy-toes to hug him.

But I'm getting ahead of myself.

The party was everything I hated—full of drunken dickheads and girls who entertained their shit. But I was there with a purpose—to meet S.

I was drinking some cheap vodka, and when E nudged me so hard, I choked on the mouthful I was downing, I knew my chance had come. I couldn't chicken out this time, but I was fucking nervous, something I never was.

I was confident, never nervous, but I guess experiencing something for the first time always makes one anxious.

S was awkward in a cool, arty way. Everyone flocked to him.

Sonnets instantly assaulted my brain because this moment right here, this was history in the making. I knew I would be changed the moment we spoke.

"You've got this," E said with a smile.

In case I didn't, however, she offered me her beer, which I happily accepted.

I was ready...but S was gone—again.

This time, I wouldn't let him go.

I searched the house, not above shouting out his name, but I found him smoking a cigarette near the pool. He stared into the water like it had the ability to solve the mysteries of life, and I wanted him to share them with me.

The walk toward him felt like the longest walk of my life. And it may have been back then. But when I was finally within a few feet away, I realized the hardest step of any journey is the first one—and I just took it.

"I like your band," I said with confidence.

S turned his cheek to see who addressed him, and I am not ashamed to admit, I swooned, and I swooned hard. His eyes were something else. Imagine gazing into the bluest ocean where you can see the bottom—that's the color of S's eyes.

"Thanks," he replied in a voice that wasn't as deep as I thought it would be.

It was elegant. It was the voice of an angel, which surprised me because I heard him sing like a possessed demon.

"What's your name?"

"Z," I replied.

He arched a dirty-blond brow. "Just Z?"

"Yup, just Z."

And just like that, over one simple initial, we fell in "love."

My friends loved S.

He drove us around as we listened to loud music with the windows rolled down, allowing the hot summer breeze in. Those are some of my fondest memories.

We were carefree and happy.

S was the hottest guy I had ever seen in my entire life, and he still is to this day. But for me, I learned very early on that looks are a tiny part of what attracts me to someone.

It's what's inside that gets me—hook, line, and sinker.

And S had the looks as well as the brains.

He wrote poetry, his favorite band was Led Zeppelin, and he read obscure texts from all over the world.

We talked for hours about everything, and I never felt more connected to anyone than I did with S.

There was one small problem—we still hadn't kissed.

I didn't know if he had friend-zoned me because back then, I didn't even know what friend-zoned meant. I just knew that every time he tried to kiss me...I would laugh.

Not exactly a romantic response, but I couldn't help it. It was my nerves. I was awkward and shy, but S was a gentleman. He never pushed.

So we hung out, holding hands and talking, which I was happy with until I mentioned this to E, who insisted I needed to do more or I would lose him.

This confused me because if I had to do something I wasn't comfortable with in fear of losing him, then was he really worth it to begin with?

The answer is no.

But you live, and you learn...

It was the night of prom, and I remember wearing a black silk dress with two large slits up the side. I had on black heels. My makeup was silver glitter eye shadow and red lips. I looked and felt good.

When S came to my door wearing a suit with scuffed black Chucks, I knew tonight was the night I would get ridiculously drunk and have my first kiss with him.

The prom exploited every stereotype, but I was okay with it because S and I made it our own. We danced out of time, and he ate (yes, ate) my corsage, and it was absolutely perfect.

He invited a few of my friends over for an after-party. I got stupidly drunk. It was fun. But when everyone crashed, I knew what was going to happen.

S asked if I wanted to come to his room. I said yes. I'd been in his room countless times, but I knew he didn't want to talk this time. He took my hand and led me down the hallway. My bare feet sank into the soft carpet.

It's weird the things our brains choose to remember—that's one thing I haven't forgotten.

He put on some music—heavy metal, of course. I sat on his bed, dizzy from the vodka and being this intimate with him. He sat near me. He smiled. He had a beautiful mouth.

I pushed back the hair from his face and stared into those eyes of his, and he allowed me. He allowed me to take my time because that's who S was. Patient, understanding, and one-of-a-kind.

He leaned in to kiss me first, and the moment our lips touched...I felt nothing.

I didn't see the proverbial stars. Nor did my heart begin to race.

It felt...nice, a word which is so wishy-washy. It's noncommittal. It's a safe word, a word used when you hate something but are too "nice" to say otherwise.

We made out for a while, laying on his bed, and he tried, he really tried to make it pleasant for me. But neither of us felt that spark, that electrical current which leaves you a heaving mess and wanting to tear one another's clothes off.

But that doesn't mean I didn't enjoy myself.

I liked kissing S, but I also like pancakes. And I found myself thinking of weird shit like whether I turned off my straightening iron or what word rhymes with orange when we continued our kissing sessions weeks after prom.

We both knew the physical chemistry fizzled compared to our emotional connection, but we still tried to make it work. He tried to make it exciting by parking his car down the street from my house and making out with me in hopes my dad would be walking my dog and catch us out.

But nothing changed the fact that I just didn't feel it.

I thought maybe it was because we had only kissed.

So one night, we were making out on his bed. He just got his eyebrow pierced, which was so hot. I focused on all the things I liked about S and hoped that would help when he slipped his hand into my jeans.

He rubbed over my underwear, and again, the word nice comes to mind. Everything he did felt nice, but I wanted naughty.

I grabbed his hand and guided it into my underwear.

"Are you sure?" he asked, those fucking blue eyes piercing my core.

I nodded.

He worked his finger into me while kissing, and it hurt. I now know my body was betraying me because I wasn't turned on how I should be, and S knew it. He could feel it.

I wasn't wet. I was the complete opposite. Not exactly the response one should have when their hot boyfriend has his hands down his girlfriend's pants.

Eventually, it felt a little nicer, but it was awful for us both. I felt guilty for not being more into it, which is stupid. There never should be any guilt associated with sex and exploration. It should be fun and liberating.

It was neither of those things.

I didn't come, no matter how hard he tried. I decided something was wrong with me because this didn't make any sense.

I confided in E, who said I needed to stop overthinking everything and just feel. But that's the thing. I was trying to feel.

Was I broken?

S was a good guy, and he was hot. So what was the matter with me?

E suggested I take control, so I did.

We were again making out, and E told me to focus on the small things that usually turn someone on—focus on his smell and the way he tastes. She said to give in to the senses, and I did.

His scent wasn't bad, but it didn't leave me salivating or wanting to take a big bite out of his neck. And he always tasted of grape candy, which wasn't a bad thing. I liked it because it was S.

S was always hard, which scared me back then. Now, I see what a fucking goddess I was. Make a man hard and he will do anything you want because they're only thinking with one head at that precise moment.

S was really riled up that night. His bedroom window was open, letting in the sea breeze because he lived near the beach. When I licked his neck, I remember I could taste the salt on his skin. He must have surfed before I came over.

I liked that.

I began rubbing over his erection, and I liked the way he arched his neck back, granting me permission to do what I wanted. I unfastened his belt, and when I slipped my hand into his jeans and gripped his dick, we both moaned.

I liked it. And so did S.

I didn't know what I was doing, but that was half the fun. It was scary and exciting, which is how exploring another person should be.

S came in my hand, and I remember how surprised I was that I made him come and also, how it felt. It was hot and wet.

I thought I had finally climbed that sexual mountain, but when S tried to get me off the week after, we were back to square one. I felt like my body was betraying me because I liked S.

So why couldn't I come?

I dated S for three months, and although our sexual history was a disaster, I think back on our time with nothing but fond memories. We broke up amicably, and just as I knew he would, S conquered the world with his very successful band.

He married once. A much older woman. But he always knew the conventional life was never for him and now lives alone, near the beach, in his hometown. We speak from time to time, but he's a memory I wish to have and not relive. Although, his foot massages were the best I've ever had.

S taught me so much.

He taught me how to swear in German, the trick to solving a Rubik's

Cube, and he taught me that even though I thought I loved him, I didn't.

I had no fucking concept of what love was back then.

Even though S was the first boy I kissed and the first boy I dated, he wasn't the man who destroyed me. He was absolutely my first crush, though.

Surprised?

As much as I "loved" S, he wasn't my first love.

He is someone else entirely...

Three

"Lover of Mine"
5 Seconds of Summer

I hit send and pass out, not even sure if what I wrote was any good.

The moment I wrote that first line, however, I knew there was no stopping me. I wanted to be honest because when it comes to matters of the heart, that's the only way to be.

But the thing is, I'm afraid that honesty is going to get me crucified.

I don't know what day it is because I literally have slept like the dead. Every time I woke up, it felt like my body went into self-preservation mode and lulled me back to sleep where it was safe.

But the incessant banging on my front door reveals it's time to face the world.

Reaching for my phone off the bedside table proves fruitless because it's dead as I forgot to plug it in. It's light outside, but honestly, that doesn't help determine the time.

"Z!"

Groaning, I reach for my spare pillow and place it over my face, hoping to drown out BOSSMAN's voice. But I know he isn't going anywhere.

When the banging and yelling continue, I kick off my blankets but keep a hold of my pillow as I stalk to the door. When I open it, I throw it at BOSSMAN's bemused face.

It backflips to the floor between us.

"What?" I bark, hands on hips. "I was trying to sleep."

"Sleep? You look like you've been in a coma for a week," he counters with a slanted grin, shoving past me and entering my apartment as he hangs up on whoever he was just speaking to.

I then realize I'm in my underwear and that my hair is the hot mess I thought it was as my fingers get snared in the bird's nest atop my head. But I roll with it.

BOSSMAN opens my fridge, but soon slams it shut. "Get dressed. I'm taking you out for breakfast."

"Excuse you," I say, folding my arms across my chest. "Since when do I listen to you?"

He mulls over my comment, moving his full lips from side to side. "True. But I think I'm about to change that."

"You're still an asshole." I finally concede only because I'm hungry and plan on ordering one of everything on the menu.

I decide to take a shower and make BOSSMAN wait. I also need a plan of attack. He is either here to grovel at my feet, or he's here to fire me.

With that thought in mind, I switch off the water and dry off. Red is my favorite color. It represents everything naughty and scandalous, and if I'm about to be fired, then it seems fitting I get fired wearing the color of the devil.

I slip into a short bodycon dress and tie my wet, dark brown hair into a messy bun. My makeup is light because my lashes are long, and as I apply my favorite shade of red lipstick appropriately named Lady Danger, it's all I need to look like I spent hours on my face, which is a complete lie.

My lips have always been plump, something which has forever enticed men to grovel for a kiss—morons. My large eyes are dark brown but can change in an instant depending on my mood. But we all know what the star of the show here is, and that's my killer red pumps.

"You never disappoint me," I affectionately say to my heels as I sit at the foot of the bed and put them on.

Memories, as always, flood my brain, memories I wish would miraculously get amnesia so I wouldn't have to think about *him* every time I put on a pair of shoes.

Sighing, I stuff my backpack full of things I will never need and enter the kitchen to see BOSSMAN peering out the window. He sure has a nice ass in those snug black jeans.

He turns when he hears me and instantly does a double take, his attention remaining on my shoes.

"Funny, I never took much notice before, but—"

I hold up my hand, demanding he stop. "Enough, you pervert. Let's go. I'm hungry."

"Pervert?" He playfully scoffs, folding his arms across his broad chest, which only emphasizes his muscles in that white tee. "Hardly. I've read what men have done to your feet."

"And that, right there," I quip, reaching for my sunglasses off the kitchen counter, "only cements my claims."

He bursts into laughter, which I can only hope is a good sign, but I can't be too sure with BOSSMAN.

As we exit my apartment, my neighbor comes waddling down the hallway. As usual, she's wearing black. She's mourning the death of her husband. He died eight years ago. Now *that* is real love.

Mourning the death of your loved one by shunning any color because your world is draped in nothing but darkness, to me, is actually really beautiful.

I wonder if I would do the same? I guess I'll never know.

I nod at my neighbor. She smiles politely, but I know what she's thinking as she clutches the gold crucifix around her throat—*puttana*. I know what she's thinking because she's seen and heard me late at night.

BOSSMAN smiles but is ignored.

I bite my lip to stop my chuckle because it's laughable she would think BOSSMAN would even stand a chance with me. I am confident, incredibly particular, and a bossy bitch. I would eat BOSSMAN alive.

My taste in men has always been select, and I've come to learn, no man can handle me. They say they can, but in the end, it always ends the same—which is why I am single.

BOSSMAN is about to press the call button on the elevator, but I shoulder open the door to the stairwell instead.

"You plan on taking ten flights of stairs in those heels?"

"Obsessed," I mischievously whisper under my breath.

BOSSMAN doesn't bother replying because he knows this is a losing battle.

We take the stairs in silence, and it suddenly becomes a race, but there's no competition. Even in heels, I make sure I beat BOSSMAN's ass because I don't like to lose. I also don't like hearing the word no. It doesn't exist in my vocabulary, which is the reason I have no idea *why* I put up with it for twenty-some years.

I really wish my brain would stop torturing me this way. It seems to enjoy persecuting me by reminding me of *him* when I give myself a ten-second reprieve.

Once we hit the foyer, I put on my sunglasses to block out the morning sun and conceal the sadness that always swells when I think about him.

I wish I could stop. Things would be so much easier if I could, but I can't, and that's the problem. *I'm* the reason I'm caught in this perpetual hell. There is no one to blame but me. And maybe Walt Disney for making me believe that happily ever afters exist. All the Disney-inspired tattoos on my legs remind me that I once believed in magic.

The sidewalk is bustling with commuters, but as I take in the chaos, it's evident we are all lost in our world. We all have a cross to bear and although grouped together, here and now, we are traveling toward our own destination—alone.

We opt for earbuds to block out the noise and not be forced to…God forbid, converse with our fellow humankind.

Imagine that? A world where we actually looked up from our phones and cared about the people in front of us, people we can actually see and touch, instead of reading about whichever Kardashian is fucking whomever six ways to Sunday.

Sometimes, I really hate technology, which is ironic, considering it's allowed me to reach readers all over the globe within seconds.

But I never claimed to be easy, and that's confirmed when I grab BOSSMAN by the arm and drag him into the small diner overlooked by most unless you're a local.

"You want to eat in here?" he asks, peering around the dingy surroundings with distaste.

"Stop being such a snob." I roll my eyes and wait in line. "They swore it was an extra raisin just that one time."

BOSSMAN pales while I burst into laughter.

I'm teasing him, of course, because he should know better than anyone not to judge a book by its cover. This place may not look like much, but they have Manhattan's best bagels and coffee. It's not fancy because it doesn't need to be.

The food speaks for itself. As does the big fat blue A on the window.

I crane my neck to see what selection of bagels we have today. "Ooh, blueberry."

"I thought you only eat gluten-free?"

"Shh, she'll hear you," I mock whisper, patting my stomach.

BOSSMAN merely shakes his head.

"*Bella*, you're up early," says the store clerk. "What do you want today?"

"That blueberry bagel and please feel free to drown it in cream cheese."

"I thought you didn't eat dairy?" BOSSMAN peers down at me, lips pursed.

"If you're here to rain on my fun parade, then you can just go wait outside."

The clerk simply smiles and goes to filling my order. I don't need to mention coffee because he pours me the largest size they have. He knows me well.

BOSSMAN orders his sesame bagel and coffee, and we take a seat at the small plastic table. BOSSMAN barely fits on the chair, and I love seeing his stuffy ass uncomfortable.

I separate my bagel and pray the gluten gods are good to me today as I take my first bite. But even if I spend the entire afternoon a bloated balloon, it'll be worth it because this is a damn good bagel.

"So—"

No conversation…ever ends well when started that way. But I let BOSSMAN continue.

"I read what you emailed me at three a.m."

In response, I stuff half the bagel into my mouth.

"It was good work. Really good. I couldn't stop reading, which is why I published it this morning."

I'm still chewing, but an amused chuckle leaves me. However, that soon turns to me choking on my bagel very loudly as I inhale it because BOSSMAN isn't joking.

"Oh my lord, are you all right?"

When he goes to stand, I shake my head animatedly. I choose death over this asshole helping me because if I don't choke to death, he will be when I throttle him for being such a dickhole.

Thumping on my chest, I dislodge the bagel, and when I can breathe, BOSSMAN knows he's in serious shit. "Please tell me this is one of your bad jokes."

"Bad jokes?" he questions, dark brow raised. "My jokes aren't bad. I had YY in stitches last week."

"I'm pretty sure she was having an anaphylactic reaction to the accidental peanut in her vegan pad Thai. Or maybe it was your joke. Either way, she is fine, while I am not. How…could you?"

I peer down at my cup of scalding coffee.

"Don't even think about it," BOSSMAN warns, reading my intentions perfectly.

"I'm not merely thinking about it. Give me a reason I shouldn't throw this in your face? Actually, I don't need one."

The moment I reach for my paper cup, BOSSMAN raises his hands in surrender and says on a rushed breath, "Because it has over one hundred thousand views…in less than an hour."

Coffee spills down the sides of the cup as I squeeze it in utter disbelief.

BOSSMAN quickly hunts for his phone in his pocket, and when he flips the screen around, my mouth falls open very ungracefully. I see that he is telling the truth.

The memoir is titled *Love Hard*, which is what I vaguely remember putting in the subject line of the email I sent when I was clearly insane. Or insan-er.

Yes, it now has over 150,000 views, but I didn't give BOSSMAN permission to print this. I didn't even read over it. Or run spell-check, for that matter.

This is a nightmare.

"This is a good thing. Stop looking at me like I just kicked a puppy," BOSSMAN says, shaking his head when he reads over the memoir. He likes it, it seems, as he can't stop looking at it.

I want to snatch his phone and throw it into the Hudson, but what about the other 150,000 cells? And this is the problem with the internet. Once it's out there, there's no turning back. Let that be a lesson learned, kids.

"I feel so…violated."

"Oh, please"—BOSSMAN rolls his eyes at my choice of words—"you had no issues licking someone's armpit."

"Bad boss," I quickly quip, tossing my bagel at his face. My aim is perfect as the cream cheese sticks to his stupid chiseled jaw.

The bagel hangs off his chin before it somersaults to the table with a plop.

He reaches for a napkin, wiping away the smear of cheese, not bothered by my weirdness because that weirdness has just landed us 150,000 hits.

I need air.

Standing abruptly, I sprint for the door, and the moment I hit the sidewalk, the urge to run is overwhelming. It's what I do best.

"Z, I need the next chapter."

"Excuse me?" I spin around because I surely misheard him.

But when he deadpans me, I know I haven't had a lapse in hearing. "We need to strike when the iron is hot. You have the journals. The material is there. It's easy."

"*Easy?*" I question, hands on hips. "That's what you think my heartache is?"

"Stop being so dramatic."

And this is why I tolerate BOSSMAN. He is one of the only men who doesn't put up with my shit.

"Can't you see you're on the cusp of changing the literary world? No one has done this before."

"I'm pretty sure that's not true," I argue because memoirs are not rare. Everybody wants their five seconds of fame—bar me.

"You know what I mean. You could be anyone. You *are* everyone. That piece got so many hits because it's relatable. Who hasn't had their heart broken? It's the only thing us human beings have in common.

"We all have a love story."

"Hold up"—I raise my hand—"did you just *quote* me?"

He ignores me. "Stop being a pain in the ass. My phone has not stopped ringing all morning. Everyone wants more. They want to know who *he* is."

I inhale…air and choke.

I can't believe I'm standing in the middle of Manhattan discussing the one thing I promised myself I would try to forget.

I hate him.

No, I really don't.

I hate myself for loving him. Or loved? Kinda sorta liked? I really don't know. The jury is still out on that one.

All I know is that now that the floodgates have opened, I want them slammed shut again. I can't do this. I haven't even written about him, and I already want to carve out my brain with an ice cream scoop.

He has been nothing but trouble—for the past one, two, twenty years, that's all he's ever been, and writing about that trouble is a very bad idea.

"Well, I want a unicorn, but we can't have everything we want. Nice talk."

I go to turn, but BOSSMAN grabs my wrist. It must be the godly early morning hour because his touch does something it's never done before—I want more.

This is bad. So very fucking bad.

"Don't you see, each chapter is a cliffhanger," he says, thankfully ignoring my moment of insanity. "And although readers hate them, it leaves them coming back for more because you have written a good fucking story.

"If it sucked, they wouldn't bother, but read the comments, Z. They want more."

"I don't know what to tell you, BOSSMAN," I reply, subtly removing my arm from his grip. I can see an outline of where his large fingers held me tight. "There *is* no more. Hooroo, mate."

"Hooroo?" he questions aloud to himself before cluing on. "Oh my god, did you learn that from your Australian online boyfriend?"

I instantly curse that chat room I innocently entered because I would have never met NT and wasted two years of my life because online relationships don't work.

"BOSSMAN, you need a hobby," I say as I walk away, leaving him standing on the sidewalk. "Preferably one that doesn't involve me."

I don't wait for a reply and am thankful he doesn't chase me.

I have no idea where I'm going, but that's what I love about New York. You never feel lost. There is always something unique and interesting to stumble on. No matter how many times I've walked these streets, I always find something new.

Taking a seat at a park bench, I watch the world pass me by. I watch as kids laugh and play naively. I wish I still had that innocence. But with age, we soon experience life and love, which begins to chip away at that purity, and before long, you're me.

I wish I could stop. It would be so much easier if I could. But love doesn't work that way. It's an uncontrollable force that takes you for a ride whether you're ready. And most times, you're not.

That's what happened to me.

Cupping my face into my palms, I tell myself to woman the fuck up. You made the choice when you wrote THE END to your story. But was it just a *to be continued…*?

"Would you like to help me feed them, ma'am?"

Facing the world through splayed fingers, I see a man has taken a seat beside me. He offers me his bag of crumbs to feed the pigeons.

"I know they say don't feed them, but they need to eat too."

I uncover my face because I look ridiculous, and I can't hide forever. But I have a feeling this stranger's kind eyes would see straight through me.

"Yes, they do." I reach my hand into the crinkled bag and toss the crumbs onto the ground.

The hungry birds peck at the food, thankful because it's apparent this man doesn't have enough food, yet here he is, selflessly feeding pigeons.

"Are you all right? I don't mean to pry, but you look sad."

"Who isn't?" I reply, not meaning to sound dismal, but it's the truth.

Every day, we wake. Some may have plans, others may not. But the common denominator here is that we all try our best to survive. And when we feel hopeless, as we all have in our lives, that one thing should keep us going.

We are trying to do better…

"Did you know there are over one million pigeons in New York," the stranger reveals as his weathered hands offer substance to his feathered friends. "They also mate for life."

I arch a brow. "I did not know that. The men of the world need to be more like pigeons, then."

The stranger bursts into a hoarse chuckle.

"I wonder how many lonely pigeons there are, though? I mean, if they mate for life, that would mean quite a few single pigeons are out there, looking for their soulmate or, rather, bird mate."

I suddenly feel a kinship to these weird-looking rats of the sky.

"One reason they survive is that they can adapt to any situation. A universal trait of being a New Yorker, some may say."

But I shake my head. "A trait of being human."

He ponders on my comment before nodding. "I suppose you're right. I try every single day. I'll get there one day. And if I don't, at least I tried."

I feel this to my very core.

I don't wish to insult him, but it's evident he's got it rough. With winter looming, I wonder where he'll sleep when it's cold. Or what he'll eat.

"I'll tell you what," I commence, pointing at the almost empty bag of crumbs. "I'll buy that from you for—" I hunt through my backpack and find a fifty—"this."

No human should ever feel worthless, regardless of their circumstances. And I'm hoping a transaction may make him feel more comfortable accepting my offering.

He appears apprehensive, but there is no judgment here, especially from someone like me.

"I don't need your charity," he kindly says, which reveals just what sort of man he is.

"I totally understand that, but this is a simple transaction. I don't expect you to give me that food for free."

This isn't me taking pity on him. I don't know him, and I don't allow his circumstances to form any opinions of him. I mean, I just learned something pretty cool, something I will always associate with him every time I see a pigeon.

And that, to me, is someone who has made an impact on my life—no matter how trivial it may seem.

He weighs over my offer before eventually accepting. "Thank you."

I don't make a fuss when he hands over the bag of feed, and we continue feeding the pigeons.

Tears prick my eyes because there is only one person I want to tell what I learned today. I could tell him anything. He would just laugh at my randomness and then tell me something just as random.

I could ask him any question, knowing he would answer.

Once upon a time, he used to give me everything I wanted. I wanted a voice message, he sent it. I wanted to watch him jerk off, he'd video call. I wanted a picture of his hands, he'd send me a picture while at work.

I loved his hands.

Seems like a ridiculous thing to obsess over, but whenever those hands touched me, I forgot everything, especially when those hands were in mine. We did so many depraved, delicious things together, but the simple act of hand-holding is still the most unforgettable memory I have.

I am a fucking chump.

"You know, pigeons are also monogamous and to keep the romance alive, they constantly do their mating dance."

When I purse my lips, confused, he goes on to explain.

"You know, when they puff out their chests and get all fluffy, that's the man trying to impress his woman. That's true love. No matter how long they've been together, they will always try, and never give up."

I look at this stranger, unsure if he is a mind reader because his pigeon analogy hits home. Or maybe I am just being a sentimental fool.

I toss the remaining crumbs to the birds before standing. I bid my new friends farewell and decide to head home.

However, two blocks away, my cell chimes. It's BUNNY.

"Do you still hate me?"

Sighing, I don't even have the energy to be mad anymore. "I never hated you. Well, maybe for a minute."

She laughs, and that's what true friendship is about—hating your friend and vowing to never speak to them again to forgetting why you were angry with them in the first place all in the same breath.

"I saw what you wrote. What changed your mind about printing it?"

"I didn't," I reply, my heels pounding the concrete, one of my favorite sounds. It reminds me of the men who have allowed me to trample all over them when wearing pumps—and I mean that in the literal sense.

"BOSSMAN did. I emailed him something I wrote in my obvious state of delirium, and the next thing I know, it's got over a hundred thousand hits."

BUNNY is silent, which is never a good thing.

"You need to write more. You need to write about *him*."

"I'm not wasting a single word on him," I reply, unsure how he's become the hot topic of discussion of late. "He can stay forgotten."

"But he's not, is he?" BUNNY wisely questions. "If it was that easy, you would have forgotten about him years ago."

She's right, and I hate it.

"What does that say about me, then? It would be so much easier if I could forget, but I can't. Something is clearly wrong with me. He is everything our mothers warned us against our entire lives, but here I am, when I know better."

"There is only one way to deal with this."

"Gin?" I offer up as a plausible response.

"Write about it."

"And what is that supposed to achieve?"

Another pregnant pause. But what BUNNY says next hits hard because I fear there is truth to her words.

"Do it and find out. It's better than not saying anything at all…that's the reason you're in this mess, right?"

That's all he and I were—a fucking climatic mess.

I don't reply because I have run out of words regarding him. No matter what word I use, it could never summarize him because he is the most confusing and infuriating man I have ever met.

"We can talk about it tonight."

"Tonight?" I ask, a pair of red slingbacks catching my eye in a storefront window.

"Yes, at my exhibition. You forgot, didn't you?"

I don't even attempt to cover my ass because everyone knows I have the worst memory—ever.

"I'll be there, and I even have the best pair of shoes to wear."

Hanging up, I enter the store, totally aware that I buy shoes whenever I'm caught in a mess—which is why I have more shoes than sense, it appears.

I'm late.

I wish I could blame traffic. Or that I had to work late, but truth be told, I'm late because it hurts to breathe.

I know that sounds melodramatic, but it's the God's honest truth.

He has always been my drug but not by choice. If I had my time again, I would tell my eighteen-year-old self that drugs are bad—very bad—and to stay away. But that day was clearly fated, and no matter how many years I've tried to "kick the habit," I always end up a junkie, hooked on him.

This is BOSSMAN's fault. If only he left me the fuck alone, I wouldn't be the unstable crybaby I currently am. I hate not being in control of my feelings because he has no right to make a mess of me.

Only I can do that.

And when I enter BUNNY's trendy gallery in Hell's Kitchen, I know tonight will not end well.

When I enter, I'm impressed with the simple interior—obscure artwork of people, places, and objects hanging from the white walls. There are no gimmicks because BUNNY's work speaks for itself.

When a server wearing baggy overalls and nothing else passes me by, I stop him and reach for his silver tray filled with champagne flutes. I take one, and just as he's about to leave, I offer him the glass as I take the tray.

It will take a lot more than one glass to help me get through the night.

No one questions me as I peruse the photos, feeling nothing but pride—my friend is so talented. She has an ability to capture moments in time so beautifully it feels like you were there. The emotions she stirs in her fans is why many seek out her work.

I stop in front of a picture of a very attractive young man—he is blond and has a body that looks like it was cut from granite.

The photograph is of him looking into the sky. It may appear simple to some, but the lighting and the way he uses his body as a conduit reveals there is nothing simple to this photo.

It is art.

And that's confirmed when I am no longer alone.

"That's my favorite."

Turning my cheek, I see the subject of the photograph is just as impressive off canvas as he is on. His sharp jaw could cut glass and his green eyes, which appear yellow in certain light, could have you forgetting your own name.

He is sure of himself but not cocky, which just makes him even hotter.

"I'm pretty sure all of them would be my favorite," I boldly reply when I know better.

I'm in no frame of mind to be flirting, but maybe that's exactly what I need because he is a cookie.

What happens when you have only one cookie that's your favorite cookie of all? You will protect that motherfucker with your life, that's what. You'll fucking starve without that cookie.

But when you have a plate of five or ten cookies that help satisfy the cravings when your favorite cookie is not replying to your texts—what happens then?

Well, those other cookies help fill the void because when you eat one, you have another to appease your select needs until your favorite cookie decides to get his head out of his ass and text you back.

Brilliant analogy, and I have BUNNY to thank for it. She has a lot of them that only make sense to us 'cause she's my kinda crazy.

This cookie is hot with full lips, which promises nothing but trouble.

All of that messy blond hair reminds me of Goldilocks. But I remind myself this isn't spring break. I am here to support my friend.

GOLDIE peers down at the drink tray, a smirk tugging at those wicked lips. "Bad day?"

"Bad decade," I counter quickly, throwing down two glasses.

He laughs, and the husky sound does nothing to help with my wrestling morals.

"I want to show you something."

He doesn't give me a chance to get a word in edgewise, as it's apparent this isn't optional.

He reaches for my hand, but I don't want to go anywhere with him. The memories resurface, just as they always do.

I'm damaged goods.

"Thank you, but no thank you." I shake my hand from his.

Such a shitty phrase to use, but that's all I can offer. That's all it'll ever be because it hurts any other way.

I don't give GOLDIE a chance to reply as I turn quickly, but my smooth exit is ruined when I bump straight into a wall of muscle.

"I am so sor—" I leave my sentence unfinished when I see the muscle belongs to BOSSMAN. "Why are you here? Gross," I add, pulling a repulsed face.

I don't believe in using tack when it comes to him.

A hoarse laughter fills the small space between us, and I only realize he's gripping my arms to stop me from face-planting when I ran into him.

"I was invited."

"BUNNY must have been desperate for numbers." I remove his hands from my arms as I am suddenly burning up.

"Why are you flushed?" he asks, his lips tipping into an amused grin.

Just as I'm about to share some smart-ass response, GOLDIE appears, wrapping an arm low around my waist.

BOSSMAN's humor soon fades when his eyes focus on GOLDIE's arm around me. I don't know what I'm seeing because if I didn't know any better, I'd say he was jealous. But that's impossible, and not to mention, yuck.

BOSSMAN is, well, my boss, and although he looks fucking hot in his black suit pants and white shirt, which reveals just enough expanse of his tanned chest to highlight what he's packing beneath, that doesn't mean it changes my opinion of him.

But why do I suddenly like the alpha vibes ricocheting between us?

I clearly need therapy.

"Research?" BOSSMAN has the nerve to quip.

"Oh, fuck you. And fuck the shitty horse you rode in on."

"Babe—"

"I am not your babe," I correct, prying GOLDIE's fingers from me.

"It didn't seem that way two minutes ago."

"Why are you still talking?"

BOSSMAN's eyes narrow into slits. "He's a little young, don't you think?"

"I think it's none of your business," I counter, stepping forward, not at all intimated by his six-foot-three frame.

"I'm twenty-three."

"Shut up!" both BOSSMAN and I say at the same time.

We square off, our eyes never wavering from the other because no one is prepared to back down. A bubble of excitement fills my belly, thrilled by the chase. Although I am alpha, I take great pleasure in watching a man trying to fight me because I always, always win.

I don't know what's about to happen, but I'm here for it.

BOSSMAN steps forward, the space between us becoming smaller and smaller, but I stand my ground.

"Nice shoes, by the way."

And just like that, BOSSMAN owns my ass because he knows what that comment does to me. He knows because he read about *him*. And he wants more…

"Isn't it a shame I can't trample all over you with them?"

"Who said you can't?"

A stunned gasp leaves my parted lips because is he…flirting with me?

"In your dreams, loser," I return quickly, refusing to submit.

"You're not the only alpha in this room."

Okay, this needs to stop. Now.

Standing on tippy-toes, I smile, but nothing is sweet about it. "Is that a challenge because all these little boys, you included, like to talk a big game, but when it comes down to it…none of you are man enough to handle someone like me."

BOSSMAN smirks, and I hate that it stirs something inside me.

"Yes, it's a challenge. Show me who's boss by giving me what I want."

"Other than a slap to the face?"

BOSSMAN's perfect straight teeth tug at his bottom lip. Is he…getting off on this banter?

"Don't make promises you don't intend to keep."

My cheeks heat because what in the ever-living fuck is going on?

Leaning forward so we're a hair's breadth away, I smirk. "You wouldn't be able to handle me, BOSSMAN."

"Could he?"

Touché…

"No," I deadpan because it's the truth.

I wanted more.

He didn't.

The end.

But why does it suddenly seem like it's just the beginning?

When BOSSMAN arches a perfectly groomed brow, I know what he's doing. He's baiting me, and it's working because I never back down from a challenge.

"Fuck you."

BOSSMAN merely smirks in response because he knows he's just won.

Let the crazy begin because it's time, it's time for me to introduce the man who ruined my life—in all of the best ways.

Four

"Love Gun"
KISS

When high school ended, I was thrown into the world without a fucking clue of who I was. Or who I wanted to be.

I, of course, didn't know that then.

I thought I had it all figured out. I was an adult.

Huzzah!

If I could give that girl any piece of advice, it would be to enjoy being young because being an adult is fucking overrated.

I went to college to study arts and humanities. I knew I wanted to pursue the avenue of writing, and arts was the way in.

I loved college. I lived at home and commuted every day. I worked at the local deli even though I was a vegetarian for five years.

It was a time I looked back on with happy memories. It was the only time in my life I ever felt completely free.

I busted my ass at work and school, went to the gym, lost the puppy fat, and ditched the black for glam. The shoes, however, were still monster pumps.

One night, E and ANGEL asked me to see a band with them in a beachy part of town. I didn't drive yet, but E had her license. It was a novelty to drive back then. Now, I avoid it like the fucking plague.

But I said yes because I had seen the band she spoke of play before.

They were glam rock, and E was obsessed with the guitarist. He did have cute pigtails.

This time, I do remember what I was wearing—a red snakeskin print halter that showed just enough cleavage, tight black PU leather pants that I had to peel from my body to remove, and a pair of red fuck-off pumps.

My brown hair was curled, and my lips were red.

We entered the bar, which was packed because the band had a pretty decent following. I remember there were a bunch of girls there. I heard the lead singer was a bit of a manwhore.

But what singer isn't?

My heels stuck to the sticky floor thanks to the spilled beer and God knows what else, and it was a hot night. The windows were open to let in the breeze, but it didn't make a difference because it was pandemonium the moment the band exploded onstage.

I use that word because this band was very flamboyant with feather boas and glitter—lots of it.

The girls rushed to the front of the stage while I waited in line for my tequila sunrise. They were squealing.

I rolled my eyes.

I didn't get it.

I still don't.

But something about a boy in a band just skyrockets their sex appeal, no matter what a jerk they are, and if they're a lead singer…they can do what or whom they want.

E waited by the side of the stage, trying to catch the guitarist's eye. He wore shiny blue pants and a short tank. I made my way over to her, elbowing past the hysterical girls singing along to the song's lyrics.

So the thing about this band is that their lyrics were filled with clever innuendos, hinting whoever penned them was, in fact, quite witty and actually pretty smart.

I stood by E, sipping my drink and half watching the band.

The lead singer didn't catch my eye. At all. He was cute enough. But he was older than me, and honestly, the fact he had women fawning all over him was a turn-off. He loved the limelight, and his confidence made me think he was a show pony jackass.

He was arrogant. And he knew he could have any woman he wanted, and at that moment, he wanted me.

The song ended, and the singer strolled over to the side of the stage and asked, "Are you enjoying the show?"

I had no idea he was talking to me until ANGEL elbowed me in the ribs and gestured with her chin to the stage where I locked eyes with him.

...MR. J.

He looked at me.

I looked at him.

And I knew then and there, MR. J was going to change my world in the worst possible way...and I was here for it.

The walls closed in on me, and I felt every fucking cliché known to humankind. My heart began to race. My mouth got dry, and the fire currently burning me from head to toe took over any coherent thought.

I nodded because he made clear he wouldn't continue the show until I answered his conceited ass. He smiled, and fuck me dead, his dimples punched me in the solar plexus with their cuteness.

"Good," he confidently said. "Because I am." And he made quite clear the show he was referring to was him looking at me.

I felt my cheeks blister, and he grinned and went back to the show like he didn't just address me in front of hundreds of people.

I didn't know what to think.

No one had ever been that forward with me before.

And just in case I had any doubts about what MR. J wanted, he sang his smutty lyrics my way any chance he got.

This is the moment I should have turned away, but I stayed because my curiosity got the better of me. In hindsight, I wish I had listened to that voice that told me to run far, far away.

By the time the band had finished, I was pretty drunk.

After MR. J was done packing up his gear, he headed straight for me, eyes only for me, which was hot. It was so hot. It made me lose all train of thought when I should have seen that he was trouble with a capital T.

He looked different up close.

His hair was dark, a little long, and wavy. He was clean-shaven, which just seemed to emphasize his beautiful mouth. His eyes were chocolate brown, and he still had some eyeliner smudged underneath.

His fingernails were painted black, and he wore gaffer tape on his wrists.

When something significant happens, those events tend to linger in your memory. Sometimes, you revisit those memories with happiness. Others may evoke less pleasant emotions.

I remember this encounter so vividly because only recently have I allowed myself to reflect on this time. It was too painful once upon a time.

I consciously tried not to think about this meeting because I wanted to forget. I wanted to forget him.

I wanted to drop the memory into a nonconscious zone and never think about it again. But it's impossible to forget the man who changed your life and stole your heart.

I remember his hair was wet like he'd just stepped out of the shower, and he smelled so fucking good. He was wearing black jeans and a red shirt. I think he had on boots. He was tall, slim, and oozed confidence and sex. He was so cool.

I needed to stay away.

But I didn't.

He leaned in close and asked, "Did you enjoy the show?"

I held my breath because being in his presence was almost suffocating. I couldn't decide if it was in a good or bad way. I still can't.

"Yes," I replied, leaning in closer as I felt his breath against my neck. God damn, he smelled like a fucking angel...an angel who was about to set my heart on fire. "I'm pretty sure you did as well."

He pulled back and laughed, and that was the moment I knew MR. J would be someone special.

He asked for my number and produced a piece of paper and pen. MR. J was and still is old-school in that sense. I don't remember seeing a cell.

I remember I was anxious writing down my number because I was drunk and also nervous. I didn't want to fuck this up. So when I was done, I held the piece over my head to show E and make sure I wrote down my number correctly.

I did.

MR. J folded the piece of paper and put it into his pocket, and again, I can't help but remember the smallest things—like how long and elegant his fingers were. And his dimples as he smiled.

There were two things I was and am still obsessed with—MR. J's hands and mouth/teeth/dimples. Okay, that's more than two, but love is a greedy bitch.

He was a conundrum, and I was hooked.

He kissed my cheek. I held my breath. And then he left.

The fact I can remember every small detail like it happened yesterday confirms what you all know to be true—MR. J was going to be my first love...and I was in so much fucking trouble.

I met MR. J on a Friday. He called me Monday morning. This showed me early on that MR. J goes in hard for something he wants. I liked that.

His voice was sexy. Not hoarse, but smooth with just the right amount of burn, like a good scotch. I honestly can't remember what we spoke about, but he gave me his address and told me to come over.

I did on Wednesday.

His house was cute. His room was at the front. I remember walking in and seeing he had a dog.

Tick.

When I asked what breed he was, MR. J said he was a red Kelpie crossed with God knows what. He guessed fox or dingo, which made me laugh. I liked his humor.

His room was filled with music paraphernalia, superheroes, and wrestling stuff. It wasn't what I expected, but I liked being surprised.

We sat on his bed and talked. He was incredibly funny and clever. We spoke about ourselves, and the more he opened up, the more intrigued I became. I really liked the way he spoke. And every time he smiled, his dimples would appear, and I would forget what I was saying.

I couldn't deny the chemistry that sparked between us. It was electric and exciting.

It was a front-runner from the moment we met. Again, I hate to be clichéd, but it's the God's honest truth.

The more time we spent talking, the harder it was to concentrate on anything other than his mouth, his smile, and the way he always held my gaze when we spoke. I liked that. I always did.

This is what I was missing with S—the capability of being set on fire by merely being in the same room with the person you want.

I knew MR. J wanted to kiss me. His eyes were fixated on my mouth. So I decided to continue to talk because if he wanted to kiss me, he would have to work for it. I wasn't going to make things easy for him. A fact I am proud of.

Mid-sentence, MR. J slammed his mouth over mine and kissed the ever-living fuck out of me—just how I knew he would.

Now this kiss is something you read about. It stole my breath. He coaxed me onto his lap and gripped my ass as we continued to kiss for what seemed like hours. This is when I realized MR. J was an ass man.

But there was something he liked even more (are we surprised?)...my feet. Stay tuned for that hot segment, kids...

He was hard immediately, and I loved that I wielded that power over him. Out of all the girls at the gig, I was the one he zeroed in on, and that got me hot.

But I soon learned MR. J likes the chase. When he gets what he wants, he grows bored and is on to the next pretty face.

But love...love is fucking blind.

Five

"Only Love Can Hurt Like This"
Paloma Faith

It's Groundhog Day when I wake to a loud rapping on my door.

Blindly reaching for a pillow, I place it over my head, hoping to drown out the noise.

It doesn't.

Groaning, I toss the pillow to the floor and kick off my blankets. Whoever is at my door is about to regret waking up this morning.

"What?" I bark, yanking open the door, but instantly regret my hostility when I see O standing on my doorstep with a large cup of coffee in hand.

"BOSSMAN sent me because he knew if he came, you would punch him in the nose," she says on a rushed breath, extending the coffee my way as a sign of peace.

A chuckle escapes me because she's right. "Come in."

She enters and smiles while I reach for the much-needed coffee. I notice her looking around my apartment, not because she is snooping, but she seems… in awe.

What in the ever-living fuck is going on?

She notices me watching her, and tears instantly spring to the surface.

"Oh my god. I'm sorry if I was a bitch. I'm not a morning person." I fail to mention I'm not usually a people person most times of the day because I don't want to make O feel any worse.

But when she shakes her head and slumps onto the sofa, it seems I have totally misread this entire thing. "I read what you wrote."

I now understand the tears. I didn't think it was *that* bad…

"It was really something, I mean—" She bursts into more tears, covering her face with her palms.

I sip my coffee, leaning against the wall because I have no idea what's going on. I usually can read people really well, all but one person, who seems to be the reason O is sobbing hysterically on my couch.

I give her some time, but we could be here all day, so I decide to play the guessing game. "It's not finished. I mean, if you hated it that much, I could—"

"Hated it?" she says, lifting her mascara-stained face to look at me. "I loved it. So much. It was…something."

And there is another noncommittal word…

O notices my confusion and reaches into her pink backpack for a tissue. "I'm sorry to come in here like a crazy person, but, Z, your words, they made me think about my first love. About *my* MR. J."

Oh, sweet baby Jesus…what have I done?

"I was sixteen, and he was thirty," she shares while I nod, never taking innocent O as a rule breaker. "I knew it was all kinds of wrong, but like you said, you knew MR. J would change your world in the worst possible way, and you were here for it."

I said that?

When I write, I go into a different world—literally—and I usually can't recall anything during the writing process because I get lost, immersed into a reality which is outside the one everyone else is living. And that is why I love being a writer.

I can escape to anywhere I want, and last night, I got lost in a past I promised never to revisit again.

Last night, I read through the tattered leopard-print Hello Kitty journal with tears in my eyes as I relived my first meeting with the man who changed my life. If only I knew the shit I would all these years later, I would have ripped up that journal and set it on fire just for good measure.

But here I am, in this fucking mess because I believed in fairy tales.

I sat down and wrote about *him*, about MR. J, not really expecting much because even though he touched me in ways I never thought anyone could, I didn't expect my ramblings to echo with anyone, but as O is detailing her affair with her English teacher, I realize how wrong I was.

BOSSMAN, he pushed my buttons, and I wanted to prove him wrong, which I apparently achieved. I should be happy, but I know I have just started something that is about to grow out of control.

"And I still love him," O concludes, looking at me for validation.

I simply nod because I wasn't listening to a word she was saying, but sometimes, that's all people want—for someone to listen without the other person waiting for their turn to talk.

"And your writing made me see that what I felt *was* love. I thought it was just puppy love, but PET, he still has my heart. The heart wants what the heart wants."

I don't want to shatter her dreams because who am I to judge, but I want to remind her of a small yet very important factor in this equation.

"Sweetie," I say, pushing off the wall and taking a seat near her. "He was your teacher. A much older teacher who abused his power. That isn't love. That's called being a dirty pervert. But hey, no judgment."

She sniffles, wiping her red nose with her tissue. "I was the one who seduced him."

I pull back with a slight smirk. "Well, what a fucking plot twist. I did not see that coming."

Her tears are soon replaced with laughter. "I just wanted to say thank you for writing that. It really touched me in ways I never expected. It was so candid, so…real. I could really relate because we've all got a MR. J."

Yes, we do…mine is just a little more complicated, frustrating, and infuriating than most.

"When can I read the next chapter? I *need* to know what happens next."

"What happens next is that I should have stopped after the first bite," I counter with a snicker. "The end."

"I don't believe that," O softly objects. "It's never the end with someone like that."

Sighing, I brush my snarled hair from my cheeks because she's right.

"BOSSMAN wants to see you. Something is happening."

"What is happening?" I ask, pursing my lips because when BOSSMAN is involved, I've learned to expect the unexpected.

Take last night, for example, because what the fuck was that? Was he *flirting* with me?

I feel vomit rising…

And not because I didn't like it…but because I did.

I.

Need.

Help.

"Okay. Give me ten minutes to get ready."

O looks at my disastrous appearance and smiles. "You may need longer than that. I'll wait."

It happens again.

The moment the elevator doors open, I get the sense everyone is looking at me. And when a few of my colleagues whisper to their neighbors behind their hand, my paranoia is confirmed.

I peer down to ensure I did, in fact, get dressed. Heels and red romper—check. So what is everyone looking at?

O takes a seat behind her desk, leaving me to fend for myself when I make my way toward BOSSMAN's office. I have no idea what I'm walking into, which isn't new, but after last night, I feel…nervous?

I scoff at the notion because since when does any man, especially BOSSMAN, make me nervous?

I am woman, hear me roar…

With that notion in mind, I burst through his door, not bothering to knock as I exclaim, "Sending O was a total dick, pussy move, but I guess you have no balls so—"

However, my rant goes down in flames when I see BOSSMAN isn't alone. Two men sit in front of him, and judging by their expensive suits and horrified looks, it's safe to assume it's not a normal day in the office for them to hear someone swear like a sailor.

BOSSMAN clears his throat, pushing his designer black-framed glasses up his nose. "Here she is. The talented author behind the memoir, which has surpassed two hundred and fifty thousand reads."

His comment drips with sarcasm, but I will address that later because now, I need a minute.

"Hold up? What the fuck? Two hundred and fifty thousand reads? You're fucking kidding me, right?"

BOSSMAN closes his eyes, not appreciating my choice of words.

But what the fuck?

One of the men stands, his attitude changing when he realizes who I am. "It is such a pleasure to meet you."

That's a load of crap, but I smile nonetheless.

"We're big fans of your work," he goes on to say. "Today's writing was genius. We are from *Now and Tomorrow*. You may have heard of us?"

He smirks arrogantly, and I already hate him. Unless you're living on Mars, us earthlings know all about New York's biggest online magazine. They write about everything, which makes them popular with everybody as they have something for everyone.

What I don't understand is why they are here.

By the pissy look on BOSSMAN's face, I have my inklings, but that's too far-fetched to fathom.

My silence is this man's cue to continue. "My colleague and I wanted to do the right thing and talk to your boss before we approached you. But we'd like you to write for us."

Now I understand why BOSSMAN looks like he just stepped in dog shit in his Italian leather boots.

The room waits for me to respond as it seems I'm now suddenly the star of the show. When did the world take a handful of crazy pills?

"Are you sure you have the right person?"

STAN, my biggest fan, breaks into joyous laughter while BOSSMAN's nostrils flare.

I hate to admit the alpha vibes he's throwing off are extremely hot. But I need to get my head in the game because I don't know what's happening.

"We want to offer you a job at *Now and Tomorrow* as editor-in-chief, as well as making an offer for exclusive rights to your memoir—*Love Hard*."

He looks at me, waiting for me to burst into happy tears. Or maybe express excitement over an incredible offer most writers would die for, but I simply look at him like he's gone mad.

"I know it's a lot to take in, so please think about it. But here is my card." He reaches into his suit jacket pocket and produces a crisp white business card.

BOSSMAN leans back in his seat, watching me closely. He knows what this means for his beloved magazine if I accept, which is why I shake my head.

"I don't need time to think about it. The answer is no."

STAN'S mouth parts while his colleague appears like I've just spoken in a different language. I guess they don't hear that word too often.

"There's no rush. Take your time to—"

"No," I repeat firmly. "Thank you for your very generous offer, but I kindly decline."

"If it's a matter of money, I can assure you—"

"Nope." I cut him off because I don't need to hear any more. "It's not the money."

"Then what is it?"

BOSSMAN also appears curious about my answer as he doesn't take those eyes off me.

"I like it here, and like a pigeon, I mate for life."

I knew that fact would come in handy one day, and when the suits look at one another utterly perplexed by my response, BOSSMAN merely smirks. He gets me, and this is why I will never leave. He may be a pain in the ass, but he's my pain in the ass.

Better the devil you know and all that.

STAN isn't happy with my decision and gestures to his colleague that it's time to leave.

"If you change your mind," he says, placing his business card into my hand.

I accept because I wouldn't want to be rude. Well, ruder. "I won't, but thank you."

They leave BOSSMAN's office, clearly offended I didn't fall to my knees and thank them. But little do they know, I never get on my knees for anyone because they're on their knees for me.

BOSSMAN is deadly quiet, but his eyes say so much. I don't know if he wants to scold…or slap me…in all the right ways.

He stands, his presence overwhelming as I almost choke on my small intake of air. I stand still as he rounds his desk and leans on the edge of it, crossing his arms and ankles. His eyes still eat me up, and I like it.

"So I think now is the time we talk about that raise," I quip, needing to fill the silence because I'm afraid of what else my lips might do.

"You do realize what you turned down?"

"Yes?" I phrase it as a question because he suddenly looks pissed off.

I thought he'd be happy, not that that influenced my decision.

"You turned down working at an elite magazine where you'd be your own boss, as well as other people's boss."

"I know. It does sound rather tedious. No offense."

BOSSMAN's perfect lips twitch. "You make it fun," he confesses, stunning me because if I didn't know any better, I'd say he was giving me a compliment. "I'm taking you out for dinner."

"I don't want to have dinner with you."

"I'm not sure why you thought that was optional."

This is the moment for me to tell BOSSMAN to go to hell because I'm the alpha, not him. But his dominance…it gets me hot.

And I hate it.

"Well, in that case, I'm only saying yes because I predict I'll be hungry later. Text me the address, and I'll meet you there."

"I'll pick you up at seven. Oh, and by the way, nice shoes." He peruses down my body slowly, and when they land on my pumps, he licks his bottom lip.

My cheeks heat, and for one of the first times in my life, I'm at a loss for words.

BOSSMAN—1.

Z—0.

But it's time to take back the power because BOSSMAN has bitten off more than he can chew—pun totally intended.

I'm sitting in one of Manhattan's most exclusive Italian restaurants, smugly sipping my two-hundred-dollar wine. I shouldn't be gloating, but I am. I can't help it. Let this be a lesson learned to BOSSMAN—don't boss me around.

He's read my journals. He knows better than to bark orders at someone like me.

O made this reservation, and then I bribed her with the first read of the next chapter of the memoir if she told me where it was. Not my finest hour, but desperate measures…

I'm surprised BOSSMAN would take me here. When he said dinner, I wasn't expecting a five-star restaurant, so I decided to meet him here against his wishes because it feels less like a date this way.

And it's not a date.

"Sir? Sir! Do you have a reservation?"

I don't need to turn around to see who is storming through this upscale restaurant. BOSSMAN has arrived, and judging by the hysterical voice of the maître d', he is not a happy camper.

BOSSMAN stands by the table while I sip my wine.

"I am so sorry, ma'am. Do you know this man?" the poor maître d' asks, wringing his hands.

I take a moment to appreciate the undertones of my wine while the throbbing vein in BOSSMAN's temple is close to exploding as he waits for me to reply.

"Z," he says between clenched teeth.

I hold up my hand, swirling the wine in my mouth very theatrically, before gulping it down with a satisfied sigh. "Yes."

The maître d' nods and scampers away while BOSSMAN takes a seat across from me. "You are the most infuriating woman."

"Thank you."

He turns the bottle of wine toward him so he can read the label.

He shakes his head while I smile broadly—butter wouldn't melt in this mouth.

"I wanted to do something nice because I really appreciated what you did today."

"What did I do?"

BOSSMAN ignores me. "If you accepted that offer, you'd be made. You'd be renown in the literary world."

"Aren't I already?" I tease, but it seems that BOSSMAN doesn't want to play.

"Why do you do that?"

"You're going to have to be a little more specific."

"That!" he exclaims, pointing his finger. "Why do you hide behind your humor? Why do you deflect whenever I try to get serious?"

All I can think of is Heath Ledger as the Joker…*why so serious?* And that's a big mistake because whenever I think of the Joker, I think of Batman who then reminds me of MR. J because Batman was his favorite.

"Tell me what you're thinking," BOSSMAN almost begs, as he must be able to read the emotion on my face.

But this is me. I learned early on that I don't like dealing with emotions. When something happens, I shut down and compress my feelings. I'll deal with it when I'm ready. Whether that be in two months or two hundred years, I will get to it when I want to wade through the bullshit in my head.

Some people like to talk about their feelings, but not me.

"I'm thinking I should have accepted their offer." I push back my chair and stand abruptly because I need to get out of here.

BOSSMAN is right.

I am well aware of my inability to deal with any kind of serious talk because that's all I ever wanted with MR. J—for him to tell me what he was feeling. But getting any kind of emotion from him was nigh on impossible.

The harder I tried, the harder he pulled back. So after a while, I just stopped.

I don't wait for BOSSMAN to lecture me any further and storm through the restaurant, ignoring the horrified gasps of the guests because I don't know why I thought agreeing to dinner would ever be a good idea.

I have clearly gone mad—for real this time.

The moment I'm engulfed by police sirens and pollution, I calm down because this is familiar. This is where I belong. Not having dinner with my boss, whom I hate.

"What did he do to you?"

"Go away, BOSSMAN." I force my way past tourists, just confirming the myth that us New Yorkers are pushy bastards who don't care who's in their way.

"No, not until you tell me why you're so…"

"So what?" I cry, spinning around to face him.

Bystanders stop and stare because I'm making a scene. But I can't help it. BOSSMAN pushed me to the breaking point, so he can deal with the repercussions because I was doing just fine until him and his fucking memoir.

But I know that's a lie. I was barely hanging on.

His temper simmers. Mine only grows.

"So evasive all the time. If I talk about anything remotely serious, you do that." He hooks his thumb toward the restaurant. "For a writer, you fucking suck at communicating. But your writing is anything but that.

"When you write, you take your readers to another world. That's a fucking skill, Z. Most writers would kill for that."

"They can have it!" I declare, squaring off with BOSSMAN in the middle of the busy sidewalk. "Most times, I don't know what's real and what's not real. I live in whatever world I create because sometimes, this world…it fucking sucks."

BOSSMAN's face softens, which only adds to my anger. "Stop shutting people out, then. Live in this world."

"No." I stubbornly fold my arms across my chest in defiance, but to also keep BOSSMAN out.

"Why? You're letting one asshole get the better of you when you deserve so much more! Why?"

"Because I'm messed up!" I scream, losing any shred of composure I was clinging to. "Because he fucking tore out my heart. And because he broke me. And he isn't the asshole…I am."

And there it is…the ugly truth.

"But the worse thing is…is that I let him break me. Time and time again. So the answer to your question is that I hide behind my humor because it's better than feeling…this." I tug at the front of my dress over the pounding of my heart, which has forever been broken.

BOSSMAN's eyes soften now, but I don't want his sympathy. I've done this to myself.

I turn on my heel and leave because this conversation is done.

BOSSMAN knows better than to follow me because this isn't over…it's only just begun. And that's what I'm afraid of.

Six

"Bad Boy for Love"
Rose Tattoo

I never made things easy for MR. J in the beginning, and that's what kept him interested. That's why he stayed.

We fooled around for months, and no matter how many times he asked if he should get protection, I said no. It frustrated him, but he never pushed. He was a gentleman in that sense.

I loved teasing him. It was something I soon learned gave me power over MR. J.

MR. J was one kinky fucker.

I discovered this one evening when we were making out hard and heavy in his bedroom, and he was completely obsessed with my feet. And when I asked if he wanted to do blasphemous things, things which ten Hail Marys could never absolve, to my feet, a small, unguarded part of MR. J shone through, and it was incredible.

MR. J was the man who kick-started this fascination most have with my feet. I like that he was the first man to do that.

He marked me in a way because you always, always remember your first time, and you especially remember a first such as that.

Everyone has a fetish, whether in the bedroom or not. We all have something that gets us hot. For MR. J, it was feet, and for me, it was shoes—a perfect combination. We were destined for a collision course the night our paths crossed.

Our chemistry was off-the-charts explosive. It still leaves me breathless to this day. Our connection was unlike anything I've ever experienced before, and I've been chasing that high ever since.

I remember one night he answered the door all wet from his shower. I didn't even get a chance to say hello before he grabbed me and made out with me on his patio, mouth fucking me in ways that should be illegal.

Another time, he had broken his ankle wrestling, and he had on a moon boot. I parked my car down the street from his house, and he insisted he walk me—well, hobbled to the car. I found it incredibly sweet.

Under the moon, in that graffitied alleyway, we made out for an eternity before he bid me good night. I remember I was giddy that night. One of the only times I ever felt those "butterflies."

When we made out, he would never stop touching me with adoration and desire. He could never get enough. It really was beautiful.

Our physical attraction was never the issue between us. It was all the other stuff.

MR. J was an emotional clam. Now that I'm older, I see that commitment wasn't for him—no matter how hard I tried.

I soon realized whenever I touched on anything remotely personal or serious, he would hide beneath his wit or evade the topic entirely. I would then not hear from him for days, and I would often wonder if he ever existed or if I made him up.

But then he would call like everything was okay, and I would go back to him because I could never stay away. I was drawn to him.

I didn't understand it.

I still don't.

I went to most of his gigs, and at first, he made clear he only had eyes for me. He made me feel like I was the only girl in that room. He would sing to me, giving me that dimpled smile that revealed secrets only he and I were privy to.

I loved those days.

When his gig was done, he would come straight over and kiss me, and kiss me indecently. He made me feel special, like he cared. He would hold my hand. He wouldn't stop smiling when we were together. He would whisper dirty words into my ear, and I loved every second of it.

My friends would always comment they had to look away when MR. J and I locked eyes because they felt like they were encroaching on a private moment. That's how explosive things were between us. They often said we set the room on fire.

I was falling hard for MR. J., and I thought he liked me too. But I never actually knew how he felt because I never asked. I was too afraid of the answer because I knew what it would be—this is on me, not MR. J.

Thinking back, I'm certain he was seeing other girls while seeing me, but I chose to believe otherwise.

I did ask once what was going on between us, which went down like a sinking ship. He evaded the question, and the only glimpse into why his walls were ten million feet high was when I asked if he was hurt in a previous relationship.

He said yes. And that's where the conversation ended. I never got anything more because the harder I pushed, the further I pushed him away.

MR. J liked me enough to make out with and see me when it suited him, but to actually see me outside his bedroom was something we never really did. I remember we went out for drinks with friends—once.

But I so badly wanted to believe he would change, and that I was the one who could change him.

But I was a naive fool.

The attraction to him was so strong, I couldn't walk away. I wanted to be with him because he made me happy. He didn't give me much, but what he did was really special and beautiful. When he was with me, he was so present. He gave me his full attention, and it honestly just felt like we were the only two people who existed in the universe.

We were holed up in his room, him educating me on wrestling and his favorite wrestlers, Roddy Piper and Randy Savage (yawn), or us watching Ren and Stimpy. Well, we didn't really watch any TV because we used to make out for hours. That is not an exaggeration either.

He liked my mouth. I liked his.

He got me hot just by kissing me, but when he actually slipped his fingers into my underwear, that was a whole different ball game because he could make me come just by using his hands.

He bit me.

He spanked my ass when I went down on him with my feet in his mouth and butt in his face.

MR. J was the first man I gave a decent blow job to, and he was the first man who made me come using his mouth on me. We were filthy together, and it was perfect for a little while.

We still hadn't had sex at this stage, and I used to love teasing him with that fact because he wanted it, but I knew if I gave in, he would grow bored.

Writing this, I am so angry with myself for not doing what I knew I should have. If this were anyone else, I would be screaming at them to walk out that door and never look back. But I didn't do that.

I kept coming back for more.

He made me feel special. He made me feel like I was the only one.

Looking back, I still don't understand why MR. J kept me around for two years.

Two fucking years.

During that time, he never called me his girlfriend. I never met his family, and he never met mine. We existed in the darkness, together in his bedroom, lost in a connection that I still can't decipher to this day.

MR. J isn't to blame.

I am.

He never made promises. I was the one who accepted what he gave me because I thought I loved him. This was my first glimpse into love, and it fucking sucked, but I couldn't walk away. I was trapped, trapped by my own hand when I could have walked away at any time.

But when in his arms, late at night, I would forget all of that because I was an addict, and MR. J was my heroin.

He would touch me in ways that showed me he cared—and in his own fucked-up way, I think he did care. I don't know what happened to him, but he is the most guarded man I have ever met. I could never read him because he held his cards close to his chest.

The stubborn woman that I am refused to give up because when he showed me glimmers of who he was and let that guard down, it was the purest, most beautiful thing I ever saw. I wanted that man always.

He was so clever.

He was irresistibly charismatic.

He was incredibly kind.

His past was paved with loss and pain.

But when I got too close, he pushed me so far away, I felt like we existed on different planets. And he once again had me doubting if the person I believed him to be was real.

But I still went back. Over and over again.

I often wish our minds could talk like bodies did because if they did, I believe MR. J and I could have overcome anything together.

But life doesn't work that way.

The first time I had sex, it hurt—not in the traditional sense, I suppose.

I felt a little pressure.

I was worried he wouldn't fit because he was very well endowed.

I didn't like it, but I didn't not like it either.

I liked the closeness between MR. J and me.

I liked the way he smelled.

I liked the way he watched me closely to see if I was okay.

I liked that he let his guard down.

It was one of the only times he let me in and I felt close to him.

I lost my virginity to a man whom I loved.

Even though he didn't feel the same way, I don't regret what I did. He made it special. He kissed me. He showed me he cared in his own way.

It was the first night I slept over.

We had sex again in the morning before I left, not feeling any different like they do in the movies. I didn't skip among the daisies. Or fantasize about our future children.

I just felt like me.

It got better after that, but it was never toe-curling amazing. MR. J had a great cock, but I was inexperienced, and I was always expecting... more.

It sounds harsh, but it wasn't that way. I don't want sympathy. I just want to express that sometimes what we read about in books is all bullshit.

This was real life, and I chose to accept it and embrace why MR. J came into my life.

My memory goes fuzzy after this. Even though I have the journals to read back on, I'm reading the entries through the eyes of a stranger because I don't remember that time. My mind went into self-preservation mode because this was my first taste of heartbreak.

But thinking back now, I see that my heart was broken, over and over, until one day, those cracks became permanent and never healed.

It wasn't long after that that MR. J and I "broke up." I use quotation marks because I still don't know if we were even together.

He came to my twenty-first birthday. I didn't think he would. He said he would try his best, which meant no, but when he surprised me, I thought maybe I was wrong.

Maybe he really did care.

I wish I could give you an answer, but I truly don't know if he did. Only MR. J knows that, and even if I asked him, he wouldn't answer because someone like MR. J doesn't change.

Something I soon learned four years later...

Seven

"Only Love"
Meg Mac

The blinking cursor stares at me. It may as well be flipping me off. I have tears in my eyes and an endless array of half-full coffee cups scattered around me.

I feel like shit.

I also feel fucking stupid.

MR. J isn't the hero in my story. But he never claimed to be. And that's why I feel stupid.

He never made any promises, but he also could have walked away. He knew how I felt, but he stayed. I don't understand why—a common factor when MR. J is involved.

As promised, I sent the newest chapter to O. I have an unread message from her in my inbox, but I can't read it. I feel sick to my stomach.

I hate that he still has the ability to make me feel this way.

I decide to go for a run because these heavy thoughts plague my mind and my heart. I wish I could run far away from them, but I could never run far enough for that to happen.

Once dressed, I do some quick warmups on the street and slip in my earbuds. I select some heavy metal and commence my run.

I have no idea what time it is because I was a woman possessed after I left BOSSMAN standing on the sidewalk, dick in hand. I came home, raided my blanket box, and read over the journals which I should have burned years ago.

But I couldn't.

They're a part of me.

Every single word was written in hopes I would learn to never feel that way again, but it seems I didn't learn a single thing…

With that thought in mind, I push harder, punishing myself because, in a sense, the pain makes me feel somewhat better. It's what I deserve for the things I've done.

I turn the corner, not looking where I'm going, and run straight into the arms of a stranger. He carries a guitar case and is dressed in black. His arms are covered in ink, and his shaggy, curly hair is dirty blond.

To make matters worse, he has a silver hoop in his left nostril.

"I'm sorry," he says in a swoony Irish accent, his hands planted on my biceps to stop me from face-planting.

This will not end well.

"I'm the one who's sorry," I reply when I find my voice. "I wasn't looking where I was going."

"And what about now?"

"What about now, what?" I ask, forgetting we were even talking.

He smiles, his bright blue eyes working me over. "Are you looking?"

He's Irish. Smooth as fuck. And he has a guitar. I don't stand a chance.

"Yes, I am, and I like what I see."

IRISH looks a little younger than me, but age has never been an issue. I like the person. That's what I'm attracted to. Everything else is secondary.

"And so do I."

He reaches into his back pocket and retrieves a black pen.

Gripping my wrist, he writes an address along my forearm. I tilt my head to read his neat left-handed handwriting.

"My band is playing tonight. You should come."

What I should do is stay away because musicians are nothing but bad news. However, my head nods before my brain can slap some sense into me.

"Awesome, I'll see you then."

And that's it.

He doesn't give me a time. The name of his band. Nothing.

He's simply given me the details, and the rest is up to me. His confidence is sexy, and I know I am in so much trouble.

BUNNY and ANGEL are my wingwomen because when I told them about the hot Irish musician I met, they insisted they tag along—ANGEL because she's worried he's a serial killer, and BUNNY because she wants to witness his hotness firsthand.

Best friends ever.

Nothing about the small building is special, but when we enter, that changes entirely. ANGEL yelps while BUNNY claps in excitement.

"Are you sure we're at the right place?" ANGEL asks, huddling into my side when she takes in the sight before us.

This is so typical of my life—something that would be innocent to most has to turn into a night of bondage and lots of latex. Luckily, I wore my short leather dress with red pumps.

We all take a moment to appreciate the sight of naked men and women suspended from the ceiling or tied to the red rubber walls. The patrons walk by casually, not bothered in the slightest.

"Why are the walls made of rubber?" ANGEL innocently asks while I try to contain my laughter.

"So it makes it easier to clean. At the end of the night, they can just hose it down."

"Why would they...oh," she says in understanding. "Oh!"

BUNNY bursts into laughter, clearly in her element. This is just another day in the office for us. I often wonder if I should tap into my female energy a little more, but what can I say...I like to make boys cry.

And when I notice IRISH at the bar, it seems he too could see that.

BUNNY follows my line of sight and nods in approval. "You weren't kidding. He is fucking hot."

IRISH has on black jeans and a snug black tee. Sounds simple, but this is simplicity at its best. He is tall, lean yet muscled, and clearly into some kinky shit—sounds like my type.

I can feel my cell vibrating in my purse, but I don't answer because I know who it is—BOSSMAN. He no doubt wants to discuss my work, which I sent into the wild when I returned after my run and never looked back.

I don't want to talk about it. I didn't even want to write about it.

But here I am...

This is what happens with MR. J. I know what I should be doing, but I do the complete opposite, which is why I like to exercise control in all aspects of my life, except when he is involved. He is the only thing I cannot control in my life, and I hate it.

ANGEL shrieks when a man parades past her on all fours led by a woman wearing a sexy fishnet dress. She tugs at his silver lead, unimpressed that he's taking so long. God, I love this shit.

There is a commotion onstage, and when I see IRISH take his place behind the microphone, I don't know whether I should curse the gods or thank them.

He adjusts his guitar strap as his band members take their places. The crowd seems interested enough to stop their pegging or spanking and pay attention to the four-piece band. The moment IRISH strums his guitar, I know he will be on his knees, worshipping my feet come morning.

This is exactly what I need.

Someone to replace the gorgeous face of the man who keeps creeping back into my thoughts when I erected a DO NOT ENTER sign months ago.

IRISH begins singing, and it's rock, it's grunge, and I am in love. As far as bondage clubs go, this one is fairly tame. But I know what's going on behind that red rope being manned by the Hulk Hogan wannabe is far from.

And I want in…

I like sex.

I like it rough.

I like it kinky.

Don't get me wrong. I also like the sex which melts your heart and makes you feel utterly connected to the other person you're with, but this right here, this is where my devious heart thrives.

I had "normal," and I always gravitate back to this.

ANGEL doesn't leave my side while BUNNY mingles with the patrons. I overhear her talking about sparkly dildos—God bless her.

ANGEL and I watch the band, and when I catch IRISH'S eye, I get that flutter in my stomach. You know the one I'm talking about. The one which throws all sensible train of thought out the window. But what's the worst that could happen?

Probably not the best question to ask in a place where whips and chains are readily accessible, but I am here for it.

"I read your memoir," ANGEL says into my ear to be heard over the sensual voice of IRISH. "It was really good. Do you think MR. J will read it?"

I scoff, but then I realize I haven't even considered that.

He knows I write. He knows my name. But surely, he wouldn't read a romance memoir.

My stomach suddenly drops.

"Fuck. Fuck!" I repeat, never factoring him into this equation.

"You should probably give him a heads-up. I mean, it's the nice thing to do."

"I would rather cut out my tongue and eat it," I reply, blanching at the thought of ever speaking to him again. The tongue-eating doesn't faze me, however.

"I know he doesn't deserve it. But—"

"No, he doesn't deserve it. I've been nothing but *nice* to him, and look where it's gotten me."

ANGEL nods as she's been with me since the beginning. She knows what a dumpster fire MR. J and I were together.

"I know. He doesn't even like cats." As always, she's trying to make me feel better. "We should have known he was bad news from the very beginning."

I feel remotely better for a few seconds and can't help but smile. "He doesn't not like cats; he's allergic."

She still doesn't seem pleased that cats aren't his favorite animal.

"As far as I'm concerned, it's *my* failings as well as his. I'm hoping to teach other women a lesson on men *not* to fall for. Besides, even if I did contact him, he would be too busy doing God knows what."

The more I speak, the angrier I become because I am such an idiot. He gave me every excuse under the sun as to why I was always last on his list of priorities, and instead of blowing him a kiss with my middle finger, I stayed.

ANGEL knows what is about to happen. She's seen it and knows better than to stop me. I have tried to move on from MR. J, but he has always been a huge roadblock, preventing me from moving forward.

The only way I know how to deal with this aching, hollowed void in my chest is to distract myself with something other than him.

And when the music stops, my eyes are on the prize. My Irish cookie.

I don't wait for IRISH to finish packing up his guitar. I head straight for the small stage, pushing past anyone who stands in the way. He opens his mouth when he sees me, probably about to say hi, as that's what most would do, but I'm not most, and I am only interested in his mouth doing one thing—and that's not talking.

"Come." One word holds so much promise, and IRISH springs up, forgetting about packing away his guitar as I walk toward Hulk Hogan.

The security guard nods once, stepping aside and unlatching the red rope for me. This place is all about dominance and control, and I exercise both with ease.

The long hallway is dim and the many rooms extending from the corridor aren't hidden behind doors, but rather, red velvet curtains. The loud music drowns out the nasties currently taking place, but I know what depraved and kinky acts are being performed.

I know because I plan on being the kinkiest of them all…

IRISH's boots sound against the red carpet, and all I want to do is have him kneel at my feet and obey. I need to take back some sense of power, and this is what I know.

The reason I can write with ease about the depraved is because I am one too.

My relationships have been interesting, to say the least. MR. J was the first relationship that showed me that I like things different. I've never been one to follow the norm, so it's no surprise that follows me into the bedroom or wherever I decide.

This is my body.

My choice.

And I won't be condemned for living the life I wish to lead.

And right now, I'm going to lead IRISH down a dark and dirty path. I can only hope he's ready.

A woman in a tight latex jumpsuit gestures with her head toward a parted curtain. There is no judgment here. And there shouldn't be.

I enter the small room, which is fitted with a red velvet chair and a few necessities you'd expect to find in a bondage club—handcuffs, a ball gag, and a whip. I grab the handcuffs, as they're my favorite.

IRISH stands by the now closed curtain, awaiting my command.

He watches as I take my time and sit in the chair. I cross my legs and am pleased I decided to wear my shiny red pumps as they are the only accent in the room, which is donned in nothing but black.

I eat IRISH up, from head to toe, and can't deny he is one handsome man. He ticks all my boxes in regard to looks, but when he slowly walks to where I sit and drops to his knees before me, his appeal just shot into dangerous territory.

He doesn't touch me.

He doesn't speak.

He merely awaits further command.

"Do you have any boundaries?"

He shakes his head, turned on by my dominance and humiliation. I don't know what it is about men and being humiliated. Not all of them enjoy it, but I do seem to attract the ones who do.

This is the thing about BDSM; it's about letting go. My kink is that I like to dominate, and IRISH's is that he likes to be dominated. It may be completely different in "real life," but right now, I am the motherfucking lion of this jungle.

"Take off my shoes."

When he eagerly lunges for my feet, I press my shoe into his chest—so hard, I am sure to leave an imprint of my heel into his flesh.

"Do it slow. I like to watch."

His fingers tremble as he unfastens the buckle of my first shoe, which is still pressed to his chest. He removes it and knows better than to toss it aside. He places it gently onto the floor.

"Now…lick."

A shiver racks his body as he cups my foot like he would the most precious jewel in the world and draws it to his delicious mouth. He sweeps his tongue over the top of my foot before sucking on my big toe.

My red glitter nail polish catches the lighting, making my feet look like the delectable treat they are, and IRISH cements this as he licks them slowly and with nothing but absolute desire.

This may be gross to some, but to me, this is what sex is about—exploring and pushing the boundaries in a safe, consensual environment where both parties are getting off. And right now, I plan on getting IRISH off and making it beyond messy.

"Next," I order, removing my foot mid-lick.

He does as I command and removes the other shoe.

I place my foot into his mouth and slip it in and out. The deeper I go, the further away I can bury my pain. I know it's fucked up, but this control gives me power I relinquished without even knowing it.

I'm not sure what it is about me, but I seem to attract men whose tastes run parallel to mine—all but one. And for the first time in forever, I think about the man who, once upon a time, I believed was my happily ever after.

He was the only man who wasn't my "norm."

And that is the reason I…married him.

Thoughts of BO throw me for a loop, and the only way for me to control them is to forget I exist in this world for a small moment in time.

Seeing IRISH fulfilling my every demand helps subdue the demons, but they are always hungry. They always want more.

IRISH is tall. I'd say six-three. I'm five-two.

So I have no qualms ordering him onto his stomach, arms splayed, so I can walk all over him—literally.

The imagery reminds me of a crucifixion, which seems appropriate considering the current situation I find myself in.

Once I am done leaving footprints all over his back, I ask not so nicely, "Take off your clothes."

IRISH peers up at me, those blue eyes setting me on fire because I like that he's getting off on this too. He stands and reaches behind his neck, taking off his shirt that sexy way guys do.

When I see his impressive body is inked and muscled, I know playtime is almost over because I want, and I want now.

I've never been a shy lover, and I take what I want as I thread my fingers through IRISH's long hair. He's a good kisser.

He fucks me with his tongue, and I wonder if this is reflective of how he gives head. If a man doesn't know what he's doing, and it feels like he's blindly fishing for God knows what, then the show is over…with no encore.

There is nothing worse than having someone's face in your crotch when they don't know your clit from your big toe. I hope IRISH is not one of those people.

But I wish that was enough because sex is fun, but sex with someone you love…that is an entirely different ball game.

And I know that's the reason I feel so empty after I have sex because I am missing that one aspect that changed everything for me.

This right now, there are no promises to call one another tomorrow. Or to ever see one another again. This is merely two consenting adults enjoying a purely physical connection. No strings attached.

I know this may seem weird to some, but this is my coping mechanism.

ANGEL has often asked how I can have sex this way—without the need to cuddle afterward.

Her question had me writing about it.

After sex, women release the "cuddle hormone"—oxytocin. Women produce more of this hormone, which means we are very likely to "fall in love" with a man after sex.

Men, on the other hand, release dopamine—the pleasure hormone.

So while us women are thinking about spending the rest of our lives with our Prince Charming, he is merely gloating in a post-orgasmic bliss.

We truly are different creatures when it comes to so many things.

The cuddle hormone can go to hell, for all it's ever done is give me a migraine. The confusion over whether what I feel is real or not has plagued me with every relationship I've ever been in.

This is easier.

But as I take what I want from IRISH, a longing hits hard because I wish it were different. I wish I weren't this broken. But I don't know how to give anymore without shattering the small shred of hope I cling to. Hope that there is more to life than…this.

Every relationship leaves a mark on us; lessons learned.

MR. J wasn't the only relationship that changed me forever. It seems I am drawn to complicated men and that I am my own worst enemy.

So sex without emotion is easy…it's all the stuff in between that hurts.

Eight

"Love Buzz"
Nirvana

I was the one who walked away from MR. J, something I am proud of doing.

It wasn't easy, but I did it.

Do I regret my time with MR. J?

No, I do not.

He taught me a lot. He taught me what I don't want in a partner. But on the flip side, he also set the bar for the chemistry I know can exist between two human beings.

I searched for that, but no one could compare. I was convinced I was broken.

MR. J had broken me, and I allowed it.

First loves, who needs them? But we have to experience them to realize the errors of the past. That's the only way we can learn.

I stayed away from men for a while because my heart was broken. I never thought it would heal. To get over MR. J, I had to go cold turkey.

There was no other way.

Every moment when I wasn't thinking about him, I was crying. I was a fucking mess. This went on for months.

That is how I know what I felt for MR. J was real because it hurt... so much. It still hurts, and I know that hurt will never go away.

But I learned from it and grew because a heart that hurts is a heart that works.

I never really "got over" MR. J, but when I met R, my feelings for him did fade.

R was another musician. Yes, I have a type, but it's honestly not a prerequisite. My circle of friends are in bands or are writers or artists. So that's the type of boys I fell for.

R was a beautiful man.

He was wounded. He was broken. He was just so damaged. And I wanted to fix him. To make things better for him.

And that right there is the worst thing one can do in any relationship.

R and I met at a party. He was painfully shy. He was also very drunk, something I learned was his go-to instead of dealing with the problems that plagued him every day.

We connected, but it saddens me because I can't remember our first kiss. I can't even remember how we got together. I think I repressed most of our relationship because when it was good, it was great, but when it was bad...it was fucking awful.

R was an alcoholic and a drug user. He couldn't survive the day without one or the other.

I do remember early on he wasn't heavily dependent, and those were the good times. He was an incredibly talented singer, and his voice was unlike anything I'd heard before. He was a true artist since he had pain and anguish to draw from.

He lived in an abusive, dysfunctional household. His father was an alcoholic, and his bipolar mother was deaf and lived a lonely life in her own medicated world.

His brother was a meth addict, and the arguments between him and R had been so violent that the police were often called.

And his sister was more like a mother to him, which put a massive strain on our relationship. She was a little too closely involved in...everything. I felt like there were three of us in our relationship—him and her, and then me.

But again, I stayed because I fell in love with R.

His family didn't define him. He was a good man. He was kind, and all I wanted to do was protect him from the pain he suffered in his life.

He moved out of his family home, which was the best thing he did. But that only lasted for a year or so before he fell into financial problems and had to move back.

Those times were tough.

Unlike with MR. J, I would say being with R was my first "normal" relationship. We did what every couple does—we went out for dinner, went on vacation, held hands in public, and he called me his girlfriend...all the time.

He was the first man to tell me he loved me.

But again, it's something I can't remember. I honestly don't know why.

At first, I liked all the perks that came with being in a relationship because this is what I was missing with MR. J. I was always so uncertain with him. I never knew if he was coming or going. But with R, he told me he loved me every day and would die without me.

And the sex with R was amazing.

He made me come almost every time. Sometimes, I would come so hard, I would cry. It's crazy, but he is the only man who has ever been able to do that. I don't know how he did it, but it was something I will never forget.

Now this sex, this sex was something you did read about in books.

Sex with MR. J was never like that. So this with R was exciting and new.

I think it was partly why I stayed because being with him was different. Not the sex, but the fact he was so open about his feelings. I wasn't used to that.

But that made me overlook the fact I was changing the sheets often because R wet the bed, too drunk to know otherwise. Or that he was drinking himself to death.

He knew he had a problem, but the thing about love is that it's blind. R loved me, but he loved his drugs and liquor more.

Those were the things he couldn't survive without, and because I loved blindly, I would buy him his poison when he couldn't afford it, which was most of the time. I was his enabler.

I don't wish to paint R in a terrible light because he wasn't a horrible person. He did have a rotten temper and was often violent. But I was the only one who could calm him down. He would go into a rage, punching holes in walls or breaking anything in sight, and only when I talked sense into him did he stop.

It was so dysfunctional.

I thought I was helping him, but I wasn't helping anyone. He was emotionally and verbally abusive toward me when drunk, but I excused it because when he was inebriated, that wasn't him.

But it was.

He would buy me flowers or jewelry the next day, apologizing that it was the last time and promising he would get help. But he never did.

R's issues stemmed back to his childhood and how a family member had done god-awful things to him as a child. He told his parents, but they didn't believe him. I wish I had done more, but I didn't know what to do.

One day, we were watching a movie, and R's bedroom door was kicked open so hard it actually flew off the hinges. R's brother stormed in and started beating R. I tried to intervene, but I was pushed into the wall and broke two ribs.

The fight continued down the stairs, and I didn't know why.

His dad was passed-out drunk. His mother was hiding under blankets, refusing to emerge. Their eight dogs ran around the large house, barking and riled up by the mayhem.

It was a mess.

Once they stopped fighting, I discovered R's brother was angry because R had asked him not to park his car in front of his as he couldn't get to work in the morning and didn't want to wake him because his brother had taken the keys.

That was all.

Brotherly love didn't exist here, and I think this was because they were never shown love or kindness growing up. Only hate. His sister loved R, but it almost stemmed into obsessive love. It's very hard to explain, but I often wondered if their love was a little too close for siblings.

But love has never made sense to me.

R had a broken nose, and he was beaten black and blue. He did fight back to defend himself, but R's brother was on a concoction of drugs, and it gave him the strength of a superhero.

I never felt more helpless in my life. I had never experienced this sort of behavior before. I thought something would happen after this because R's brother needed help. He was out of control. But the next day, they acted like nothing had happened.

I asked R why he would allow this type of violence, and he said, "He's my brother. What am I supposed to do?"

After everything, R still loved his brother. He thought he was helping him by ignoring the issue, but it made things so much worse.

R then started injecting methamphetamine after that. He was so talented, but he needed an escape. I tried to stop him, but he was too far gone. He was broken, and my love wasn't enough.

Things with R eventually got worse, but for a few years, I didn't think about MR. J. I had enough to deal with, and in a way, I think I got into an abusive relationship because it helped me forget about MR. J. I know that might not make any sense, but R's feelings for me were clear when MR. J's weren't.

But one day, I met a new friend. Her name was B. She was the breath of fresh air I needed, and we hit it off immediately.

One night, we were out, and I saw a poster for MR. J's band. That's all it took.

One fucking poster.

B saw my reaction, and I spilled out my history over way too many tequilas. When I was done, I knew I wanted to see MR. J again.

I was still in a relationship with R, no matter how fractured it was, but I didn't care. R wasn't seeing anyone, but drugs and alcohol were his mistresses, and he happily chose them over me every day.

He often crawled into bed with a bottle to help him sleep. Once that was finished, he would smoke joint after joint to pass out. When I expressed my anguish over this, he would call me every name under the sun and kick me out of bed.

I couldn't go home as it was late, and my parents would ask questions. So often, I would sleep in my car.

This is why I decided to see MR. J.

If things with R were happy, I would have never made that move. But I hadn't felt happiness or self-worth in a very long time.

I turned up at MR. J's show, and when he saw me, it was like mere minutes had passed, not years.

The feelings I felt returned because I realized they never left. They simply were in hibernation, and now that they were awake, they were hungry.

I relished in the way he watched me. He was nervous and fumbling over his words, which was unlike him. My cool, composed cat was flustered because I had grown.

And that fucking dimple when he smiled at me—it smacked me so hard, I barely saw straight.

He still wanted me. And I wanted him.

But I had to be smart this time.

I couldn't give him what he wanted. That was the reason we didn't work last time. I made it too easy for him.

So I left before the show was over, without saying hello or goodbye. It worked like a charm because he called me the next day.

And just like that, I fell back into the cycle that I knew would break me even harder this time.

We flirted over text but never committed to seeing one another because it was different this time. I was dating someone, and MR. J was fucking anything in a skirt.

The years made his philandering even worse. I remember countless girls thinking they were his girlfriend, very typical of falling under the spell of MR. J.

One girl, in particular, G, was a fucking piranha and made clear he was hers whenever I turned up at one of his shows. He would go home with her, so she had every right to assume they were dating. When she told me he was her boyfriend, a part of me died.

I was standing in the bathroom, putting on my lipstick, and she very loudly spoke about MR. J and his very private tattoo that only someone he is intimate with would know about.

That right there should have been my out, but I saw it as a challenge. I am an overachiever, after all.

G wasn't MR. J's usual type, but I didn't know anything about him anymore because those walls were even higher than before. He was harder this time. I don't know what happened, but he lost something.

I don't want to say innocence, but he was different. He wasn't the kind MR. J I knew. But that didn't matter because the moment he wrapped his arms around me, I was fucking lost again.

We made plans to meet up, not at his house this time, but at an apartment. We talked for a little, but we both wanted the same thing.

The moment we kissed, nothing else existed but us. It was like I had been starved for years, and only now was I being fed. We made out how we used to. My lips were bruised, my body ached.

We fooled around, and when I said those magical words, "Do you want to (fill in the blanks) my feet?" I knew I had left a mark on MR. J.

I didn't think I had, but I see that I did.

We were adults now, or so I thought.

We didn't have sex that night because he didn't have a condom. I liked that he didn't assume, but I often wonder if that was because he never used protection.

He left in the wee hours of the morning, and I instantly felt history repeating itself, and I wasn't wrong.

We often sent texts and kept in contact, but he never made plans to see me. We only saw one another when I was at a show. He wouldn't kiss me like he once did.

Everything was in secret. I was just another groupie his friends would laugh at.

His friends were not nice people.

One evening, I received a text message from MR. J's phone, telling me to meet him at an address. It was a brothel. This continued throughout the night, and I soon realized it was his friends messaging me.

When I confronted MR. J about the deplorable behavior, he said his friends did that often.

Red flag, my friends, but still, I stayed.

We saw one another on and off for a year while I was still dating R. I'm not proud of that time in my life, but I want you to see that love can be ugly as well.

I played MR. J's games as I thought that would somehow work in my favor. All it did was leave me ashamed of the person who stared back at me in the mirror.

B, my "best friend," flirted with MR. J, and when he called her, I knew it was time to get out. She told me he had asked her out and that just ruined me in ways I can't even explain. I don't know if he did, and I was too afraid to ask.

This is a time in my life that I wish I could relive because I would do every...single...thing differently.

This time, I had a love/hate relationship with MR. J. He wasn't devoted to me as he once was, which allowed me to see that this time was different. My feelings for him weren't as strong and that was because most of the time, my love for him made me sad.

The first innocent love I felt for him was gone...and only when I accepted that could I let him go. I accepted he didn't want me. He was attracted to me, but that was all I would ever be.

One year was spent trying to find a man who didn't want to be found.

For three years, I tried so fucking hard with MR. J, but it wasn't enough. I was never enough for him. I found out he had been in committed relationships since me, but he just couldn't commit to me.

I wasn't who he wanted to settle with. I was okay to fuck and do filthy things with. But to take to the movies or have dinner with, I wasn't good enough for.

It really hurt.

It still does.

To love someone who doesn't feel the same way is one of the worst feelings in the world. All I could think was, what's wrong with me?

I would have done anything for MR. J, and that was the problem—I lost myself by trying to "save" him.

I never wanted to play his games. I just wanted him. But I was the one always making an effort. I was the one who wanted to see him while he seemed okay with not seeing me.

That isn't love. That's the complete opposite of what love entails.

I left both R and MR. J, as both were as toxic as the other. I left a message on MR. J's voicemail because that's all he deserved.

The message simply said, "You've been made redundant."

And then, I swore off men...that was until I met BO.

It wasn't the best time to be meeting anyone, but love doesn't give a damn if you're ready or not. It throws you into the deep end, expecting you to know how to swim.

I didn't...but I soon learned how.

Nine

"Love Her Madly"
The Doors

I decide to beat BOSSMAN to it and go to work before he pounds on my door.

After IRISH and I went our separate ways, I had the sudden urge to write. It's no lie, I am drawn to complicated men, and as I was fucking IRISH, it got me thinking about the man after MR. J.

He was by far the most wounded man I have ever dated. With R, I know his upbringing shaped him into the man he grew into. He suffered from depression because of not dealing with his past, and his dependency on alcohol was a way to cope with everything.

He was devastated when I broke up with him. He chased me hard, but it was too late. The feelings were no longer there. His pleas became desperate, and the police needed to intervene. It was a horrible end to our love.

I often wonder if R was a Band-Aid to help close over a wound that needed a thousand stitches instead.

I read over some journals, surprised that I couldn't recall living through the events I had.

When something traumatic happens, we often deal with it at the time, then push aside those memories, hoping to never reopen those wounds again. That's how I feel with R.

My entire relationship with him was a sore and it never healed.

The thing about hindsight is that it's useless. I can't go back, only forward, hoping to learn something from my mistakes. I've not spoken to R since we broke up.

And I like to keep it that way.

After writing about him, I did feel somewhat better as he often feels like the forgotten relationship, when, in reality, he was a very important part in shaping who I've become.

But he's not someone I wish to see again.

After sending the chapter to BOSSMAN, I showered and passed out.

I woke a few hours later, deciding to bite the bullet and go see him.

And alas…here I am.

The moment the elevator doors part, I know every person in the office has read my chapter. I knew this piece would either make me the hero or villain because I did cheat, no matter how you look at it.

Regardless of the circumstances, I was still in a relationship with R when I made the choice to pursue MR. J—again.

I rub over my chest because my heart tingles—heartburn or heartache? The jury is still out on that one.

When I see O behind her desk, tears instantly spring to her eyes as she jumps up from her seat. "I loved it so much," she says, throwing her arms around me.

I stand rigid, arms by my sides because I honestly don't know what to do. Safe to say she sees me as the hero, but when PL walks past us, nose in the air, it's clear she doesn't share the same sentiment.

And this is why I never wanted to air my dirty laundry.

It's not paved with unrealistic expectations. It's ruthless, unfair, and at times, bordering on insanity, but that's what life is about because I don't do boring.

Well, not anymore, anyway.

I manage to subtly maneuver out from O's grip and smile because thank you seems kind of weird to say when someone is bawling their eyes out over something you did. I leave her as she pulls out handfuls of tissues from the box behind her desk.

I don't even ask if BOSSMAN is free when I open his door and let myself in. He's on the phone, so I take a look around his office. He has literary awards displayed on the shelf, which I never took notice of before. I run my finger over the glass, impressed, but of course, I would never let BOSSMAN know.

I wonder why he pushed so hard for me to write this memoir. I mean, I don't see it as anything special. Just the life of a girl who has experienced some crazy things. My life seems to be full of drama, but as I turn to look at BOSSMAN, who watches me closely, and I heat from head to toe, I wonder if maybe I *am* the drama.

He hangs up but doesn't speak.

He rocks backward and forward in his leather seat, his long fingers steepled against his mouth, deep in thought. This would be the time I would drop a smart-ass comment, but I've suddenly forgotten how to speak.

The morning sun beaming behind him only emphasizes his broad shoulders beneath that fitted white shirt. I have come to terms with the fact that I am attracted to BOSSMAN.

I don't know when this happened, but I want it to stop.

He is smug and annoying, and I don't even really like him...which seems to make no difference when he stands to his full six-three height, and I envision making out with that chiseled face.

"So that was some piece."

His evasiveness slaps some sense into me. "Is that a good or bad thing? Not that I care about your opinion," I add sharply.

A smirk tugs at that stupid, sexy mouth. "Well, considering I just got off the phone with *Love Your Life* magazine, I'd say it's a good thing."

"Why are they calling *you*?" I can't keep the distaste from my tone because why is the chicest magazine in New York calling him?

A laugh rumbles from BOSSMAN, not at all offended by my insult—shame, that. "They want to run an exposé on you."

It's my turn to laugh this time. But I realize BOSSMAN is serious when he doesn't join in with the laughter. "What's going on?"

BOSSMAN rounds his desk and leans against it, crossing his arms and ankles. Those black pants should be illegal as they cling to all the right parts, which has me forgetting that I'm supposed to hate him.

"I was undecided about publishing your chapter today. But I'm glad that I did. It showed that love comes in many different forms. This is the first piece of yours where we have received mixed reviews. Some good. Some bad."

I shrug, as I knew it would ruffle some feathers.

"But the consensus is they want more. I don't know what it is, but this has struck a chord with so many—globally. I mean, it's not even well written."

"Fuck you," I chime in, not appreciating him attacking my work.

But he ignores me.

"But I think that's why it's doing so well. It's so…raw. People can relate as they are you. Most people have had their hearts broken or broken hearts. They've cheated or been cheated on. The way you write, there is no judgment, merely a story about a woman baring her soul.

"You knew the repercussions when you wrote that last night. You knew that some would see you as a martyr while others would crucify you. You went back to the one man you should have stayed away from.

"But in reality, your curiosity got the better of you because I know you like a challenge."

I hate that he's right.

"And that now you've introduced your ex-husband, BO...you know they want more."

I swallow past the lump in my throat.

I knew what would happen when writing about BO.

But there is no way I can write about my life without including the man who was in it for over a decade. I try not to have any regrets in my life, but he is one. I don't know what I would have done differently; I just know I would have done things differently with him.

"He's your Achilles' heel," BOSSMAN says, and it's not a question. He can read the turmoil on my face.

"You don't know what you're talking about." But it's weak.

When I started writing for BOSSMAN, it was about five years into my marriage. I kept business and personal life separate. It was easier that way.

But now, here I am, venting for all to see.

"You know what I find extremely interesting? The fact you were married for so long, yet I have a feeling MR. J was the one you really wanted all along. He was the one who got away, so to speak."

"Well, isn't it lucky I don't care what you think?"

This conversation needs to end. Now.

"What is it about him? I mean, you're funny, incredibly smart, and infuriatingly beautiful." The words are out before he can stop himself, but it doesn't seem like he wants to take them back.

"Thanks. I think," I reply, needing to say something before I ponder too closely on what he just said.

"Why does he have this...hold over you?"

I ask myself this every single day, and it would be so much easier if I could forget him. But I can't. No matter how hard I try.

"You need to let this go. He isn't good for you."

"And you need to stop thinking you can tell me what to do. Or what is good for me," I snap, not appreciating his tone.

"I know that he's a selfish idiot who doesn't want you but can't seem to leave you alone."

Of course, he knows this because he's read my journals. He knows what's coming, and he knows it won't be pretty.

"That's not entirely true," I counter because it runs both ways.

Not talking to him has been a new form of hell, but I have to try. I keep making the same mistakes over and over again. But when it comes to him, I never seem to learn.

No matter how badly it hurts, I keep coming back for more.

"Which part?" BOSSMAN questions, and I suddenly don't like that he seems to think he's some expert about my life.

The air between us becomes heated, and I know shit is about to go down.

I storm toward him, ignoring his personal space when I get into his. "Don't you dare think you know anything about me!" I exclaim, inches from his face, shaking in rage. "You may have read the best-of, but you know nothing about me.

"So fuck you and your smug—"

He doesn't give me a chance to finish because he does something that I would have never guessed, not in a million years.

He slams his mouth against mine, robbing me of words and air.

For a split second, I think I'm dreaming, but when BOSSMAN wraps his hand around my waist and presses me against his warm, hard chest, I know that this is really happening. And that I really am in fucking trouble.

I need this to stop, but when BOSSMAN parts my mouth with his tongue and slips it into mine, I know stopping will be impossible. He kisses me hard, almost with an edge of anger, and I like his aggression.

I tug at his hair, taking great pleasure in messing up his perfect locks, which feel just as divine as they look.

He growls—yes, growls—into my mouth, only kissing me harder and deeper. He shows no mercy, and I take everything he gives. He bites my bottom lip. He sucks on my tongue. He kisses me so passionately I almost forget to breathe.

Everything he does feels incredible when it shouldn't—and that's why it does. I am attracted to the unattainable and complicated because I like a challenge, just like BOSSMAN said.

He towers over me, and I can't lie, I like it. I like that I know he could hurt me, though I know he won't. I never thought I would be comfortable handing over the reins, but here I am going from dominant to submissive all because BOSSMAN's tongue is mouth fucking me in ways that would have me clawing at his shirt, demanding more.

And more he gives me when he lifts the hem of my dress, bypasses my underwear, and sinks a finger into my sex. He doesn't stop kissing me and begins fucking me with his finger in sync with his tongue.

I buck my hips because everywhere he touches feels like nothing before. I know it's because this is new and unfamiliar, but if not careful, I could become addicted to this taste.

Opening my legs wider, BOSSMAN reads my needs clearly and adds another finger. I moan into his mouth and sag forward, but he holds me up.

He is everywhere.

I am swimming in his smell.

In him.

I attempt to rub over his erection, but he nudges my hand away. I'm too far gone to protest.

We continue kissing passionately, with his fingers working me into a heaving, needy mess. I usually can't get off this way, but I'm beginning to think that's because I've never had BOSSMAN's fingers inside me.

"Are you going to write about this?"

His cockiness should be a turn-off, but it's not.

"You wish." I gasp when he circles his thumb over my throbbing clit. "You're merely something to pass the time."

"Oh, in that case…" He thrusts his fingers deeper and quicker, the rhythm so fast I feel it pulsate all the way to my toes.

I like that he doesn't break our kiss.

This could be totally sordid, but it's not because this isn't a casual fling. BOSSMAN has felt this spark between us too, and now that it's been set on fire, I'm afraid of what comes next.

I'm so incredibly turned on, and I hate that BOSSMAN can feel it. He knows he is the cause of me being unable to see straight. But he wants me to beg.

Each time he works me up to the point of almost coming, he slows down or eases the pressure against my clit.

Bastard.

If I wasn't so wound up, I would walk away.

But I can't.

I want to come, and I want it to be by, and in, BOSSMAN's hand.

I bite his tongue before sucking it into my mouth. He isn't the only one who can play this game. When he sinks his fingers into me, I clench my muscles and thank my Kegel exercises when he hisses into my mouth.

I rub against his body, circling his mouth with my tongue, and place my hand against his, coaxing him to go in deeper. "Make me come."

It's an order, and BOSSMAN groans.

With my hand affixed to his, I control the movement of how I like to get off. I handed over the reins for a few moments, but I'm back in the driver's seat as I use his fingers to how I please.

BOSSMAN is good with his fingers and mouth, but that's not the thing that gets me hot—the fact he maintains eye contact with me, watching me just as closely as I watch him, is what has me shifting my hips and demanding more.

"He's a fucking fool," he breathes against my mouth.

I don't know who he's referring to, but I honestly don't care because the only thing I care about is coming.

"Shh, stop talking," I pant, gripping his hair and yanking hard. "It's hard to imagine someone else."

BOSSMAN chuckles. "No one else can make you come this way, baby."

And that's when I slam the brakes on because that term of endearment, it just reminds me of him—the bastard who not only ruined my life, he's now ruining my orgasm as well.

"I can't," I say, my body giving me the middle finger as I untangle myself from BOSSMAN.

He senses my shift and doesn't say a word as I discreetly rearrange my clothes.

I can't even look at him, which is ironic, seeing as I had no issues with his hands down my pants five seconds ago.

I need help.

He clears his throat and takes a seat behind his desk, busying himself on his computer. If this isn't fifty shades of awkward, then I don't know what is.

"I'll email you the details for the *Love Your Life* gig. They want to take pictures, do interviews, and have a day-in-the-life kind of deal."

"They have no idea what they're in for," I quip, trying to lighten the mood. It doesn't work.

"Indeed." That's BOSSMAN's clipped response as he continues typing, and I can't help but think those long fingers were inside me seconds ago, and I liked it—a lot.

Now is the time to leave with some shred of dignity left. "I'll work on the next chapter. That one might take a little longer."

Reason being I have to open up some old wounds which are going to hurt like a bitch.

BOSSMAN merely nods.

I don't know why his detachment bothers me. I was the one who told him to stop.

And this is why I can't do relationships.

Anyone who tells you it gets easier or that you'll get your shit together when you're an adult is a fucking liar.

"Okay, well, see ya."

BOSSMAN grunts.

The moment I leave his office, I lean against the door and take three deep breaths. Why do I feel so…shitty? It's not like I even like BOSSMAN to care enough about his feelings, but that's clearly a lie.

I don't know when this happened, but it needs to stop now.

Hunting through my bag, I eventually find my cell under six shades of red lipsticks and reason with myself as to why messaging MR. J is a very bad idea.

This bastard has ruined me. He deserves an earful. But then I remember what happens when we talk. I forget everything else exists and fall back into bad habits that I wish I could kick.

Sighing, I toss my phone back into my bag, thankfully listening to sanity. "Not today, Satan."

I've met my people quota for the week, so I decide to go home and write. Not my memoir, but rather, write in my journal about what a fucking idiot I am.

When a knock sounds at my door, I think two things—who the fuck is at my door, and am I wearing pants?

Peering down, I'm thankful I remembered to dress after I came home and scrubbed my skin raw before collapsing face down on the bed, unbelieving BOSSMAN had his hands all up in my bits, and I liked it.

Groaning, I decide to join the land of the living because whoever is pounding on my door won't go away. I quickly tuck my journal under my pillow as I do not want anyone reading about my encounter with BOSSMAN today.

I hate that my body still tingles thinking about his touch.

I open the door, ready to tell whoever it is to go away, but when I see the faces of my two best friends, I smile because it's like they could smell my woes a mile away.

"We brought pizza!" ANGEL says, waving two boxes as proof that they didn't just drop over to make sure I wasn't rocking in a corner somewhere, crying into my dairy-free gallon of ice cream.

I step aside and let them in.

BUNNY stops and looks at me with her lips pursed. She so knows. "You so fucked your boss."

ANGEL's mouth drops open, stunned. "BUNNY!" she scolds. "Z knows better than to—"

But she soon stops when she reads the guilt all over my face.

This is one of the many things I love about ANGEL—she is the first person to defend my honor, even when I've fucked up to biblical proportions.

"I didn't fuck him," I state, and ANGEL's shoulders sag in relief. That's short-lived, however, when I add, "But he fucked me with his fingers and tongue."

ANGEL pales while BUNNY waves imaginary pom-poms in the air.

"Luckily, I brought this." BUNNY walks into the kitchen and hunts for the wine opener as she senses she will need a glass before I divulge all the sordid details.

I slump onto my couch, not even sure where to start because I don't even know how it happened. ANGEL opens the pizza box, and I smile when I see she got me my favorite—vegan on a gluten-free base.

"Here."

I accept the slice of pizza, and when BUNNY sits across from me in the La-Z-Boy, eyebrow raised, I stuff half of it into my mouth. Hopefully, I'll choke on it and won't be forced to tell them what went down today.

No such luck, however.

"So..." BUNNY says, passing out plates.

"So..." I repeat after BUNNY, so wishing we could discuss anything but this.

"Cut the bullshit. I want to know everything."

I look over at ANGEL, who is chewing her pizza slowly. "You may want to cover your ears."

A snort gets caught in BUNNY's throat while ANGEL places the slice of pizza onto the plate, knowing it's best to listen to this tale without food in her mouth since it's likely to go down the wrong way.

"I went to see BOSSMAN, and we were talking about my memoir. He said *Love Your Life* magazine wants to do an exposé on me."

"No shit," BUNNY says, shaking her head in awe. "Congratulations. That's fucking awesome. Now stop stalling."

I can't help but laugh at her candor. "One minute, we were talking, and he was being his usual annoying self. And then the next…talking was replaced with kissing, leading to other things."

BUNNY looks like all her Christmases have come at once, while ANGEL looks like I just told her Santa isn't real.

"Did you?" BUNNY uses her hands to coax me along while I wonder if saying it aloud will sound as shitty as it felt.

"No." Yup. It felt even shittier.

"What?" BUNNY's shock is written all over her face. "I thought he'd know his way around. I mean, he *is* a cocky jerk which means he should be dynamite in bed."

"That's not it," I correct, feeling my cheeks flush. "I stopped him before he could finish."

"Why in the ever-loving fuck would you do that?" BUNNY asks while ANGEL shakes her head, understanding my dilemma. "Oh, for fuck's sake. Not this fucker again."

I sigh, wishing I wasn't so transparent…and pathetic.

"Z, why? Why are you letting him ruin your life?"

And that's the million-dollar question.

I shrug because I got nothing. "He isn't the one ruining my life. I am. I wish I could forget him. But my heart is a sadistic whore."

"I guess now isn't a good time to tell you BO has been posting very publicly about how happy he is. I think it's only time before he gets engaged. They're living together."

ANGEL closes her eyes and slaps her forehead, while I stare at BUNNY like she just recited the alphabet in Chinese. "Engaged to another person?"

"No, a goat. Of course, another person," she replies while I suddenly regret stuffing half a slice of pizza down my throat as it's about to come back up.

I don't know how to feel. Getting engaged means he's moving on…with another person. While here I am, obsessing over an ex who doesn't give a fuck and being fingered by my boss, whom I hate, in his office.

Good times.

"I thought you'd be relieved?"

"I am," I reply because I guess I am.

There is no love lost between us because he's the one who left, but it's still a hard pill to swallow because while he is getting on with his life, I feel like I haven't even passed GO.

"Who is it?"

"Why does it matter?" BUNNY asks, but I know that's code for I don't want to know.

Which is why I press.

"Who?" This time, I direct my question at ANGEL, who confirms it's as bad as I suspect when she folds the pizza in half and shoves it into her mouth.

I reach for my cell off the coffee table because if my friends won't tell me, social media will.

"I really miss the days when someone would go away, and you'd never see a scrap of them again," BUNNY says with a sigh.

"That can still happen," I reply blankly, scrolling through Facebook. "If we kill them and dissolve their bodies in a vat of acid."

I prepare myself for anything; well, almost anything because when I see the smiling faces of BO and his new girlfriend, I realize I prepared for anything but that.

"No fucking way," I gasp, shaking my head, convinced I've been sent to hell to repent for the sins I committed. And there are many.

BUNNY gives me a sympathetic smile while I refrain from gouging out my eyeballs because nothing will ever rid my brain of the memory of seeing my ex-husband with some blonde bimbo. Their exchanges of 'babe,' 'you give me fireworks,' combining their names to make a cute wittle acronym and other disgusting, unoriginal soppy bullshit, makes me want to hurl.

Her name is LARS—polar opposite to me. Blonde. Gym junkie. And from her posts, uncouth and probably loves NASCAR as much as him.

"Z, don't," BUNNY says, but it's too late. I've fallen down the rabbit hole they call social media.

I've been told by friends and family who still follow BO what he's been up to. But actually seeing it, I don't know how to feel.

He is still a conceited gym junkie who thinks he will be TikTok famous, judging by his lame videos. I have no idea who this man is because who I see is a stranger.

I am not attracted to any part of him in any way, shape, or form. I literally feel nothing. Maybe I really am broken.

His profile photo is a shot taken by LARS, and the caption is about how he should be a model. The comments reveal LARS was the author of this post, which means she has access to his socials.

He wouldn't even let me look at his phone, and his new beau knows his Facebook password.

Wow, she must have a magical vagina to convince the control freak to surrender his password to her.

When I get to one video, however, I am angered and wounded in the same breath. It's a photo of him when we were married, which then morphs into him now, the happier, more improved version according to his post, which says, "It's amazing what happens when you're happy."

I scroll through his previous posts and see LARS has commented on every single one when we were still "happily" married. It's not hard to see where this is going.

I've seen enough.

"That motherfucker," I curse under my breath. "So if he wasn't happy when we were together, why did he stay? This is just fucking insulting."

"You're pissed off?" BUNNY asks, but it's more a statement than a question.

I don't know what I am.

"I guess it's just a shock, that's all. I mean, it's been over for years. Someone once told me, by the time a person ends a relationship, they've checked out months, even years prior. And in my case, that's very true. But I guess it's just… why her?"

"Does it matter who she is?" ANGEL asks, reaching for a bottle of water and offering it to me.

I must look like I'm seconds away from bursting into tears, and I don't even know why. "No, it doesn't, but I guess it's just hard to accept he would love someone so quickly. I mean, I knew—"

But I don't finish that sentence because I know if I do, I will definitely cry.

I don't know what this is, but I know the next thing I write will likely break me.

BUNNY wisely said that even though the marriage ended, I would still be sad. At the time, I scoffed and thought the only thing I would be sad about was the fact it didn't end sooner.

But she's right.

This is an end of a chapter, so to speak.

Looking at the picture of BO and LARS, I don't feel jealousy or sadness. I feel closure…and it's what'll help me write the hardest thing of my life.

Ten

"Love at First Feel"
AC/DC

My ex-husband is a bastard.

I wish I could dazzle you with eloquent words and phrases, but I can't, and that's because BO is a fucking bastard. He left me when I needed him the most. In sickness and in health, my left foot.

He left the moment things got rough. I asked for space, and his space equated to him finding space in someone's vagina.

I had the balls to do what he couldn't because...sing it with me...HE'S A FUCKING BASTARD.

I guess, in the end, my feelings for him were stronger than his were for me because I never gave up. I wanted to fight, but when the going got tough, he ran into the arms of another, leaving me heartbroken as well as broke—period.

He was only nice to me while waiting for his money, and the moment he got it, it was like I didn't exist. He told me he'd fight for us when I asked for space to sort out my head. But it was all lies. He gave up and moved on to some blonde who likes to stalk my socials.

Yes, LARS, I see you.

You can have him. But just remember me when looking at the ink on his leg (regardless of the new addition of a sunflower). Tattoos are forever. But love clearly is not.

After so many years together, his one-word response spoke volumes. I deserved more than that. And I would never treat him that way. But he didn't even have the decency to reply when I all but bled in one final message, asking him to give us another chance.

If this is what love is, then it can fuck right off and leave me alone.

He played the victim because I was the one who spoke up. He gaslighted me, as he never had any intention of getting back together. He made me feel horrible for needing space. All the while, he was seeing other women because BO can never be single.

We weren't divorced. We weren't even separated. We didn't even have the talk that things were over.

All I did was ask for space, and he decided space meant it was okay to fuck another woman. And then he said he had the "decency" to tell me this in case I saw it online because he took her on a lovely little holiday while I was crying my eyes out over what went wrong.

And you want to know the kicker—he told me this the moment he signed a separation agreement I had drawn up in his favor as I felt sorry for him. I felt sorry for him because he gave me some sob story about how he was doing it tough, living with his...parents...in their very cushy home where, no doubt, his mom made his bed and did his laundry.

Oh, cue the violins.

I signed away more than he deserved because I didn't owe him anything until the divorce, but like an idiot, I tried to make his life easier, and in return, the moment he signed on the dotted line, he told me he was seeing someone.

A week later, he was moving his things out of my house.

And to the day, a year and a day to be precise that he left, that is when I was served my divorce papers. It took me a while to sign because regardless of what happened, BO was a big part of my life. A month later, BO texts and bluntly demands I send the papers back so he can skip among the sunflowers with LARS it seems.

Fuck you very much.

I've cried so many tears over this. I think I always will. But I know in my heart of hearts that I tried...I really fucking tried to make things work. But he gave up because that's the thing about love...just because you love relentlessly, that doesn't mean it has to love you back.

Let's cut back to "happier" times...

I met BO through friends, and yes, he was another musician. Thankfully, not a lead singer this time.

He was really sweet, so damn tall, and had beautiful blue eyes.

R didn't take the breakup well, and BO really helped me through it.

I told BO about what I had done with MR. J because there was something different about BO. He knew what he wanted, and that was me. There were no games with BO.

He was independent, worked a steady job, and had a large circle of friends, friends he introduced me to immediately. He was the man all the girls wanted because he was kind as well as attractive—a winning combination.

R eventually accepted it was over between us, but he turned stalker for a few months after we broke up.

I didn't understand why the love I chose thus far was so destructive. Most of my friends were in steady, committed relationships, while I often wondered what was wrong with me.

Why did I fall in love with men who drove me crazy—and not in a good way?

Love ♡ Hard

MR. J didn't just break me this time, he destroyed me. I was angry, and BO was the one who suffered because looking back, I see I lost an innocence within myself. I used to believe everyone was good, or at least, tried to be good, but love taught me that isn't the case.

BO and I took things slow.

He lived about two hours away from me, which was what made things work between us. I didn't want to be smothered after R, but on the flip side, I didn't want to be abandoned either like MR. J had done to me.

I wanted a happy medium, and I found that with BO.

We took things slow because I was wounded. Sometimes, I believed beyond repair. But the more time I spent with BO, the more I saw that I needed time to heal.

I had spent several years with toxic men. So I didn't know any different. I expected BO to fly into a rage at times or want to fuck my friends, but he never did that. But BO wasn't an angel either.

He stopped partying and being a fuckboy before he met me, and when I asked why, he said he wanted to be a better man for me.

He confessed he had seen me at gigs and was instantly intrigued. I didn't even know he existed, and here he was, wanting to better himself for a woman he'd never met.

I want you to see that we aren't aware of the impact we have on the world most of the time, and I think that unguarded innocence is a beautiful thing.

We got to know one another, and six months later, we bought a house together.

I know it may seem fast, but after the hell I had been through, BO made me feel safe. Something I never felt in my previous relationships.

And I soon learned that love and safety go hand in hand.

Everything was going great. BO and I made our home a safe place filled with animals and love. He worked hard and never complained when

I worked late at night, finishing the piece I was writing for whatever freelance magazine I was working for.

I wanted to write romance because I still believed in love. BO was proof that it existed. I was just looking in all the wrong places for it.

BO loved and supported me. So it came as no surprise when I said yes when he proposed.

I want to add a little sidenote here about another love I experienced in my life, and that was with my Chihuahua, BW.

BW played an important part in this proposal because BO tied the ring to his collar and asked me to marry him that way. I was so emotional that BW was involved because BW was possibly the love of my life—in K9 form, of course.

I adopted him when he was one from a shelter. He had been returned three times. He was on death row. The moment I saw him, it was literal love at first sight. He stayed by my side for eighteen years. He never left me. Even when I was up at all hours of the night writing, he'd sleep by my feet until I carried him to bed.

If that isn't true love, then I don't know what is.

The day he died, he died in my arms, and I can honestly say the pain was as profound as losing my father.

A day doesn't pass me by that I don't think of my baby boy. His love was selfless because he lived for me and I for him. For me, my animals are as important to me as people are. I also wanted to mention my baby girl, DCA—the German shepherd who changed my life. I know you and BW are hanging out together now, barking at the mailman in doggy heaven.

For the first time in my life, I was happy, and that was thanks to BO. So it shouldn't surprise you when I say, out of the blue, MR. J sent me a text. It was like he could sense this massive shift in my life and wanted to remind me he still existed even though I had tried very hard to forget him.

I hadn't heard from him in over a year, and for him to text me was unheard of. I sat on it for a little while, unsure what to do.

The text simply said I miss you.

Again, something he never said—ever.

I wanted to ignore him. I should have. But I didn't.

I texted him back.

My message was very cordial. I wanted to keep it brief and not fall back into old habits.

At first, he was polite, but I know MR. J. He was testing the waters. He asked if I was seeing anyone. I said yes. I didn't ask him if he was because I honestly didn't care. It was the first time in my life when I actually didn't want to talk to him.

He began to flirt and reminisce, and that was when I took my power back. He had three years to tell me he missed me. Three fucking years to give me some sort of answer to how he felt about me.

He was too late.

And I told him that with a reply that said, "Thanks for the memories... because that's all you'll ever have." He chases hard when he wants something, and I know he didn't want me enough to chase.

And I deleted his number.

If you're asking why I didn't block him, the answer is because I actually knew MR. J better than I thought I did.

I knew he wouldn't chase me. That isn't his style.

And that was the last time I heard from MR. J...well, for a little while anyway.

BO and I got married a year and a half later. It was a beautiful, small ceremony. My parents loved him, especially my dad. They bonded over everything.

Life was good.

My career took off, and I began writing for elite romance magazines, making a name for myself with my candid topics. I was a full-time writer. My dream come true.

BO and I tried to have children for many years, but it just never happened. I often wonder if this was the reason for our demise. When I asked him if he wanted kids, he would say it was up to me. Hardly the response one wants from their spouse, especially someone who is a control freak because it's so noncommittal.

But to have kids, you had to have sex, and I would rather poke out my eyes with a fork than engage in that two-second activity with BO.

We didn't see one another a lot as I was writing, and BO worked late hours, but we made it work. We spent the weekends together, going to the beach to walk the dogs or taking road trips. We were a "normal" couple, and for a while, it was enough.

BO and I were very different in how we did things.

I was carefree and spontaneous, which drove BO mad. He liked structure. If we were a minute late anywhere, he would be incredibly grumpy for the day. He wanted to stick to a schedule while I didn't.

I was the main breadwinner in the family, and at first, we split the bills, groceries, et cetera...but after a while, BO assumed because I was making more money, I should be paying for most things. I didn't mind because it was our home, but when BO started spending his money on sports paraphernalia and things he didn't need, I started to feel like I was being taken for a ride.

He never paid for dinner or movies. He expected me to pay for everything.

Our bank accounts were separate, so the money I used was money I earned.

I didn't say anything because I loved BO. He was my husband, and marriage is about sharing. I did wonder where BO's money went because he never seemed to have any.

We didn't fight, however. He treated me with love and respect, so I overlooked this small oversight because money comes and goes. But love, true love doesn't.

However, true love shouldn't leave you with a hole in your chest.

It was two days before Christmas, and I went to the store to buy ingredients for a carrot cake. I decided to check the PO box beforehand. There was a letter addressed to me.

The swirly handwriting on the front of the envelope had me guessing the sender was female.

I opened it and simply stared at the piece of paper in my hands because staring back at me was a photocopied picture of BO and a blonde woman I had never seen before.

The letter was sent anonymously by someone from BO's work.

This was his coworker, and they were having an affair.

It goes without saying the carrot cake went unmade.

I went home and read the letter countless times. It said they had been sleeping with one another for months and that the company was rife with rumors. I thought back on BO's behavior.

Did I miss something?

Sex between us was really passionate and frequent at first. The honeymoon phase was rampant for us. But there was one thing I never could achieve with BO: he could never make me come.

He never gave me oral sex, as it was something he didn't like. I'm not a huge fan of it because most men have no idea what they're doing down there. But he didn't even attempt it, not even once, because it was something he didn't enjoy.

Sex was frequent, but I just could never get there.

Sad, but true.

But that didn't matter because everything else between us was so great. I was willing to sacrifice the sexual spark because I had that with MR. J, and look where that got me because unlike my husband, MR. J made me come every single time.

I had the sex without love, and now, I had the love without sex, and I wondered if maybe that wasn't enough for BO.

Is that why he cheated?

When he came home, I showed him the letter, looking for any signs of deceit. All I saw was shock.

He explained she was someone he worked with and that they were just friends.

I remembered he went to a birthday party a few weeks back. He confessed it was hers, and he stayed at her house—something he failed to mention.

He said others also stayed over, but I suddenly felt uneasy. Was my stable marriage not so stable after all?

For weeks, I had received calls from a private number, but they would never leave a message. I didn't think much of it, but when my phone rang as I was talking to BO, I just knew it was her.

She was Scottish. And she was the girl in the photo.

I knew she was the one who sent the letter even though she claimed it wasn't her. She detailed many intimate details about BO that no one should know. She said she had a miscarriage. It was BO's. We spoke for over an hour, and during that time, I switched back and forth, back and forth.

I thought BO was lying.

I thought BO was telling me the truth.

I just didn't know.

How could you do that to someone you loved?

I ended the call, convinced BO had cheated. I asked him to explain his side. And he did.

He said she asked lots of questions and stalked his social media. I needed time.

The one thing SCOTTISH did say was to check BO's phone bills. She gave me her number. When he was at work, I checked and was horrified to see how many times he texted and called her throughout the day. This went on for months.

Other phone bills, I couldn't find. They were the dates SCOTTISH told me that he texted her late at night, telling her he was frustrated because we weren't having regular sex. I was troubled he told SCOTTISH something so personal as he never mentioned it to me.

She just knew too much, and personal things which no man should ever share with another woman if they were merely work colleagues.

A few days later, she sent an email with more damning evidence. I didn't understand why a woman would go to this much trouble if she wasn't a woman scorned.

That was the day I questioned love...again.

Love had done nothing but coax me into making bad decisions. I thought love conquered all, but love seemed to be the problem and not the solution.

I asked BO to leave. He didn't.

He pushed and pushed and had an answer for everything. I was tired. My heart hurt. The possibility of being screwed over by love again had me slowly backing down, and eventually, I believed BO.

Don't shake your head at me. I know what you're thinking.

But without physical proof, I decided to believe my husband.

When I asked BO's work colleagues, they all played dumb. No one wanted to get involved. I had to trust my gut. I had to trust love.

And that's what I did.

We moved on, but it always, always played at the back of my mind. If faced with the same situation now, what would I do? Would I make the same choice?

The answer is no. I would have left him because I believe that he did all the things SCOTTISH said he did. Why would she go to the effort she did? She was a lover scorned.

It's ironic, he used to tell me he disliked blondes. But all the "other women" in his life have/are blonde. BO is a liar, and I was a lovestruck fool for not seeing it sooner.

I was a fool for doing many things like rolling over when it's not in my nature to submit. But I did with him. Something simple as buying smooth peanut butter instead of crunchy reminded me that it was always BO's way.

Years passed, and we moved closer to my parents as my father was diagnosed with cancer. It was the hardest time of my life. The man who had taught me about love withered away before my eyes. But he smiled until the very end.

During one of the last talks we had, he held my hand and said, "Never make apologies for who you are. Never be afraid because being afraid stops you from taking risks, and I taught you better than that."

He then said, "Never rely on a man to make you happy because they come and go, but you have to live with yourself until the day you die. Never forget who you are."

He passed away two days later.

The love I felt for my father was something beautiful. He loved me no matter what, and that is how love should be.

BO was there when my dad died because they were very close. We had been married for many years, and he was such a great support to me during that time. I felt like my entire life had just stopped. I couldn't believe he was gone, but I had to be strong for my mom and family.

I didn't grieve how I should have.

There isn't a right way to deal with death, but I know I didn't process what happened because soon after, things for me changed.

I started to change.

On the outside, I was smiling, but on the inside, I was clawing at my skin, desperate to break free from this pain, this sadness, this... nothingness.

But I continued living because that's what we are trained to do—we live, or we at least try.

I went about my every day like normal. I looked like I was coping, but I wasn't.

The only real love I felt had been snatched out from under me, and instead of things getting better, they got worse.

Six months later, I went overseas to see a friend, but I now see that was the start of my transformation—like a butterfly, I suppose.

Things with BO were crumbling, but neither of us said anything. We had grown comfortable after being together for such a long time.

And that was when I made a friend who soon became my soulmate.

BUNNY was unlike anyone I had ever met before.

I had many friends throughout my life, but none of them stayed. They were there for a season, not a reason, unlike BUNNY. I met BUNNY, and she changed everything.

She allowed me to see beauty in things that most would not see. She too was wounded as love had hurt her in cruel ways. Love bonded us, and it allowed me to see that love does come in many different shapes and sizes.

I loved BUNNY with all of my heart because I felt like I had found something I didn't even know I was looking for.

We laughed. We cried. We did everything together. BUNNY was my saving grace.

By this time, I realized I was spending a lot of time with her because I didn't want to be at home. BO was becoming jealous, irritable, and selfish. However, I now see that he always was.

He too felt the shift between us but didn't address it. Because why would he?

We had a very comfortable life where my job provided for us, and I never stood in his way of doing anything. He came and went as he pleased, and when he went, I realized that was when I was most happy.

I knew that was because I had fallen out of love with BO.

When you fall out of love, where does the love go? Was it ever there to begin with?

Thinking back to how we met, I realize that I don't think I ever really loved BO.

He was safe. He offered me stability and was kind. I thought that was love, and maybe it was something like love.

But it wasn't enough.

I had changed—looks, personality, needs—but BO had remained the same. Apparently, favoring red lipstick is a reason for concern, according to BO and his mother. They were "worried" about me because of this fact.

We grew apart, and the divide only got bigger and bigger.

BO wanted me to remain the same, but I wanted to grow. And I wanted to explore. But I felt guilty for wanting this.

BO was a good guy (most of the time and when sober), but it wasn't enough. I couldn't stay with him because he was a nice man.

I stayed for two years too long.

And when I spoke to BO about our failing marriage, he just disregarded it.

But he was secretive—hiding his phone, taking calls in private. I always suspected he was seeing someone else. And on New Year's Eve when he was passed out in his own vomit, I saw his screen light up on the stroke of midnight.

It was from a girl, and oh wow, what a coincidence (not) that that girl was LARS. I didn't think anything of it at the time, but if it walks like a duck and that duck is named LARS...

I spoke to BUNNY, who offered advice and support. She never pushed. She asked me did I love BO, and I answered honestly.

I said I don't know.

She asked, "Have you ever been in love?"

I pondered on her question because the answer wasn't as clear-cut as I believed it to be. When I was with my partner at the time, I thought I loved them, but could I live without them? Did I love them so much it hurt to breathe?

Does that love even exist?

I suddenly felt an overwhelming sadness because I realized I had never experienced that love because I never really loved myself. Self-love is the first step toward loving—period. If you don't love yourself, then how can you love?

You are the most important person in your life. No one else other than you.

BO and I hadn't had sex in over a year. We were barely talking. We were roommates who were married. That's how it felt. We never saw one another; we were nothing but strangers.

I should have left; I should have left so many times. But I stayed because I'm a coward? I thought I would grow to love him again?

I wish I had the answers. But love doesn't come with a manual.

I see that BO was with me because I was easy. I let him do what he wanted, no questions asked. And that's because I trusted him.

I shouldn't have.

I felt like an utter idiot for not leaving him sooner. I wasted time because...I don't fucking know why.

Love shouldn't evoke those emotions. Love didn't live here anymore and hadn't for a very long time.

Therefore, I asked BO to leave. I needed time to heal. Or maybe to understand where the love had gone. Yes, our marriage was fractured. But when I made those vows, I meant them. I didn't know what to do, so I asked for space.

To add to the final insult, BO told me I should leave my house.

What a guy!

And well, you know the rest.

Our "friends" called me every name under the sun as I was the one to blame. I HATE the phrase slut. It is beyond disgusting, especially since it's associated with females.

And that's what I was branded. A big ole letter S sewed to my chest.

But guess what?

Men can be "sluts" too. And BO...you're the biggest one of them all.

If you ever read this, I want you to know that I had the balls to do what you didn't, and I'll wear that title with pride. The only thing I can thank you for is being a decent human being with my father.

But apart from that, you suck.

I soon realized all the mistakes I had made throughout my life. I felt like I had wasted years, and I wouldn't waste a second more.

So I did what I shouldn't have.

But it was the only thing that made sense.

I had to go back to the beginning to understand where the love went wrong.

Social media had come a long way, and by liking one single tweet...he came back to me, and I was in so much fucking trouble.

But what's new?

Eleven

"Tainted Love"
Soft Cell

Three Days Later

"So when can we expect the next chapter to *Love Hard*? I am dying...d*ying* to know what happens next."

In response, I take a large swig of my Red Bull because I have a feeling I'll be needing it.

I have no idea why I thought this would be a good idea.

I could blame the lack of sleep. Or the frozen burrito I had at 3 a.m. But the fact BOSSMAN is glaring at me like I'm the antichrist incarnate cements the fact that I should have stayed in bed and never agreed to this exposé. I'm afraid I will *expose* a little too much in the shitty mood I'm in.

I knew this would happen. The moment I hit send on my email, I knew it would evoke these feelings in me, ones I've tried so hard to suppress. It's not that I haven't dealt with my marriage breakup. I have.

I just didn't want the entire world telling me where I went wrong. Or what a fucking idiot I am because there is no guessing what the next chapter will be about.

As I risk a side glance at BOSSMAN, I see that his resting bitch face is still set in stone. I have no idea what his problem is. Surely, he can't be angry that I hit the road before things got messy—well, messier because right now, this is a fucking mess.

"I hope soon," I reply to SHAN, the interviewer from *Love Your Life* magazine.

The moment I entered this posh mansion, I haven't been able to shake the feeling that everyone has been staring at me. Not how BOSSMAN is because he looks like I just kicked his puppy, but they are looking at me in almost…awe.

And I know that's because of this memoir, which has created a shitstorm overnight.

Who would have thought my miserable love life could be so relatable? I suppose everyone has their own MR. J, and the woes that come with loving the unattainable.

"We all want to know what happens with MR. J. Are you two back together?"

Were we ever together—period? That's the better question here.

On cue, I feel the heat creep up my neck.

BOSSMAN clears his throat an octave way too high, hinting this topic isn't part of the exposé.

I narrow my eyes at him because fuck him and whatever crawled up his perfect ass and died. If he has a problem, like an adult, he should tell me what it is instead of being a total buzzkill.

But I can't deny that the pissed-off look suits him.

His usual groomed hair is ruffled like he's run those long fingers through it. Those long fingers which—

Shaking my head, I focus on anything but *that* because that's the reason I'm in this predicament in the first place. I give SHAN a sympathetic smile because the saying rings true in this case—it's not you, it's me.

"Let's take some photos while we have good light."

This is a total bullshit excuse to escape BOSSMAN, who is raining on my parade, which is why I decide to give him a piece of my mind.

Nodding, I stand but don't follow SHAN as she practically runs out of the room. I instead close the door, sealing my fate. I lean against the door, folding my arms and looking at BOSSMAN, raising a brow.

He has the audacity to look down at his gold Rolex.

"Oh, don't let me keep you," I quip, my temper rising. "In fact, I think we would all prefer it if you went back to the office and took your bad mood with you."

He snickers.

This is not going to end well…for him.

"I don't need a babysitter. I think you do, however, with all the sulking you've been doing. What's your problem?"

The white shirt he wears is unbuttoned mid-chest, revealing the thin gold chain that hangs from his thick neck, and on anyone else, they would look utterly ridiculous, but BOSSMAN looks so hot, I can't stand it. And I don't even want to touch on the topic of his black jeans which are ripped at the knee.

This look isn't his usual style, but he could make wearing a paper bag look hot AF.

The sunlight streaming in from the large bay window highlights that strong jaw and the dark, dirty-blond whiskers accentuating his stupid, perfect face. Against my better judgment, my attention shifts to his full mouth, and memories of when he kissed me slam into me, leaving me winded.

I dig my fingernails into my palms to remind myself that this little fantasy will only end in tears—the proof is in the pudding, and I am suddenly pudding in his hands as he saunters toward me.

The room is suddenly not big enough for us both.

"My problem is"—he stops inches away, peering down his regal nose at me—"you."

"Leave then," I bark, but there's no bite to it, and that's because I am currently drowning in BOSSMAN's delectable scent, and it's not his cologne—it's all him.

But I don't allow that to distract me.

"You'd be doing me a favor because it's apparent you'd rather be anywhere but here."

"You can't be trusted," he replies while I blink once, hoping to make sense of his comment. But to no avail.

"What the hell does that mean?"

"It means I don't trust you."

"Did you smoke crack today?" I question, deadly serious because I am not entirely sure why he wouldn't trust me doing an interview that benefits us both.

"No, but I wish I did," he counters without missing a beat. "Your last chapter wasn't a hit."

"*Excuse me*?" He may as well have slapped me with that comment.

"I didn't want to say anything, but a lot of readers have had issues with your…infidelities."

"My what now? What infidelities?" I've not even written about them—yet.

"Well, it doesn't take a genius to piece together what's going to happen."

"Oh, is that right?" I mock, glaring up at BOSSMAN. "Enlighten me then. I want to know."

He realizes playtime is over and just as he's about to retreat, I stand on tippy-toes so our lips are a hair's breadth away. "Because I call bullshit. I think your gigantic ego is bruised, and you're upset."

"Upset?" he scoffs, his exhalations becoming heavy. "Why would I be upset? I don't fancy becoming one of your science projects for you to write about."

Oh my fucking god, he *is* salty.

"Oh, BOSSMAN," I taunt. "Watch your nose grow. What happened between us was a mistake. Stop acting like a pubescent teen and get over it. You got rejected. Big deal. I know it stings—but there's a first time for everything."

I know my sarcasm isn't helping, but I don't appreciate him criticizing my work, especially when he was the one who forced me to write this fucking memoir in the first place.

"I plead temporary insanity," he states calmly. "I guess, I was curious to see what the fuss was about. But…I've had better."

Oh no, he didn't.

I don't even think twice before I knee BOSSMAN in the balls. He drops to the carpet, cupping his privates, eyes wide as he gasps for air. I don't give him time to recover as I bend low and grip him by the collar of his shirt.

"Don't you ever speak to me that way again," I warn, drawing him close. "You do, and I walk. We clear?"

The threat isn't empty, and after being scouted, he knows I have options.

His chest is heaving, and I know it has nothing to do with the fact his junk is probably on fire. "Very," he finally replies through clenched teeth.

"Good." I let him go and turn on my heel, then decide to use this anger for good. I'm going to write the next chapter and make it my bitch because no one makes a mess outta me.

Again…

Thankfully, BOSSMAN got the hint and left; I guess kneeing someone in the balls does that. But in what universe did he think insulting me was okay? I am a little surprised he's acting this way, though. If I didn't know any better, I'd say he was upset because he cares.

But that's just crazy talk.

With him gone, I could focus on the interview and took some photos I didn't hate. SHAN said she would run everything by me before publication and I can't help but think this memoir has elevated me in ways I never imagined.

I hate to say BOSSMAN was right, but he was.

This memoir has touched so many people because it's relatable. Everyone has a MR. J. Mine, however, he is a rare find—and that's not a good thing.

Once I was done for the day, I decided to grab something to eat at my favorite place. And alas, here I am, looking at my gluten-free vegan sandwich, wondering if I can stomach another bite.

I don't know why I've allowed BOSSMAN to get under my skin. I don't even know when this happened. But this seems to be a running theme in my life. I think I'm in control, or that I have an inkling to what's going on, but then I get thrown on my ass, wondering where I went wrong.

My cell is glaring at me from the table because I have a foolish, irrational urge to text MR. J.

And welcome to my life.

Whenever something turns to shit, I go back to him because, why? Because I'm a fucking masochist, that's why.

Groaning, I quickly yank out handfuls of napkins from the chrome holder and dump my cell in the center of the pile. Ignoring the inquisitive stares of my fellow diners, I commence to wrap my phone in the napkins until it looks like a cheap, badly wrapped present.

I then shove it between the pages of the menu before slamming it shut.

Out of sight. Out of mind.

But when I hear it vibrating, I realize this plan would have worked better if I turned off my cell.

"I'm losing my mind," I mutter under my breath.

This would be the time I visit the local corner store, purchase my favorite bottle of gin, and sleep for a week. But no such luck.

"You are a hard woman to track down," says a young man with bright blue hair and a snakeskin piercing.

When my phone continues vibrating from within the menu, I subtly push it aside with my elbow in hopes I can convince this hot stranger that I'm not totally insane.

"Do I know you?" I ask because I don't remember him, and I'm sure I'd remember someone like him.

He takes a seat, and I like that he didn't ask. I like confident men, and BLUE reeks of it.

"No, but I know you. I've been following your writing for years," he replies, looking for a server.

I push my half-eaten sandwich his way, and he gratefully accepts.

As he chews the huge bite he just took, he slides his business card across the table. My opinion of him soon changes because anyone who carries around a business card in this day and age is an utter dick.

But when I see who he is, and more importantly, who he works for, I realize *I'm* the dick.

"You're shitting me," I manage to push out through my heavy breathing. "You work at Incognito?"

He nods, still chewing.

"As in the largest publishing house in the world, Incognito?"

He nods again, grinning.

I suddenly wish I hadn't offered him my sandwich because I need to hear him confirm with words and not gestures that he's here to see me.

BLUE is the slowest chewer in the whole world, but the moment he finally swallows, he puts me out of my misery. "May I be frank?"

"You can be whoever the hell you want to be," I counter, which has him laughing. "Just tell me why someone from Incognito is here, in this shitty diner, wanting to talk to me."

When my usual server walks past, unimpressed with my choice of words, I hold up a hand in apology. "You know I say that with the utmost love and affection."

Thankfully, BLUE starts talking so I can stop. "We want to offer you a book deal. Your memoir deserves a lot more than being in some mediocre online magazine."

Mediocre seems harsh, but I allow him to continue.

"My boss is a big fan and wants to publish your memoir. He wants to include the publications you've already written, but from here on in, all new writings are to be published by Incognito."

And there's the catch.

"To do that, I would have to stop writing for *Love Me, Love You Not*," I say in case we're not on the same page.

But when he nods, it seems that we are.

"Your talent is wasted writing for a magazine. Being published means a bigger reach. Book tours, local and abroad. My boss thinks with the right marketing, this could be huge."

I know he isn't talking shit because it's unheard of for Incognito to approach anyone. They are the elite of the elite. And here they are, eating my hand-me-down gluten-free sandwich while talking about book deals.

I need a minute.

BLUE reads my need for a time-out and retrieves his business card from me, only to scribble a figure on the back of it. When he offers it to me again, I curl my lip.

"What's this? A 1-800 number?"

BLUE chews on his left snakebite, looking all devious. "No, that's the advance Incognito is offering to buy the rights to *Love Hard*."

I almost fall off my chair because that's a lot of zeros.

"You're fucking with me?"

"No, I'm not. We want you, and my boss will do anything to get you to sign with us."

"I don't have an agent," I stupidly say because this would be when he or she would swoop in and tell me not to agree to the first offer they put on the table. But here I am, visualizing all the shoes I could buy with that very generous advance.

I need to get my head out of my shoe closet and into the game.

"This is a shock," I confess, staring at the figure on the business card to ensure I read it right. "I need time to think about it."

"What's there to think about?"

BOSSMAN, my subconscious screams…

I can't do this to him. Can I? That's something awful people do, and I'm not a horrible person. Well, most of the time I'm not. This feels like a slap in the face. I mean, he was the one who pushed me to write this memoir.

"They're your words, Z," BLUE wisely says, reading my thoughts. "You're the one who has bared her soul and connected with millions of readers worldwide. Don't let this opportunity pass you by. My boss won't offer this again."

"Your boss sounds like an arrogant asshole," I state, leaning back in my seat and folding my arms.

BLUE bursts into laughter. "An arrogant asshole who wants to help change your life. Don't take too long."

He stands, hinting we're done. He's thrown his grenade, and now he's running away to avoid the shrapnel once it explodes.

"I'll check in with you tomorrow and remember, this offer is only valid if you don't publish any more. We want exclusive rights on everything you write from now on. We don't have a deal otherwise."

"I don't like rules," I say with a sarcastic smile.

He places his hands on the edge of the table and leans in close while I almost forget my name. "Oh, I know. When I said I've been following your writing for years, I meant it. Talk soon."

I am stunned into silence because I'm liking the stalker vibe.

He leaves me with a nice view of his ass as he exits, but nice ass or not, I need not to be fooled—he's a honeytrap. And I want to bathe in the sugary goodness.

The table vibrates, and I wonder if it's my body responding to the hotness of BLUE, but then I remember wrapping my phone like a Christmas ham before the devil presented me with an offer.

I can't avoid the inevitable, so I reach for my cell and unwrap it, and when I see why it's been ringing off the hook, I peer over my shoulder, paranoid he's here in disguise.

BOSSMAN has called me numerous times, but it's the text that gets me because BOSSMAN is ancient, and I'm surprised he even knows how to text. But regardless of this fact, what he's written makes me feel like the world is suddenly making me choose.

I'm a dick. You're right. I am upset. I'm upset that you're not. I'm sorry x

I read the message endless times because this is the first time BOSSMAN has shared his feelings with me. We bicker like an old married couple because that's who we are, but for him to be vulnerable this way is something new.

I fold my arms on the tabletop and bury my head in the nook as I wish this day would kindly fuck off. But no such luck because when "You've Got to Hide Your Love Away" by The Beatles comes on over the radio, I take that as a sign to finish what I started.

This song reminds me of MR. J. When I asked him what his favorite songs were, he listed off a few, and this was one of them.

Damn him for giving me everything I wanted, bar the one thing I wanted the most—him.

Twelve

"Love On the Brain"
Rihanna

I hadn't thought about MR. J in years. I didn't even stalk him online. I just shut off, and for a while, it worked.

But I don't know what it is about him that has me coming back to him when things are bad.

Is it because I associate happy memories with him? But that doesn't make sense. You've read our history. There is more bad than good.

But does that good outweigh the bad?

There was only one way I could find out.

It was over a decade since I last saw MR. J.

A lifetime.

So much had changed.

I had changed. So much.

I wasn't the timid girl I once was.

I knew exactly what I was doing the moment I liked MR. J's tweet. The ball was now in his court.

From the limited pictures online, MR. J looked the same—older, but he was still MR. J. I wasn't instantly attracted to him this time, which made me happy.

Maybe I had finally conquered that beast, but the next day when there was an awaiting message from him in my inbox, I knew the beast had merely been sleeping.

The message was short and polite, with impeccable grammar. It was hard to believe this was MR. J. I made peace with the fact that he was in the past, but here he was, able to set those butterflies off in my stomach once again through one measly message.

I spoke to BUNNY who suggested I mirror his message. Don't give him too much. So I didn't.

He responded immediately. And his reply this time was long. I had never heard him "speak" so much. It threw me for a loop.

I responded with a short reply, and he came back with an even longer message, ending it with a question, passing the conversation baton over to me.

I could have stopped it right there. I knew MR. J was interested. He was active on my social media, a subtle nudge to make himself seen. And I liked it.

He never did this before. He never showed this sort of interest.

The messages were polite and funny, but MR. J hadn't changed—he comes in hard when he wants something, and he made it clear he wanted me. Again.

I didn't know how to react.

Even though separated, I didn't tell MR. J I was married at first, but I didn't hide it either. All he had to do was look at my socials to see pictures of BO and me during our happier times.

One day, we were sending messages back and forth, and he was subtly flirting, which was new. He had mellowed, I guess, and he definitely was different.

He commented about his mouth being sweet like cake because he had always been a sweet-talker, and I took a chance because it felt right and exciting.

I messaged back that I liked cake and his mouth, so we all won.

And that's when he called me baby.

I detest that term of endearment. But coming from MR. J, I liked it.

That one comment then triggered a chain reaction, and we fell into old habits.

It took one week. That was all.

We messaged every day. So many messages filled with smut and laughter and getting to know one another again.

He sent me a voice message, and the moment I heard his voice, a rush of emotion overcame me, and I needed a moment to catch my breath. I knew I was a goner.

We sent filthy messages, and I loved waking up to them. He messaged me every single morning, and I loved he sent those messages as soon as he woke up. He messaged when he was at work. He sent me anything I asked for. He answered any question I asked.

I asked. And he gave me what I wanted.

He was the MR. J I always wanted.

We spoke about meeting up, and his response had shown me how much he had grown. He told me he didn't like crowds and preferred his own company these days—so unlike the man I knew.

But he shared that that was due to his past job in a strip club. Those late nights over the last ten years had just gotten worse and worse for him, and he got drunk to get through the night. When the sun rose, he went to sleep, only to rise when it was dusk to do it all again.

MR. J has always been a creature of the night, so working those hours came naturally to him, which is why working a nine-to-five job was a major life change for him.

He told me the one thing he appreciates now more than ever are sunrises because he's starting his day, not ending it how he once did.

It's apparent that that job took its toll on him. He doesn't like crowds, loud noise, or drinking because they're all a reminder of the life he lived. He wanted a change, which is why he's up at three a.m. running the streets, starting the day.

I admire him for that because it takes guts to change your life that way, especially a job that has left a permanent scar. That place sounded like hell, and honestly, after the tenth set of boobs, you'd be indifferent.

However, before we saw one another, I needed to tell him about BO.

He thanked me for my honesty but said it didn't make a difference—he wanted me. As long as I wasn't uncomfortable or he was putting any pressure on me, he wanted to see me.

And we did.

I was so damn nervous.

We had spoken for weeks, every single day since he sent that first message that he sent on my dad's one-year anniversary. I like to think it's a sign from my father. But actually seeing him, that was a whole different ball game.

I got ready and went to the address MR. J had organized to meet. It was a beautiful hotel because we both made clear a coffee date wasn't what we wanted.

I messaged beforehand to tell him I was nervous. He replied that he was too.

My heart hurt, but in a good way this time.

I was certain I was seconds away from having a heart attack when I texted him that I had arrived, but the moment he came downstairs, those nerves disappeared because standing before me was MR. J, and he did something which I will never forget for as long as I live—he held my hand and never let go.

We went to the room and talked. We talked so much.

He was now in his forties. He had silver sprinkled throughout his groomed beard and in his hair, which was still long. He looked wiser, but his eyes carried such sadness, and I didn't understand why.

Being in his presence has always calmed me, but this time was different. He was mellow. Soft, not hard. He wouldn't stop smiling and his dimples...those fucking dimples.

He was simply beautiful.

He didn't play guitar anymore as he had broken his hand and was now working a nine-to-five office job. It was hard to believe he was so different.

But I liked it.

There wasn't a thing I didn't like, which is why I leaned forward and told him to kiss me.

He was taken aback by my forwardness and dominance, but he soon learned what a boss I had become in the bedroom. I wasn't the naive girl I once was, and I was about to make his life hell.

We made out for hours, exploring and reacquainting ourselves. It was the first time in a long time that I was happy.

He smelled the same.

He kissed the same.

But he wasn't the same...he was open, unguarded, and he made his feelings for me clear.

I teased him for hours, which destroyed us both. I loved it. And he loved it.

I loved that I was the one calling the shots. I was the one in control.

I bit him.

Tormented him with my feet.

I watched on with an amused grin as he tried so desperately not to come because he was so turned on.

He wouldn't stop complimenting me, eyes locked as we got lost in a world where only we existed.

That chemistry was still there, but it had grown—tenfold. It was hard to breathe at times.

When we finally had sex, that was the sex that I knew we were supposed to have. We were both open and accepting, and that is why it was beyond explosive. He whispered filth to me, and I loved every single word because the smut was filled with feeling—the best kind.

He held my arms above my head, leaving bruises behind, while I reared up and bit his neck, wishing to brand him for all the world to see.

We lay in one another's arms for a long time after, talking and catching up on years lost. MR. J stroked my back, my arm, my leg. He held my hand.

This was everything I ever wanted from him, and when he asked if he could see me again, I knew I was in trouble because I didn't expect our reunion to be this way.

I knew what would happen, but I didn't anticipate all the other stuff.

He kissed me when I left, but not before slapping my ass.

It was perfect.

Did I feel regret?

No, I didn't.

I felt sadness because ending things with BO was a major life-changing event, but I didn't regret a single thing.

MR. J texted me afterward, and we spoke all night. It was simply beautiful.

We continued our texts and voice messages for weeks, and I couldn't believe he would message every day. This was different, and I liked it so much. He told me he missed me. He told me what the smutty videos I sent did to him, which I loved. I loved that I got him off.

I told him what I wanted, and he gave it to me. It was that simple. I was honest, forthright, and dominant, and MR. J did everything I asked.

I didn't want BO. I wanted MR. J. I always had.

Leaving BO was the scariest thing I ever did in my life, but I don't regret it. By leaving him, I found myself, the real me, and I loved that person. For the first time in my life, I loved me.

I loved my independence because I realized I didn't need a man in my life to feel complete—I completed myself. And ironically, it was rekindling with MR. J that helped me realize that. He helped me find the real me, and I will love him always for that.

MR. J and I had plans to see one another again when something tragic happened to him. I gave him space because I understand loss too well.

But he became distant again, and that triggered me.

I couldn't help but think history has a way of repeating itself. This time, however, I didn't quit. I pestered MR. J every day to open up and not shut me out. I was forward. Bossy. I laid everything out on the table. I wouldn't make the same mistake again.

"Talk to me."

"Tell me if you want me to leave you alone."

He said no, he didn't want that. He just needed time to sort through things alone.

And day by day, I saw those walls re-erecting. I was watching MR. J leave me in slow motion.

I knew he liked me. He wouldn't have put up with me scolding him if he didn't. He wouldn't have messaged every day if he didn't.

Or I like to believe that he did.

Eventually, we saw one another again, and this time, it was even better. We fooled around for hours, but we didn't have sex. Instead, MR. J simply allowed me to touch him—touch his forehead, over his eyes, his mouth.

He fell into an almost slumber, and that was the first time he really ever let his guard down. He was tired, so tired, but not just because he couldn't sleep.

Something was plaguing him.

And I wanted to know what it was.

I continued to push because I could see he had a wall there for a reason. Something heartbreaking had happened to him, and I wouldn't stop until he told me what it was.

He could have walked away at any time, but he never did.

He stayed, just how I once did. And I still don't understand why.

I wasn't a booty call. We were forming an emotional connection without the sex, which was the opposite of what we once experienced. We were pen pals in a sense, and to a writer, stimulating my mind is as good as sex.

But I was insecure. And I hated it.

The more I pushed to see him, the grander the excuses became, yet he still didn't leave.

He stayed.

Until one day, I snapped.

I demanded he tell me what was going on. The ball was in his court.

And finally...he did.

He had wanted to tell me for months that his past relationship had ended horribly, in the worst possible way, and because of this, he believed he was broken and could never love again. He could never see himself "going there" again.

He was happy to discuss anything I asked but, of course, remained respectful.

MR. J thought his revelation would scare me away.

It didn't.

BUNNY was once again my angel. Once I stopped crying because I thought he wanted to end things, she told me that MR. J had finally done what I had always wanted. He opened up and shared something that he never shared with anyone before.

The emotional clam had opened, and inside was a beautiful, rare pearl.

The next day, I asked him endless questions, which he answered. I liked that he confided in me when he hadn't spoken to anyone about it before.

He confessed it was awful dealing with this alone as he didn't know how to handle something so tragic. It explained so much.

We grew closer after that.

Our connection was amazing because MR. J had laid his cards on the table, and I was still here. I didn't run away because, who isn't broken? Who doesn't have baggage?

It doesn't define us, though. It teaches us how to survive. It shows us that we were stronger than whatever tried to beat us. But that thing that tried to beat us is still shady as fuck.

I loved when he told me how our chemistry was always fire, but it only seemed like "more" this time. It validated what I felt and what I was feeling.

MR. J didn't often talk about his feelings, but when he did, the words he chose sang to my very soul. They touched me more than his tender touch ever could because he stimulated me intellectually as well as physically.

However, the question was...did I love MR. J?

And the answer is—no.

Hard to believe?

But I didn't.

I didn't love him because I was re-learning what love was. I had just fallen in love with myself. So falling in love with someone else was still a learning curve.

However, although he had changed so much, love has a long memory. It may forgive, but it doesn't forget. And I would never forget what it felt like to love MR. J.

He doesn't ask for anything, but you want to give and give and give.

That's his allure. I suppose some women want to "fix" a broken man.

MR. J and I had been talking for months, and things were like a roller coaster. Some days, he was amazing. Others, not so much.

He was an emotional yo-yo, and I think that was because he didn't know what he wanted.

I always felt he wanted me, but on the flip side, he didn't. But he didn't want to let me go either. It didn't make sense. But MR. J never made sense to me. I never knew what he was thinking.

I don't know if that's because I pushed him to feel, and he didn't like that. It's always easier to switch off your emotions than it is to feel. I challenged him, and I will never make excuses for the fact because that's who I am.

The messages soon became less frequent, and sometimes, I wouldn't hear from him for days. But then he would appear. It made my head and heart hurt.

I was always in a state of confusion with MR. J.

My overthinking brain loved keeping me awake at night, throwing scenarios at me that he was seeing other girls. That he was speaking to them as he was to me.

I didn't sleep much during those months.

I'm jealous. Very jealous. Especially with MR. J.

He occasionally said he too was jealous of other men, but it was because they were touching something he wanted.

I didn't understand it. He could touch, but he didn't.

One day, he would give me so much. Others, nothing at all.

See why I was confused? Every day was like climbing a mountain, only to see there was another higher peak when I thought I had reached the top.

It was exhausting. He was the most frustrating man I had ever met. He was regimented and wouldn't stray from his schedule. Something

I left my husband for.

I accepted that was MR. J. But why?

I hated that I couldn't let him go when I knew I should. Day by day, I felt us fading. He was pulling away. I asked to see him so many times, I lost count. But he was always busy, which showed me that he would put anything before seeing me.

But this time, I wasn't standing for it.

He texted me once or twice a day to appease me. But when he chose not to reply, his silence spoke volumes. His half-assed attempts were not good enough anymore. I wanted more. I deserved more.

I always did.

MR. J may have given me what I asked for, but he never gave me what I always wanted the most—him. He never gave me his time.

I'm certain his past is the reason he hid behind his walls. I can't be angry with him for that. We all have a past, and MR. J's changed him.

He was always very patient and kind. But was he too kind to tell me that he didn't want what I did? I was demanding, and he didn't like pressure—we would never work.

We should have, but the past has shown me that we can't—no matter how amazing the connection.

All I could do was stand back and watch something so beautiful crumble before my eyes, powerless to stop it.

There are no villains in this story. MR. J was never cruel to me. On the contrary. He made me feel beautiful and special because his texts were always filled with compliments. He made time for me through text.

But it wasn't enough because they were just words, and I soon learned that if he makes you cry more than he makes you smile, run, my friends.

FUCKING RUN!

When I asked him what his favorite songs were, or what his favorite poem was, which is "Gossamer Wings" by Juan Olivarez—so tragically beautiful and a reflection of who MR. J is—he replied without asking.

He trusted me.

He never asked for anything in return.

When I asked what his favorite memory was of us, and he replied the last time we saw one another, as was the time before that, I knew he felt that spark too. Something that monumental is hard to ignore.

But I wanted to see him, to touch him, and not live through memories because I chose him. But he was most content being alone. If he wanted to see me, he would have.

It's that simple.

There are no excuses when it comes to love.

I tried, I really did. But love shouldn't be this hard, right?

Wrong.

Nothing worth fighting for is easy. And MR. J was worth it. To me, he was, anyway.

But I was fighting a losing battle.

I like to believe he pulled away because I evoked feelings he didn't want to deal with. I tell myself that. I think we could have changed the world. But I'll never know.

I wish he saw what I did when I looked at him. He was smart. Funny. So clever. He was gentle. But instead, he closed himself off in fear of... being hurt? Or maybe he just hasn't found the right person to love yet?

What I do know is that I am not that person. I never was.

And that's where our story ends...for now.

Thirteen

"Love"
Lana Del Rey

BLUE's "rule" only incited me to write and write. I wrote so much. I couldn't stop. But I knew that would be the case. And that's why I didn't want to start because I knew once I did, it would be over.

A secret isn't a secret once it's told, and I was so used to MR. J being a secret that it felt like a chapter was closing once I divulged what I had done.

But that's the thing about life—it's forever changing. *We* are forever changing and evolving.

Staring at my screen, I'm not so sure my readers will be awfully forgiving if they read what I had done. I doubt their love for my memoir would continue because BO was the "perfect" man on paper, so why didn't it work?

Was I to blame for not trying harder?

MR. J is anything but perfect. Whatever perfect is, he is on a completely different planet to it. But that didn't stop me from pursuing something I knew would never eventuate.

I'm a fucking glutton for punishment because the need to text him is almost suffocating. When this happened in the past, I would force myself into an exhausted heap because when I woke, I would wake to a message from him.

But when they stopped, I just learned to deal with the loss. It never went away, but I guess I got used to it. Sometimes, to deal with the rejection and pain, I would pretend he had moved to a different country so we can never be together.

Or if it hurt too much, it was just easier to pretend he was dead. That's how messed up I am.

It's amazing what we grow to accept as normal.

I guess we do this to avoid heartache and further disappointment, which is all I seem to have with MR. J.

So why can't I stop wanting him?

Groaning, I fall back onto my pillows, wishing I could silence the voices, but they've been screaming at me for years. But I don't want to go back there. What would be the point? I know what happens whenever I see him.

A fucking, painful mess.

I think about the last time I saw him, and that's what I don't understand—it was amazing. We spoke for hours, and even though he was still guarded, he opened up a little, revealing a man I had never met but knew was there all along.

The situation with his ex had changed him. He lowered his walls and let someone in, and it pains me to think the person he chose had horrible demons plaguing her—which wasn't her fault.

He had helped her as best he could, and when he detailed their relationship, I couldn't help but fall harder for him because he really fucking tried. He wanted me to know him, so telling me her story wasn't about him; it was her story.

But it was how she made him feel, which is why it was his story as well.

He was broken, and I don't even think he knew how badly so, and again, all I wanted to do was fix him. But that's been my problem my whole life—some people don't want to be fixed.

They are happy with their decisions, even if you're not. And MR. J was happy being alone. But I couldn't accept it.

I saw, I felt the way he was when we were together. He looked…happy, and he looked at peace. He often told me how he took on too much, trying to please everyone but himself because he was constantly burned out.

And when that would happen, he would retreat further and further away.

He needed time to regroup. I didn't understand why he didn't just say no, and many times, I would send him messages saying I was done. But three days later, I would be back because I just couldn't stay away.

He never expected anything. I was the one who wanted more than he could give. But he could have told me when I asked him endless times if he wanted me to leave him alone. I often wish he did.

But MR. J never wanted to hurt me. I know this for a fact because during one of my many "what the fuck is going on" moments, he sent me a text which summed up our entire "relationship."

I am so sorry I have upset you…this was never my intention x

It was never his intention to hurt me, but what he didn't understand was that I wasn't upset; I was confused. I was in a constant state of confusion with him. I don't even know what he was sorry for, as that was his response to me asking why he suddenly became detached.

I just never understood how he could switch off his emotions that way. How he could just not…feel. Or maybe he felt too much once upon a time, which is the reason he is the way he is.

And that was the third wheel for our entire relationship—I never understood him.

I hate this.

This would be so much easier if I could forget about him. It's clear he's forgotten about me. And here I am, wasting more time on someone who just doesn't care.

"There is something wrong with me," I say under my breath, staring at the ceiling.

Why do we do this to ourselves? Why do we want the ones we can't have?

In my defense, I did think I "had" him. I didn't understand why he would bother entertaining me if he wasn't interested. I gave him so many "outs," but he never took them. He could have so many times.

Tears leak from the corners of my eyes because this still hurts as it did the day I decided to "end it." I told him what I wanted, knowing how it would end, but I couldn't go on. It was killing me inside.

Late last night, I realized you'll never give me what I want—you.

Whether you can't or won't, I don't know, but what I do know is that I want more, but I need to accept that you don't.

I'll always want you.

I think the past year and then some has confirmed that, which is why I need to stay away from you if you don't want what I do.

I often wish you'd see how great things are between us. And how they could be better if only you'd let me in. I would never hurt you as I know you've been hurt in the past. I would be loyal because after traveling the world and meeting so many different people, it's you I still want.

It's you I'll always want.

This isn't me giving up. It's me fighting for what I want. It's now your turn to fight for what you want, whatever that may be x

He never fought for me, for us…so I walked away.

Tears continue to fall because I just don't understand how we could communicate so well physically, but emotionally, we spoke completely different languages.

Most would say he's just a fuck buddy, and I'm a hopeless romantic, but fuck buddies don't want to form a friendship with you and message random shit daily. They want to fuck. And that was my problem…I could never get MR. J to come over to do any of that.

He would text me cute messages every day and ask how I was, instead of taking me up on my offer to fuck him senseless. Anyone would think he had something against blow jobs, and my insecurities often screamed at me that maybe I didn't do it for him anymore.

But when he sent me those filthy texts that were filled with so much passion and desire, I knew that wasn't the case.

I found it so hot he did that, that I got him off just by looking at my pictures and thinking about the things we had done. There was one thing he used to text me, and he used to text me this often.

I would get a text saying, *You just made me come.*

It was hot.

MR. J using me as spank bank material is sexy AF. Who says romance is dead?

But BUNNY wanted me to explore and play. I wasn't lacking attention from the opposite sex, but I am fussy. I mean, I'm fussy with the shoes I wear…and they just go on my feet. Having random sex isn't something I can do.

I need to like the person in some sense, or there needs to be something that really stands out for it to happen. I've never been a fan of a one-night kinda deal. Hard to believe, considering what I've been up to of late.

But I'm really trying to forget MR. J—for good, this time, and I'm willing to try something different in hopes it'll help.

It's not looking good so far.

However, I know what my problem is, besides the obvious, that is.

We human beings just want to connect. We are a social species, and love and belonging are the most important needs we must fulfill.

Don't believe me?

Google Harry Harlow and the Wire Mother Experiment.

And this is why I don't understand how MR. J could be so closed off to his feelings. Or maybe he was just this way with me. I don't know because I never asked.

If I had my time again, I would have asked a million questions because what's the worst he could do? Not reply, which is what he did anyway.

A knock sounds on my door, interrupting this pity party for one. There is no way I'm answering it. The thumping continues, so I turn up Spotify and hope whoever they are gets the hint and leaves.

Sadly, that's not the case as the knocking becomes louder and even more obnoxious, which can only mean one thing…

Jumping up from the bed, I don't even bother to see if I'm wearing pants and charge through my apartment, ready to start World War III.

Yanking open the door, I don't bother with pretenses because I know who it is. "I really wish you'd lose this address!"

BOSSMAN snickers, not at all insulted by my quip. "I said sorry."

A laugh explodes from me, and it's not of the humorous kind. "Would you like a medal? I know this may come as a surprise to you, but that's what most people do when they're being a dick! And for the record, you are the biggest dick I've ever met, and trust me, I've met a lot of dicks!"

BOSSMAN attempts to enter, but I use my arm as a barricade across the doorjamb. "I'm not sure what part of you being a dick you misunderstood, but that usually means you're not welcome in someone's space. So would you please be so kind and fuck off?"

Of course he doesn't listen and storms past me, totally ignoring my wishes because deep down, I don't want him to go. For once in my life, I want someone to fight me…and win.

"Where's my memoir?" he has the audacity to ask, and I wonder if maybe he's caught wind of my offer from Incognito.

But I know he wouldn't bother with playing games if he had.

"You couldn't text that?" I question, slamming the door shut. "Instead, you had to come down here and ruin my day."

My day was already ruined, but he doesn't need to know that.

I expect him to bite back, but he doesn't. He simply stands in the middle of my apartment, appearing to either want to throttle me or kiss me, and I'm not sure which I prefer.

"You are the most infuriating woman!"

"Well, you are the most infuriating man, so we're even!"

BOSSMAN runs his fingers through his unruly hair, which looks like he's been yanking on it as it stands in all different directions. The look suits him.

"If this were anyone else, I would fire them. But—"

"Don't you dare pull that shit on me." I shake my head. "I'm your best writer. That's why you haven't fired me. This idea was yours, but I put everything on the line to write it. That has nothing to do with you.

"So don't threaten me with talks of being fired because, you know what?" I throw my hands up. "I quit. I don't have to put up with your bullshit. Quite frankly, I'm sick to death of your moods. Us women get shit for being the moodier sex, but that is so far from the truth.

"I am so done. I don't need this bullshit."

"There you go," he has the gall to say. "Causing drama because you can't seem to survive without it."

I take a step back because he may as well have punched me in the solar plexus with that comment. "What the hell does that mean?"

"It means, you can't be happy," he replies, the room suddenly closing in on me. "You had a husband who was boring as dog shit, yes, but he was stable. But it wasn't enough for you. You had to go and create drama because you thrive on it.

"You self-sabotage your happiness because nothing is ever good enough for you! You knew what you were in for the moment you contacted MR. J, because men like him never change. Yet you put up with his shit instead of telling him to fuck off like he deserved because actually being happy scares you.

"You think you love him, but how can you love someone who treats you like shit? He couldn't text you because he was working? Where was his work? Antarctica? I'm pretty sure even they still have cell service, so there is no excuse not to text someone back if they can text you back in fucking Antarctica!

"Or when he did finally reply, it took over a day to respond to a single text?

And his response was something so lame and aloof, it had you questioning if maybe *you* said something wrong!

"For fuck's sake, Z! Why do you allow this asshole to control you? He doesn't care about you! He never did. I hate to be the one to break it to you, but if he did, it wouldn't be over a decade later, and you're still questioning his feelings!

"He entertained you because you did everything for that fucker, yet he couldn't see what was right in front of him. And now, look at you. You're waiting for something that'll never happen because MR. J doesn't love you! He never did!"

BOSSMAN's chest deflates as he spits out his last words, but when he sees the betrayal tears in my eyes, he realizes that he actually said those words rattling around in his head aloud.

"Z—"

But it's too late.

"Get out," I whisper, wishing I could counter with something witty, but I can't because everything BOSSMAN just said is true.

I self-sabotage because there is no worse feeling in the world than loving someone who doesn't love you back. You love them with your entire heart, yet it's still not enough.

You are not enough.

I can feel the ugly tears approaching, and I know it won't be pretty. BOSSMAN can't be here when they fall.

"I'm sorry, I didn't—"

"No, don't be sorry," I defiantly oppose. "You meant every word, and you should never apologize for how you feel. Which is why, right now, I feel like stabbing you in the jugular."

I eye the red ballpoint pen on the coffee table.

"You're right, I'm not sorry." He stands tall, knowing shit is about to get ugly.

"Nice to know you think I'm a pathetic loser," I scoff, wishing I never wrote this fucking memoir. Nothing good has come out of it.

Just as I'm about to throw BOSSMAN out, he swoops forward and cups my cheeks in his hands. I try to fight him, but he won't let me go.

"You're not the loser, he is!" he yells, his frustration clear. "And I wish you'd see that. You've put him up on this pedestal for so many years when the truth is, he doesn't deserve you. He never did.

"You deserve someone who will text you back within seconds. You deserve someone who would drop everything to see you. And you deserve someone who will love you back. You don't have to be alone, but you choose to be because you're afraid of finding someone who will actually stay—no matter what."

"Stop it," I manage to say because the floodgates are seconds away from opening.

"No," he stubbornly argues. "Not this time. Not until I tell you…not until I tell you how I feel."

"Feel about what?"

BOSSMAN sighs, his beautiful eyes turning soft, something I've never seen before. It takes my breath away. "Feel about you."

I don't know what's going on, but I don't have time to question it when BOSSMAN slams his mouth over mine and kisses the ever-living fuck out of me. It suddenly feels like my first kiss because I don't know what to do with my mouth or tongue.

I've forgotten everything because this can't be happening—again.

But as I tug at BOSSMAN's hair and press my body into his, it's evident this is happening, and unlike last time, I won't stop.

If only kissing BOSSMAN was awful, it would be easy to stop this insanity, but kissing BOSSMAN is unlike kissing anyone…ever. He is dominant and submissive, rough and soft; he is every kissing cliché because when he kisses me, nothing else exists but his mouth on mine.

He makes me forget…everything with one single kiss. And that scares the living hell out of me.

He walks me backward and pushes me onto the couch. I expect him to follow. But he doesn't. He simply looks down at me with an expression I've not seen before.

He is tall, rugged, and dominant, and I want him all over me.

I wait with breathless anticipation because this is his show, and I honestly don't know what he has planned next. This has escalated from us fighting to… this, whatever this is.

Those eyes eat me up from head to toe, and when they remain on my feet, I know that BOSSMAN is thinking about the dirty things he read in my journals.

"You don't realize the power you wield," BOSSMAN says, surprising me. "Yes, your feet are fucking delicious, but it's what's attached to them, both inside and out, that has men falling to their knees—literally, wanting to worship you how you deserve."

All but one…

BOSSMAN reads my thoughts and shakes his head. "Time to make hotter memories where it's my mouth you remember…and not his."

I don't have time to get a word in edgewise as he spins me around and drops to his knees between my splayed legs. He runs his hands up my legs, which sends my body into overdrive. He doesn't waver, which I like as he loops those deft fingers into the waistband of my blue silk pajama shorts and slides them down my legs.

I'm not wearing any underwear so he can see me in the flesh, and when the green in his eyes is eaten up by a dangerous black, it's evident he likes what he sees.

He pulls me forward so my ass is on the edge of the sofa, and when he coaxes me to lean back by pressing a large hand against my stomach, I know things are going to get messy. He lowers his mouth to my sex and eats me out.

There's nothing quite like a man who knows his way around a woman's body, and the way BOSSMAN licks, sucks, and fucks me with that mouth, it's fair to say he has mastered the art of it because he is setting me on fire.

I fall back against the sofa, but I never take my eyes off him as he continues eating me with such passion, I can feel my climax racing for the finish line—already, which is a first as it usually takes a lot more for me to come.

I thread my fingers through his hair and tug at it, needing to anchor myself to something as I don't want to come just yet. I want to enjoy this because it feels incredible. BOSSMAN uses his tongue in ways that should be illegal.

When he sucks over my clit, I literally go blind for a second before my vision returns, and I watch as BOSSMAN makes a meal out of me. I can't look away and am utterly mesmerized by the sight of him between my legs, owning me in ways I didn't even know I wanted to be owned.

He isn't gentle, but I don't want gentle, and I make that clear when I open my legs wider and arch my back, so I can fuck his face as his mouth consumes me whole. The noises coming from him warm my flesh, and knowing he is enjoying himself as much as I am turns me on.

This is all about me because the position I'm in doesn't allow me to reciprocate, but I plan on returning the favor as the impressive swelling in the front of BOSSMAN's pants hints that his cock is as glorious as I assume it to be.

BOSSMAN uses a finger to coincide with the movement of his tongue, and I suddenly feel so full, I want to explode. It's sensory overload and I don't know what to focus on first. But when BOSSMAN pulls away only to stand and remove his shirt, it seems my eyes win as it would be a crime to look away.

The way he takes his time unbuttoning his white shirt would grate on my nerves if this were anyone else, but this is my own private strip tease as he reveals sliver after sliver of hardened flesh. The shirt splits open, showcasing a body that rivals a Michelangelo sculpture.

His chest is broad, sprinkled with soft hair which I like because I like men with scruff. His abs are carved out of granite, his waist tapered, but if that isn't enough to slay me, his V muscle which is my favorite thing on a man is so defined, all I can think of is running my tongue up and down it before I take that beautiful cock into my mouth.

I've not seen it yet, but I just know it will be as impressive as the rest of him.

Once he removes his shirt, I need a moment to appreciate his broad shoulders and, if possible, how being bare-chested only seems to emphasize the sharpness of his chiseled jaw. He waits for permission, and if that isn't the hottest thing ever, then I don't know what is.

"Those too," I say, pointing at his pants.

A wicked smirk mars his handsome face.

He unfastens the top button before lowering the zipper. The moment his dick springs free, I lean back into the couch cushions because it's everything I was expecting and then some. It's thick and long and shaved clean.

He steps out of his shoes. The pants and socks follow soon after. He's standing before me naked, and all I can do is stare because BOSSMAN is the hottest man I've ever seen.

He points at the sports bra I'm wearing. "Your turn."

I don't hesitate to remove it as gracefully as I can because it's tight, and I wasn't expecting company, which is what happens in the real world. If this were a movie or a romance novel, I would be in the finest lace and silk, but this is what love is about—the imperfect moments that make life real.

I toss the bra aside and bask in BOSSMAN's approval of me sitting naked before him.

My boobs aren't huge, nor are they pert and perky because I'm not in my twenties. This is who I am, and I'm not ashamed of my stretch marks or my curves. I am a woman, and I embrace my shape as I stopped caring what others thought about me long ago. The only opinion that matters is mine.

But BOSSMAN likes what he sees, and I like what I see when he grips his cock and starts jerking off.

Something is utterly mesmerizing watching a man jerk himself off as he watches you. It's like a drug to me. It's my kink, I guess you could say. Or maybe I'm just a pervert who likes to watch others get themselves off.

Whatever it is, watching BOSSMAN inspires me to write, so I record this in my memory. I never want to forget this moment in time.

"Do I make the cut?" he asks, reading my thoughts.

"Yes, but I still hate you."

A husky laugh leaves those full lips, and when I remember what they felt like pressed between my thighs, a whimper escapes me because I want more.

"It doesn't seem fair," I say, unable to tear my eyes away from his big hand wrapped around his dick. "You know what I like, you've read it. You have the home ground advantage."

"Don't you see?" he breathlessly replies, his tempo quickening. "You won the fucking game the moment we met."

His confession robs me of words and air because I did *not* see that coming.

"Don't look so surprised. I didn't stand a chance. I never did. I tried to be respectful, but I had to stop myself on so many occasions from kissing that fucking gorgeous mouth or dropping to my knees and worshipping those sexy feet.

"Every time you wore a pair of heels into the office, I had to jerk off in the bathroom to stop myself from fucking you in every position, wearing nothing but those goddamn heels."

I gulp. "I wore heels almost every day."

"*I know*," he says between clenched teeth, pumping his fist faster and faster.

Again, I circle back to the point of never underestimating the impact you have on the world. We don't see ourselves how others do, and it's a damn shame.

We are our own worst enemies.

BOSSMAN is opening up, and I don't know what to do because no man has ever done this before—not even BO, who was nonvocal in the bedroom. So I say the only thing I can. I start something that will surely break my heart, but I'm ready for it, or at least I'll try.

"Fuck me."

BOSSMAN growls, which excites me because I want this to be rough.

He picks me up and robs me of breath as he kisses me passionately. He tastes and smells amazing, and I almost beg him to give me what I want because every part of me throbs in need.

He sits on the couch, resting on the edge, and surprises me as he coaxes me to lean forward. He positions me so that my butt is in his lap while I'm face down with my hands planted on the floor. I bend my knees on either side of his legs as BOSSMAN holds my thighs.

I'm glad I'm not shy because this position doesn't leave much to the imagination. With my ass on full display for BOSSMAN, he spanks me hard. Before I have a chance to cuss, he positions himself at my sex and sinks into me in one fluid stroke.

He's not wearing a condom, which is very irresponsible, but I'll scold myself tomorrow because right now, I've forgotten my own name as BOSSMAN fucks me brutally. He controls the speed and the depth, but this angle is incredible for deep penetration because each stroke hits me hard.

BOSSMAN holds my waist, encouraging me to rock back and forth, and at first, I'm a total rookie because I've never had sex this way. But it doesn't take long for me to catch up to speed. Our bodies work in unison, and I know that's because of our chemistry.

That's what makes sex for me—it wouldn't matter if BOSSMAN was the hottest man to walk this earth with the biggest dick known to humankind; if the chemistry isn't there, it would not feel this good. But everything he does feels beyond incredible.

BOSSMAN holds me tight and does all the work. I don't fail to see that. Even though this is far from lovemaking, his touch still has a tenderness.

However, I push that thought out of my mind because I can't deal with it.

I focus on BOSSMAN's sated breaths as he sinks in and out of me and the frenzied slapping of our flesh. He hits me hard with every stroke because of his size, and when he opens me wider, a cry leaves me because it feels so fucking good.

"What a view," he hums, running his thumb along the pleat of my ass.

"Are you an ass man, BOSSMAN?" I ask, giggling.

That turns into a winded moan when he grips my hips and fucks me wildly. I lose myself to the rhythm and let go, and when his adroit cock continues stroking my clit in just the right way, I have no other choice but to surrender.

I come loud and hard, losing myself and riding this wave, which makes no sense—but the best things never do. I rarely come this hard, but when I do, I know what it means…I'm so fucking screwed.

And when BOSSMAN pulls out, spilling his seed on my lower back with a satisfied groan, I know that he feels it too.

We are so fucking screwed.

Fourteen

"My Love"
Florence + The Machine

I wake deliciously sore, which can only mean one thing...I didn't dream about having sex, and not mediocre sex with BOSSMAN—twice. I had the best sex of my life with my boss, who is sleeping soundly beside me.

There is so much wrong with this picture.

I have no idea when we made it to my bedroom. I do, however, remember him fucking me on my bed before I passed out in a legless mess.

And alas, here I am, wondering what the hell I'm to do.

I curse the early morning sunlight streaming in from my window because it only confirms that he looks as good as I remember. He felt even better, though.

Groaning in disgust, I slap a hand over my mouth as I don't want to wake him. Thankfully, there was no spooning or cuddling, and I can escape because there is no way I can be here when he wakes up.

With absolute precision, I measure my movements and slide across my silk sheets, inch by inch, as rigid as a board because I cannot afford any wrong moves. The mattress squeaks, and I freeze, never taking my eyes off BOSSMAN.

A sated breath leaves his parted lips which only look even more delicious than usual because of the heavier growth he sports. Just as I reach for the pillow, prepared to smother him to death, he rolls over and begins snoring lightly.

This should be a relief, but now, all I can focus on is his tight ass, and memories assault me of when I dug my feet into them as he fucked me senseless.

I need a lobotomy.

Right now, however, I need to split.

But it feels like I'm traveling across the country as my bed is never-ending. I continue shuffling along, certain I'm at the edge of it, and just as I'm about to turn over my shoulder to see if the end is nigh, I roll off the mattress and fall flat onto my face.

Thankfully, my rumpled clothes smothered my yelp, and they also provide me with an out as I don't have time to hunt through my closet for something to wear. So this pj romper onesie, which is a baby blue with white clouds printed all over it, is my attire for the day as I slip into it and then crawl on hands and knees across my floor to put on my black high-top Chucks.

I do all this with my eyes glued to BOSSMAN, who is still asleep.

I know this is ridiculous, but what's even more ridiculous is the morning-after talk, because what is there to say? Thanks for a nice time?

Vomit rises, and I know I need to leave before I do something stupid and stay.

Still on my hands and knees, I exhale in relief when I see my backpack and phone on the coffee table. Grabbing what I need, I don't look back and make my way out the door, crawling toward freedom.

Once out in the hall, I stop and raise my face to the ceiling, a sigh leaving me that turns into a strangled gasp when I see my neighbor, looking at me and shaking her head.

"*Buongiorno*," I say casually, like crawling out my apartment is just a normal day for me.

When she nods unmoved and unlocks her front door, I realize that it is.

Coming to a stand, I quickly sprint down the hallway and bounce on the spot as I wait for the elevator. I press the call button like that's supposed to make it come faster. But I can't get the vision of T-1000 in *Terminator* out of my head, but instead of Robert Patrick chasing me, it's BOSSMAN.

When the doors open, I lunge inside and frantically press the button for the foyer. Once I'm safe inside, I lean my head against the glass wall and exhale.

"You need help," I mumble.

Last night is proof of that.

When the elevator finally arrives on my floor, I burst into the foyer, and my Chucks squeak across the polished floor. I run out the glass doors, never looking back. The moment the smoggy air fills my lungs, I know I'm free and will worry about going back home when I have to because right now, I need to talk to my girls.

I send an SOS text to both BUNNY and ANGEL, which we only send when shit has hit the fan, and my current predicament is a shit show.

I can't stop running as it seems my body takes the flight in the fight-or-flight response very seriously. Only when I enter our favorite diner do I calm the fuck down.

Sliding into a booth, I yank out handfuls of napkins to wipe down the sweat from my brow. The server doesn't even ask if I want coffee. She turns the white mug upright and fills it to the brim. I must remember to tip her well.

Twenty minutes and three cups of coffee later, my friends barge through the door. Both look like they've just woken up, and I wonder what time it is. I suddenly feel guilty for involving them in my drama.

BUNNY leaves her sunglasses on as she slides into the booth across from me, stealing my coffee. ANGEL sits beside me, her face riddled with concern. At this point, they would expect me to confess almost anything.

Once BUNNY finishes my coffee, she lifts her shades and takes a close look at me. She can sniff the depravity on me. "Oh my fucking god, you got laid… and laid good."

ANGEL blanches, but when I don't deny it, she alerts the server that we need more coffee.

"The fact that you're in your pajamas, however, has me guessing you…you did the walk of shame…out of your own apartment?" Her lips twitch before she bursts into laughter. "I swear to God, you can't make this shit up."

Groaning, I cover my face, embarrassed, because she's right. I did do the walk of shame out of my own home. If this wasn't happening to me, I would find it quite comical and be writing about it for my memoir.

But I can't even think about what I did without wanting to be sick.

"Please don't tell me it was him." ANGEL doesn't need to clarify who he is.

"No," I reply, and they both sigh until I add, "it was BOSSMAN."

Silence is never a good sign, especially when that silence is drawn out. I knew this was bad, but the fact my friends are speechless confirms this is a dumpster fire.

"Was it any good?" BUNNY asks, finally breaking the silence. Although, I wish it was with any other question but that one.

I don't need to answer. She can read it all over my face.

"I have no idea how you get yourself into these situations," she says, hiding her smirk behind her coffee cup. "At least when you were married to Captain Boring, you had some sort of order, but lately—"

She doesn't need to finish.

"I know." I sink low, wishing I could disappear.

ANGEL surprises me when she asks, "Apart from the fact he's your boss, why is this a bad thing? As I see it, you showing interest in someone other than him is a good thing."

"It's not good," I correct. "It's a bad, a very bad thing. I don't like BOSSMAN, remember?"

"I think you want to believe that, but I call bullshit."

BUNNY once again inhales her coffee, thumping on her chest to breathe again.

"I think you're afraid of opening yourself up to BOSSMAN because you know you could actually like him. It's obvious he likes you."

I arch a brow and look at ANGEL like she just smoked a huge joint. "Obvious to who? I'm pretty sure he feels the opposite to like. More like tolerates because I make him money."

"I disagree. I just think you're making excuses and hoping that MR. J will stop being a crybaby and come to his senses and text you."

Well, then there is that.

I look at BUNNY, who shrugs.

She agrees?

Oh my god. My friends have turned into traitorous wenches overnight.

"Have you checked his social media?" ANGEL asks, and when she retrieves her cell from her bag, I almost tackle her to the ground.

But she's faster and holds the phone high above her head. "We are putting an end to this right now. Let's see if MR. J is putting his life on hold for you."

"I'm not putting my life on hold for him. I fucked my boss, in case you've forgotten," I argue, but it's weak because she's right.

I can't stomach seeing his stories or reading his tweets because I don't want to know if he's moved on. What would that say about me if he has? I want him to be as miserable as I am so that he finally comes to his senses and sees what's right in front of him.

But history has shown me that won't happen.

When an unimpressed hmph leaves BUNNY, I realize I've just been played because ANGEL wasn't the mastermind behind this, but rather, BUNNY as she scrolls through her phone, looking at no guessing what.

"I don't want to know," I almost beg, interlacing my hands. "If he's in pain or crying, then tell me."

"I can't believe you're in love with someone who listens to superhero podcasts. How can you like this man?"

This is going as expected—a fucking nightmare.

"But there doesn't seem to be any sign of love on the horizon. No surprise there, seeing as he wouldn't post that shit as he's more secretive than the Secret Service."

BUNNY is right.

MR. J would never post anything personal on his social media.

"Has he looked at any of your stories? Or *liked* any of your posts since you stopped talking?"

I shake my head.

Once upon a time, he would stalk my socials—good times. When that faded, I knew his interest would too. And I was right. I hate that he can be so predictable at times, and others, he's a fucking Rubik's Cube.

"Let this go," ANGEL says, and I sigh, wishing it was that easy. "He's not good for you, Z. He never has been. You deserve so much better."

I've heard it all before, but it doesn't make a difference.

I want him, and I don't know how to make it stop.

BUNNY makes the mistake of tossing her cell onto the table because I see him—I see MR. J looking up at me with that dimpled smirk from her screen. I've not looked at his pictures in a long time because it's just torture, but seeing him again, I can't deny my happiness.

It's hard to forget years' worth of history, especially the past year's worth of memories. We really connected, and I honestly thought he was going to be my happily ever after. But he thought differently.

"How can I make this stop?" I almost beg them to reveal the magical potion I'm not privy to.

BUNNY shrugs because her love life has been just as sucky as mine. We both look at ANGEL who has been married for a gazillion years and is actually happy.

She is clearly a unicorn.

"There is no formula," she wisely says. "Just find a man who isn't a dick."

Both BUNNY and I are on the edge our seats, waiting for more, but there is no more.

If only it were that simple.

BOSSMAN is a dick. But MR. J, he isn't, and that's my problem. If he were a dick, I could forget about him, but he never treated me badly. He just didn't want what I did. I don't understand it, and that's why I can't let him go.

"I'm so sorry to interrupt, but you're Z, right? I love your writing so much. *Love Hard* is the best thing I have read. Ever."

Lifting my head from my perch off the tabletop, I see a young woman standing by my table with a pen in hand.

"That's me," I reply with a smile.

Regardless of my emo mood, I'll never turn a reader away.

She smiles and nervously offers a notepad my way. "Could you sign this for me?"

"Of course." She tells me her name, and I think of something witty to write.

When MR. J's handsome face flashes at me from BUNNY's screen, the message writes itself.

Love hits you when you least expect it...are you ready for the fall?

Tears fill her eyes when she reads what I wrote, and BUNNY alerts the server that we'll need more coffee.

An hour later, RED is wiping her eyes after purging her relationship woes.

BUNNY and ANGEL stayed and listened because we all know what a broken heart feels like. Sometimes, all we need is someone to listen, really listen, and not wait until it's their turn to talk.

"Your memoir has connected with so many," she says, giving me another hug. "It's because it's so real. You don't sugarcoat anything. You tell it how it is."

"Yup, life can eat a giant dick," I reply, looking at BUNNY over RED's shoulder, who muffles a chuckle behind her hand.

"Can I take a photo?"

Peering down at my pajama onesie and Chucks, I shrug. "Sure."

We take a few selfies, all of which I look like I escaped a traveling circus. But anything for the readers, right?

RED waves goodbye, and when she's gone, I slide into the booth, my cheeks billowing as I exhale. "I can't believe my pain has resonated with so many people. This world is full of sadistic assholes," I add, shaking my head.

"Speaking of assholes," BUNNY says, arching a brow.

"You're going to have to be a little more specific," I say around a mouthful of waffles.

"Go home and deal with BOSSMAN."

I had forgotten about him for a full minute. But the nausea returns, and I push away my breakfast, afraid I'll vomit if I take another bite. "Surely, he's gone by now."

I look at my friends for reassurance, but all I get is a big fat nothing in return.

"Go." ANGEL shoos me out of the booth, confirming I need new friends. "You'll see what a great guy he is."

"Oh please, you'd say that about Satan," I reply, shouldering my backpack. "As long as he's not MR. J, right?"

She nods without apology. "How many times does he have to break your heart until you learn your lesson?"

"Did you know fish don't have eyelids," I reply with a wide smile.

ANGEL gets the hint. "I love you, but you drive me to drink."

I place a hand over my heart. "Thank you."

Leaving my friends, I put on my big girl panties and make my way back home. I take the long way even though I'm doubtful BOSSMAN would still be there.

He's probably thankful I left because I saved us both the embarrassment of having to deal with the repercussions of our actions in the daylight. Everything looks a lot more drastic in the stark light of day, like my hair for example.

I blanch when I see my reflection in a shop window and decide to stop dawdling and go home in case I meet the man of my dreams looking like a crazy person. History, however, proves this is very unlikely. But I've totally not given up on life—yet.

I ride the elevator to my apartment relatively calm, and when I check my phone, I see RED has tagged me in her story on IG. The photo is cute, and I don't expect my readers to bat an eyelash when they see me traipsing the streets of New York in my onesie.

Unlocking my door, I'm not focusing on where I'm going because it is my home and all, but it's a total rookie move.

"Nice pajamas."

Screaming in complete shock, I throw my phone in the air. It skates under the kitchen table and is in no way helpful to me to call for help, but not even Jesus Christ could help me right now.

BOSSMAN sits on a stool at the breakfast bar, his designer glasses perched on the bridge of his nose, and he casually looks at me over the top of them. In his hands, he holds my journal.

"Motherfucker!" I cry, storming over, totally forgetting etiquette as I attempt to tackle him to the floor.

"Can't keep your hands off me." He laughs, fending me off with one arm while using the other to hold my journal above his head.

My attempts to reach it are pathetic because I've forgotten how tall he is… and also, how good he smells.

I don't know who I hate more right now—me or him.

Giving up, I take a step back, blowing my matted hair off my face. "Why are you still here?"

He frowns. "I thought you were getting us coffee."

"Ha ha, you're so fucking funny." I clutch my sides, unimpressed with his lame-ass jokes.

"Who said I was joking?" he counters playfully, arm still high above his head because he knows the moment he drops it, I'm all over him like a rash. "But I am a little hurt. I mean, usually it's the man doing the fucking and fleeing."

"Stereotype much?" I roll my eyes. "And gross."

BOSSMAN is only saying this to lighten the mood because he is in no way, shape, or form sexist. He's simply trying to stop me from freaking out—again.

"So…his dick was the biggest dick you've seen? Will you need to update that after last night?" He deadpans me, not at all joking because he knows his cock is awfully nice.

Groaning, I turn my back and decide to shower, hoping I can scrub away my sins. Slamming the door shut, I lock it and undress. But BOSSMAN doesn't take the hint and takes perch outside the door.

"I want to see who this man with the magical dick is," he says while I toss my Chuck at the door.

"Why are you still here?"

A laugh follows.

Stepping under the spray, I don't wait for the water to warm because I clearly need a cold shower to wash away my indecent thoughts.

A small, insane part of me actually liked seeing BOSSMAN in my home. Not many one-night stands usually stick around, but I'm fooling myself if I think that's what BOSSMAN is. He's dangerous because he makes me want things I can't have.

I don't want a future with BOSSMAN, right?

I mean, I want to slap his face most days. That's hardly the recipe for a healthy relationship, which gets me thinking; if there was a recipe, what would it be?

A dash of jealousy.

A teaspoon of trust.

And a cup of love.

Placing my hands against the tiles, I lower my head and stand under the spray. I have no idea how I find myself in these situations. I like being challenged, but fuck me dead. If I don't end up with an ulcer by the end of this, it'll be a fucking miracle.

"Can we talk?"

Vomit rises, but I need to approach this like an adult. "No."

Hardly adult-worthy, but whoever said being an adult is enjoyable needs to rethink their choice of words.

"Z…I had fun with you, and I know you had fun with me. I can still hear how much fun you had."

My cheeks heat, and it has nothing to do with the hot shower.

"But I get it."

I'm glad he does, but I sure as hell don't.

"I know you hate me for it, but I read some of your journals, and seeing him through your eyes has helped me understand you a little better."

I turn my cheek, desperate for the punchline.

"You've put him on a pedestal for so many years when, in reality, he should be the one appreciating how lucky he is to have your love because I know you don't love many people…but when you do…you love hard.

"He doesn't deserve you. He never did."

Silent tears fall, coalescing with the shower spray, and soon, I don't know what's what.

I wait for more, but there is no more and that's because BOSSMAN has gone. He could have left, but he didn't because he wanted me to know that I mean more to him than that. He wanted to show me that he isn't like every other guy.

I'm so fucking screwed.

Once clean, I turn off the shower and dry off.

Wrapping the towel around myself, I open the door cautiously, just in case he decided to come back, but he hasn't, and I hate that I'm disappointed. I haven't been this messed up over a man since MR. J.

And I think that's why I settled down with BO—I never felt this apprehension with him. He was predictable and provided me with safety, but I learned the hard way that that isn't what I want because…I clearly want to be tormented to death.

I see my cell light up from under the table and guess it's probably ANGEL texting to see if I made it home in one piece. Getting onto my hands and knees, I retrieve it, and when I unlock it, I see that the last app I was in was Instagram and thanks to BOSSMAN catching me unawares, I accidentally shared the picture of RED and I in my stories.

I decide to see who viewed my story. I scroll through the hundreds of names and faces, feeling incredibly blessed these people chose my story to view. However, that soon turns to something I can't describe because I'm surely dreaming when I see a face who should not be in my feed—ever.

But here he is…a little red love heart near his picture, which has just shattered mine.

MR. J is back, and I don't know why. But what I do know is that our story isn't done…not by a long shot.

Fifteen

"Lovestruck Lobotomy"
VOILÀ

MR. J has always surprised me.

When I thought we were going strong, he would retreat.

When I was convinced I was done, he would come back to me and make me forget why we didn't work.

Being with MR. J is like riding a roller coaster with my eyes closed. I never see the twists or the turns. The steady climb. Or the massive drops. But I can't get off because I'm addicted to the rush.

MR. J intrigued me, and a part of me believes that's why I haven't been able to let him go. All I ever wanted was for him to give us a go, and if we didn't work, I could walk away without regret. But I hoped he could see what I did each time I saw him.

But he never did.

We had an amazing time together, but the moment he left, it was back to guessing when or if I would ever see him again.

So today's musings are a little different.

I'm not going to lie, the response to my neurotic ramblings has thrown me for a loop. I didn't know what to expect when I began writing, but no writer does. All we can do is be honest and hope we connect to at least one person because that's what most of us want to find—a connection.

And that's what I had with MR. J.

Sure, I've dated my fair share of men, but there is always one who stands out in one way or another. Whether they're the one who was the best kisser or the one who made you safe, there is always one you'll never forget.

For me, MR. J is the one who got away. I always felt like it was the wrong time for us because that was something we never had enough of—time.

We keep missing one another. Missed chances for one reason or another. We constantly fell in and out of sync, and I never understood why the dynamics changed so drastically.

I often wondered if it was because he found someone new. But then he would come back to me, confusing me even further.

We just don't work, and I don't know why.

I never understood why we never saw one another more often. He could have come over any time he wanted, but he didn't. And I still don't understand it.

I loved when he messaged early in the morning because at least I knew he was thinking of me. He was never over-the-top affectionate, but in his own way, he was. He used to send voice messages, pictures, and videos just because.

He used to tell me what his day was like.

But when all that stopped, the chemistry subsided and gave birth to overthinking. I need the everyday talking and the smut to continue the physical attraction. But when it stops, I grow bored—idle hands and all that.

The one thing I asked MR. J was that for this to work for me, I needed him to communicate, which seems like a normal occurrence for most, but for someone who would rather cut out his own tongue and eat it than talk, this was our downfall.

But our past isn't filled with merely heartbreak.

We had some amazing times, times which somehow overshadowed the bad.

When we first started seeing one another, he played it cool, but when he let go, we wouldn't stop talking or making out. Those were good times.

I used to love lying with him on his bed, watching TV in silence because it wasn't uncomfortable. It was comforting to be able to sit with someone and not have to fill the space with unnecessary small talk.

But when he did talk, I was hooked because he stimulated every part of me—mind and body.

I guess I divide my time with MR. J into three parts—the beginning, which was my favorite time with him, the middle, which I often wish I never commenced, and the end, which seems not to be the end, after all.

I'm not sure if he and I will ever "end."

He once told me once he's hooked, he's hooked, and that our chemistry will never fade, which sounds romantic and like we're meant to be, but life doesn't work that way.

Remember when I said love doesn't make sense?

This is the perfect example of it. Use me as the blueprint of things not to do.

I do have many regrets about MR. J, but I don't regret meeting him. He's taught me so much.

When we rekindled after so many years apart, of not even speaking, it was incredible that we gravitated back to where things fell into an old, familiar rhythm. He confessed he could feel the chemistry the moment we started messaging. Even if I wanted to stop it, I couldn't.

When we were together, he was so affectionate in his own ways, and

I loved it because he wasn't aware of it, and that's the best affection of all. When I asked him if he realized he would lean down and kiss my arm randomly, he said he didn't know he was doing it and that's because it was innate.

The moment he would come to my door, I would throw myself into his arms, and we would kiss for so long. But it was never enough.

I remember when I would kiss his neck, he would close his eyes in complete surrender and whisper he would feel better. It wasn't just sex; it was always something more.

And the more we saw one another, the more it grew.

Every time we fooled around, he would look at me, really look at me deep in my eyes, and I could see that he felt it too—this ever-present spark was sure to burn us both alive.

After sex, we would both lie in a breathless heap, but without fail, he would always drag my leg over him and caress it while we chatted for hours. Or he would take my hand.

That killed me. It still does because, again, he was so unaware of his affections. If our hands ever unlocked because we needed to get up and use the bathroom or get a drink, the moment either of us returned, he would reach for my hand—without fail.

My boy always held my hand.

He was the one to instigate our kisses goodbye, always coming back for more. The more we saw one another, the more the kisses grew. He would say goodbye to me outside my car as I dropped him home, only to lean back in and kiss me so many times.

I can still remember those sweet kisses...they were my favorite kisses of all.

He often said I could do whatever I wanted to him, and I know he meant it because I did. Not just in the bedroom, but when we were together, he was mine to do with as I pleased.

He once told me he never falls asleep at people's houses; he's a creature of habit, remember. But he fell asleep at mine. His sated soft breaths touched me so profoundly because I wish he could see what I did. He trusted me, but sometimes, I think maybe he didn't trust himself.

We were filthy together, but that was always filled with respect, desire, and...love because that love, now love is the thing you read about in books. Or see in the movies.

I will always be drawn to him, and I like to believe he feels the same way.

Writing this, I read over the thousands of messages we sent to one another.

They made me laugh.

They got me hot.

But they also made me sad.

There is so much left unspoken between us, which is why I can't write THE END.

He's made his feelings perfectly clear because if he wanted me, he wouldn't have let me go. He would have met me halfway because he knew how I felt about him. Regardless of the fact that I knew he'd break my heart, I had to try.

And let that be a lesson learned...never go through this life with regrets because sometimes, we don't have a chance to make amends.

MR. J didn't want me, but he also wouldn't let me go. I gave him ample opportunity to, and whenever I thought it was really it this time, he'd come back to me—in his own way.

I wouldn't talk to him for a few days, and his response would be him sending me some love on my socials, like a little nudge hello, I'm here.

If he didn't want me in his life, he would let me go, but he didn't. And that is something I don't understand.

My beautiful friend KAT once said he and I were in a situationship, and she's right. If only I did something about it...

I thought MR. J retreated when anything emotional was involved, but now I wonder if it's because I didn't ask the right questions?

I've established being in a state of confusion when MR. J is involved is a common occurrence, but when he dropped those walls, things were so clear. I wish they stayed that way, but then he retreated, his own worst enemy at times.

I've never made apologies for being headstrong, and MR. J was the only man I really had to fight hard for and that's because I wanted him. He was worth every heartbreak I felt because when we were good, we were fucking on fire.

And that made it worth the pain.

Love isn't easy. I had that, and look what happened.

I'm still a pupil when it comes to love, but I wanted to share with you, dear reader, that I'm still learning, just as you are.

So let's learn together because I'm about to do something which I'm surely to regret.

Stay tuned...

Sixteen

"Love is Embarrassing"
Olivia Rodrigo

"**A**re you sure you want to do this?" ANGEL asks, and it suddenly feels like we're teenagers again.

"No," I reply honestly, peering at the corner building in front of me.

This place holds many memories—some good, some bad. But tonight, I need to forget all of that, as I'm here for answers.

Or something like that.

This place is where I saw MR. J after years of no contact, the place where I saw that time had changed him. It had changed us both.

But I refuse to believe I'm that unlucky. No way can that happen—again.

MR. J's love for wrestling never wavered as it's as much a part of him as breathing. He commentates for the local shows, shows which he puts together. He combines his love for wrestling and music into one event, and it's doing really well.

The one thing about MR. J is that when he really likes something, he likes it for life. For example, his love for KISS, superheroes, and wrestling hasn't changed since I met him.

When he loves, he loves hard.

BUNNY has never seen MR. J in the flesh. She's not giving anything away, but I dare say she's not impressed. When I told her my plan, she said I was a fucking masochist but wanted to come along for the ride.

However, ANGEL is prepared for anything because she's been there, and she knows this can get ugly real fast.

The moment we enter the foyer, I'm hit with an influx of memories that leave me unsteady.

"We don't have to do this," BUNNY says, latching onto my hand. ANGEL grabs the other—my forever wingwomen.

"I really do," I counter, loving my friends more than anything, but I can't back out, not now.

A black star is stamped on our wrists, and the moment of truth arrives when we enter through the double black doors. Everything looks the same—same red decor, same sticky floor, but what's different is me.

I don't care what the dress code is. I wear whatever I feel on the day. Some days it's Chucks and denim, others, short shorts and a tank, but tonight, I'm dressed in a red silk strapless dress and of course, red glitter pumps.

I don't really blend in, but I don't want to. I never have, and when we walk to the bar, it's evident even if we wanted to fit a mold, we don't because three hot, confident women will always turn heads, no matter their attire.

I order our drinks, keeping my eyes peeled to the mirror behind the bartender. It's a reflection of the wooden commentary table—MR. J's post for the night.

He told me he never attended these things early. And he never stayed once it was over. He was out the back door before the final count. This wasn't because he was antisocial. It was because he didn't like crowds.

He did his job and went home, hoping to catch some sleep, but never could, thanks to his insomnia.

MR. J is such a complex creature. I'm always learning something new.

With our drinks in hand, we decide to stand in a darkened corner because I don't want MR. J to think this is an ambush. It's not, per se.

The lights dim, and the band takes to the stage.

Once upon a time, I would enjoy the show, but now, all I can do is look at the time. No wonder MR. J doesn't like to stick around at these events. I just want this done so I can go home, put on my pj's, and apply the new pink clay mask I bought online.

How times have changed.

When the band finally finishes, the butterflies begin to take flight because I know MR. J will appear at any moment. It's been months since things fizzled, but it feels like mere seconds when music blares over the speakers.

ANGEL shoves another drink into my hand, which I down in one mouthful. But when the gold glitter curtains on the stage part and MR. J emerges, I almost gag on it because my memory, the traitorous whore, has done a poor job at remembering him.

Has he always looked so…hot?

He's wearing black jeans, boots, a white shirt that is open at the collar, a vest, and a black suit jacket. He has on dark sunglasses and a bandanna, and my god, I need to wipe away the drool when I see he wears his beard just how I like it—the dark scruff groomed with gray scattered throughout it.

There is one word I've always associated with him and that's cool. MR. J has swagger, and when I see the women in the crowd noticing this too, it takes all my willpower not to tackle them to the ground.

MR. J and his colleague greet the fans, putting on a show as they part the ropes on the wrestling ring in the middle of the room and step into the center of it.

The room is filled with hollering and catcalls as MR. J and his friend shake hands. He's such a showman, but I've always believed him to be an extroverted introvert. He plays to the audience when the time is right, but in reality, I know he's most content being in his own space—I understand this well.

But no one would guess that just by looking at him.

He takes the microphone, and I brace myself because his voice has always been my kryptonite.

"Are you people ready to party? I said, are you people ready to party?" He amps the already feverish crowd up. "If you're ready to party, if you're ready to rock…gimme a fuck yeah!"

The audience is under his spell as they comply. But MR. J wants more.

"I said, gimme a fuck yeah!"

The room erupts into pandemonium, while I want to cry.

The moment I hear him, a flood of emotion overcomes me. I miss him… that bastard. I hate that his voice still has the power to stir such longing in me. But it does, and that's because of the history we share.

BUNNY nudges me in the ribs, breaking my stupor. "I thought he'd be taller."

I know she doesn't mean it because MR. J is tall. She's just trying to make me feel better. But the only better in this situation is to step out of the shadows and make myself known…which is what I do.

The moment I do, the light above me draws attention to my presence, and just like always, MR. J seems to be in sync with me.

He pauses mid-sentence, and when our eyes lock, I'm done for.

"Oh, here we go," I vaguely hear ANGEL say because she knows what comes next.

Nothing else exists but this moment in time—this beautiful, untouched moment between two human beings.

A dimpled smirk hits me in the solar plexus because no matter how many times I've seen it, it always feels like the first time. MR. J doesn't hide his appraisal as he examines me from head to toe, and when his astute gaze lands on my feet, I know he's thinking about what these feet have done to him.

A secret only we're privy to.

A woman turns over her shoulder to look at me, confirming that the entire room is wondering what the fuck is going on. But this isn't an uncommon occurrence for us. When that energy bounces between two people, it's impossible to ignore. I can taste it—it lingers on my tongue, as does the taste of MR. J, who was always the finest delicacy.

I wet my lips, and MR. J grins.

I actually can't stand how handsome he is. He may not be big and tanned like BOSSMAN, but he has spunk. He holds himself with such confidence, one cannot help but fall for his appeal. And I have fallen. Boy, how I've fallen.

MR. J is quick to recover, but I know things are about to get messy…and I am so here for the show.

I don't really get wrestling.

Sure, it looks cool, but so much effort and so much pain for so little reward seems kind of pointless. But who am I to judge?

Look where I am.

MR. J has played it cool and professional and kept to the script. But his eyes have followed my movements—like a predator, watching his prey.

The final match is about done, and so is my shot of tequila. So with that as an incentive, I gesture it's time to bounce.

BUNNY mouths, "What the fuck?" while ANGEL claps.

She was done an hour ago.

I know this may seem immature, but fuck MR. J. I made the first move—as usual, it's now his turn. I don't even bother looking at him, but I know he's watching. I leave with my head held high and wait.

Once outside, we walk in silence until BUNNY addresses the big pink elephant. "What the fuck was that? We came all this way and sat through meatheads throwing one another around, for what? For us to leave? I don't get it."

But when I hear it, I smile. Sometimes, MR. J is so unpredictable. But other times, he's not—like right now.

"Baby!"

ANGEL rolls her eyes while BUNNY turns over her shoulder, mouth agape. Me…I just relish in that term of endearment because it's been so long since I've heard it.

My heart and mind are racing, but that always goes hand in hand when MR. J is involved. This is what you read about in books. Or see in the movies. That feeling of utter surrender to the one you…love.

I think I've loved MR. J since the moment I met him, and the stupid thing is, I've never told him. An epiphany hits, and that is, I'm just as emotionally inept as MR. J. I can't move on because I don't want to—because it's him I want.

It's him I've always wanted.

And when I turn around and see him feet away, it just cements that I'm where I'm supposed to be.

At first, we don't speak. We merely look at one another, re-familiarizing ourselves with a past that won't let go. There is something about one another that won't allow it. It would be easier if we could.

But when I remember what it feels like being in his presence, being lost in his kisses, I realize I don't want easy. I never have.

Love is worth fighting for, and MR. J is worth it to me.

He looks at me just how he always does—with that dimpled smile that promises me the world. He doesn't shy away from openly checking me out, and I know he likes what he sees.

I often asked what he was looking at when I caught him. And he would appear genuinely taken off guard, as if not aware that he was looking at me with that look that set me on fire.

If this was "back in the day," I would throw myself in his arms and hug him as tightly as he hugged me before his hand slid to my ass. I would then kiss the left side of his neck before detouring to his mouth where we would then make out until I could no longer stand it because I wanted more.

"Hi."

"Hi," he replies.

The world tunnels into a whirlwind of color and the only focus is MR. J and I.

I want to say more, but what do you say to the man you've loved since you were eighteen years old? Sometimes, that love lay dormant, and I didn't give it light to grow. But it never went away. And seeing him now is proof of that.

It doesn't matter if it's six months or six years, this between us will never burn out.

"Did you enjoy the show?" So reflective of our first conversation when we were just kids.

"No," I reply with a smile.

MR. J laughs. "Well, I'm sorry about that. What can I do to help make your night not a total waste of time, then?"

"You know better than to ask a question like that."

He nods, his eyes dancing with mischief. "I do, which is why I asked."

Oh boy…we're in trouble.

"What can I have?"

"Whatever you want. You know you can do anything to me."

"Whatever I want?"

He nods, those dimples appearing.

"Well, there is one thing I want," I reply, taking a step toward him.

He stands his ground.

Even though I'm in heels, he's still taller than me, which is just hot because tall guys are my weakness. But let's face facts—MR. J is my weakness—period.

Standing on tippy-toes, I grip his shoulder and whisper into his ear, "What do you think of my shoes?"

A low moan leaves him and just like that, I know he never checked out.

This is headed for a collision course flooded in tears, but I don't care.

He places his arm low around my waist and kisses the side of my throat. "Sensational...as always."

Surely, he can feel this between us as I'm fairly certain even people in Australia could feel this pulsating energy vibrating between us. The history we share paves a path of desire and euphoria because I know what he does to me, and he knows what I do to him.

So on instinct, I step into his arms as he draws me in close and hugs me.

It's not just a hug—he embraces me and makes me feel safe. He makes me feel wanted as he runs his hand up and down my back, caressing me softly. It's a union I've missed. No one hugs how a lover does.

Kisses are grand.

So is getting fucked six ways to Sunday.

But being hugged by the one you want is indescribable.

See, I'm a romantic at heart.

We don't break apart. We simply stand in the middle of Manhattan, embracing—two lost lovers who never seem to find their way home.

"I missed you," I whisper into the crook of his neck.

"I missed you too, baby."

God, my heart hurts; it hurts because I know this will end in tears, just like every time before. But I welcome the chaos for one final taste, which is never really the final time. There will never be an end to MR. J and I.

Our paths will continue to cross until one of us finds someone else. But I don't want anyone else. As for him, I don't know what he wants.

BUNNY clears her throat, and just when I think she's about to tear him to shreds, she smiles. "Fucking finally. I have been waiting forever to meet you."

Both she and ANGEL have seen how I lose all good sense when it comes to this man. They are protective of me. But she can see what he does to me.

Everyone can.

He breaks our embrace only to kiss her on the cheek.

She takes one look at me and sees something that she's not seen in a long time—I'm happy.

When we're on, MR. J and I are on fire. But when we're not, we're a smoking pile of ashes.

MR. J smiles when he sees ANGEL. She doesn't smile back. God bless her.

He owns it and doesn't retreat. He knows my friends are aware of our turbulent past. But he stands by me and interlaces his fingers through mine. "Can you wait five minutes?"

The answer should be *haven't I waited long enough?* But I nod.

He kisses my cheek and jogs back to the venue.

ANGEL scoffs and shakes her head. "No, do not fall for this shit again. He's all in for a few minutes, and then you're back to walking on eggshells."

"It'll be different this time."

I realize how ridiculous I sound, but I want to believe it. I want to believe in love. Love prevails all. It has to.

"No, it won't. History has proven this. He needs to be more proactive if he wants to keep you in his life. He's a big baby, so we know that he won't. He needs to grow up and see what's right in front of his face!

"Actually, I take it back. He's a baby turtle—when something scares him, he hides."

I look at BUNNY, who shrugs. "Look, I get it. You two are on fire together. I see that now. But I still think you need an exorcism."

I burst into laughter because this is all true, yet it doesn't make a lick of difference.

MR. J returns with his backpack in tow and wearing black-rimmed glasses. My Clark Kent. "Wanna talk?"

He holds my hand and smiles.

ANGEL shakes her head, begging I see reason. BUNNY simply hails a cab. She knows what my choice is—it's him.

It's always him.

"Sure. Come back to mine?"

"Sounds amazing."

I bid my friends goodbye and basically have to pry myself from ANGEL's clutches. I know she means well, but this is what I came here for.

MR. J and I take off into the night, hands linked as we walk toward my home. This shouldn't feel so natural, but it does. It always does with him.

I remember reading an article about the psychological effects of your first love. No one could really explain why we can't forget them. No matter how much time has passed or how many other relationships one has had since, it's hard to forget your first love.

They all agreed, however, that falling in love with someone for the first time is a life-changing experience and that first love is the first dose of addiction.

If love is an addiction, your first love is the first hit, and when I look at MR. J, I know I am fucking hooked.

Heartbreak is a complex and emotional thing—there is no "right" way to deal with it. But there is nothing quite like your first heartbreak. It shapes you for future relationships. It changes you.

But holding MR. J's hand as he guides me through the streets of New York, I know that even though I have changed, my feelings have not.

We enter my building in silence. We enter the elevator in silence. That silence continues as we walk down the hallway toward my apartment. My hands are steady as I unlock my door.

I welcome MR. J inside, and he takes a moment to look around; always the observer. I want to lay a thousand and one kisses all over his face like I usually would, but I refrain.

He places his bag on the floor and removes his bandanna.

His hair has grown. It has an unruly wave and sits curled at his nape. Visions of yanking it as I fucked him senseless assault my brain. So I quickly make my way to the fridge as I need some water. I would usually go for the vodka in the freezer, but alcohol is not a good idea at this point.

Grabbing two bottles of water, I turn and am about to offer one to MR. J, but one bottle bounces onto the floor as it slips from my hand. MR. J is right behind me. He bends down to pick it up, and I watch as he unscrews the top and offers me the bottle.

Suddenly, water is the last thing that will quench this thirst.

"My boss thought it would be a good idea to write a memoir using my journals as material, and well, one chapter has turned into five or six, and now I've been offered a publishing deal to write a memoir based on my journals. Seeing as you're a big part of them, you're in it…a lot, and once I started, I couldn't stop. So I was wondering what you thought about it?"

And only then do I take a breath.

MR. J processes over what I just told him, and I'm fearful I've said too much—as usual. Why is he always so composed, giving nothing away, when I'm a chaotic mess?

"Well," he starts with a slow nod. "Thank you for telling me that. I do have one question."

I gulp.

"Who's going to play me in the movie?"

And just like that, I can breathe again.

"You're not mad?"

"Of course not. I'm flattered I made the cut."

Little does he know how the entire thing is based on him. It was never meant to start out that way, but here we are, me questioning my sanity, yet again.

"Can I read it?"

I guzzle down half the bottle of water before I smile. "I'm sure you'd rather read something else."

"No, I think I'd like to read your memoir, please."

Shit…

"Can you read it when I'm not here?" *Maybe in fifty years' time when I'm dead would be the preferable option.*

His beautiful mouth twitches. "Why?"

"Because I..." I tongue my cheek, searching for the right word, but all have escaped me.

"You what, baby?" He steps closer while I have nowhere to go as the counter is at my back.

"I don't want to see your face when you read it."

He bursts into a husky laugh. "Now I really need to read it."

He digs into his pocket, and when he produces his phone, I know I have about two seconds to smash it into smithereens before he reads me spilling my guts all over his screen.

I lunge for it, but he's faster and holds his arm in the air. "Whatcha gonna do?" he challenges, and that's all it takes for me to wave goodbye to my heart because it's about to be broken.

The air is filled with that familiar spark, and I surrender because I've waited so long to feel it again.

I don't know who lunges for who first, but the moment our mouths meet, nothing else matters but consuming the other whole. MR. J doesn't just kiss; he devours. He kisses with such intensity I almost forget I need air to survive.

His tongue delves in deep, challenging mine to meet him halfway, and it's one I happily accept as I fucking eat him alive.

I shove him backward and lead him toward my bedroom because we're not doing this in the kitchen. We kiss like it's a race—it's frantic, it's passionate, it's everything I want and more. MR. J has always been an amazing kisser, and when starved of it, it reminds me how much so.

When we enter my bedroom, reality collides into me, reminding me how many tears I've shed in this room because of this man. That has me severing our kiss because, what the fuck am I doing?

MR. J's confusion is clear, but I soon clear up any misunderstanding. "On your knees, MR. J."

A shiver racks him from head to toe because I know he likes it when I order him around.

He does as he's done a thousand times before and undresses as I take a seat at the foot of the bed, watching him. I take great pleasure in watching because he is remarkable. The soft hair on his chest, which leads down to his navel, has me eager to run my tongue across his collarbones, before licking down and down…

When he takes off his pants and I see that he's hard, I quash down my moan because holy fuck, his dick is perfect. He's groomed and clean, and it's what I like. But I know it's *him* I like. Everything else is just along for the ride.

He does as I order and kneels before me, awaiting further command.

I've never understood why he's so obedient in the bedroom, but out of it, it's impossible to get him to do anything I ask. But I guess this has never been our issue.

Crossing my legs, I lean back on my hands and smile. "We're going to play a little game."

He listens intently.

"You're going to take off my shoes and tell me why you deserve to kneel at my feet. I mean, what makes you any different from any of the other men who have asked to be where you are?"

His Adam's apple undulates as he swallows deeply.

"If you please me, then you can *(BLEEP!)* my feet. How's that sound? How long do you think until you come? Twenty seconds?"

His throbbing dick is all the response I need.

"Go on then"—I bend low, getting into his face—"show me what you got."

His eyes come alive as I rub over his dick with my shoe. But I know he'll come if I keep going, so I back off.

His long fingers carefully remove one shoe, and when he touches my foot, I see the excitement and longing hits him hard. It's hard to find someone who ticks all the boxes sexually, especially when you have a specific kink.

But there's no judgment here. We both get off on this.

"Come on now," I scold, pursing my lips. "I think you can do better than that. I mean, one guy—"

But I leave my sentence hanging, and MR. J takes the bait as I knew he would.

"What did he do?"

Another kink of MR. J—he likes to hear all about his predecessors and compare notes. He likes knowing he has something they want because he knows how fussy I am and that I don't just fuck anybody. It gets him off knowing they want what he has in his hands and mouth—soon enough.

"Well, he licked every toe so goddamn slowly and when he was done licking them, he took each one and fucked them with his mouth and tongue."

A low moan slips past MR. J's lips. "Did you like it?"

"Yes, very much. I liked it even more when I slipped his dick between my feet and jerked him off."

This, in fact, did happen, and it was hot because the power us women wield is an aphrodisiac. And now is no exception.

MR. J continues touching my foot while I fondle his dick with my other foot. I know it's taking all his willpower not to come as the way his cock throbs is a sure sign he's barely holding on.

"Miss them?" I ask, watching the way he caresses me with that untamed look in his eye.

"Yes."

"Why? Tell me what exactly about them you missed."

I like being verbal as well as vocal in the bedroom and with MR. J's eloquence, I could do this all day. "Yes, your feet are perfect, but that's not why I like them."

My red glitter toes catch the light proudly.

"Why do you like them, then?"

He smiles before rendering me speechless. "'Cause they're attached to you.

Has anyone else touched what's mine?"

His question ruins the mood because it reminds me of the last man who rocked my world—BOSSMAN.

"Yes," I reply honestly.

MR. J frowns, but he has no right to be jealous. He's the one who made it clear we wanted different things. But am I doing to BOSSMAN what MR. J is doing to me?

I mean, BOSSMAN could have left the morning after, but that was me. Instead, he stayed. He waited for me to return.

Oh god, what the fuck am I doing?

But when I look at MR. J, my heart flips me off because it's clearly a masochist.

"Other shoe." I offer my other foot, suddenly needing to quicken the pace before I have time to think.

MR. J takes this heel off with as much desire as the other, and when he cradles it to his chest, like it's his most prized possession, I see that he lowers his guard and is just so present in the moment. And I love it.

"Okay, show me why your mouth is better than anyone else's."

His eyes drop to half-mast as I choose my words wisely. I know what turns him on. He brings one foot to his mouth and begins licking and sucking, and I watch closely, enjoying the way I turn him on.

I don't have this chemistry with anyone else. I guess that's why I put up with MR. J's bullshit when I know I shouldn't.

It's these unguarded moments that make me forget.

We never break eye contact because this is about trust and respect. His hands move higher and higher up my legs, and I know he likes my ink.

I can see the way he appraises every inch of my skin.

I'm driving him crazy because I know what he wants, but he can wait, just as he's made me wait for years.

"Eight out of ten," I say, removing my feet from his mouth and hands. "But

I am impressed with your stamina."

He looks disappointed.

"Let's make it a ten out of ten. Stand in front of the mirror."

He doesn't hesitate and does as I say.

And this is the reason MR. J is my favorite lover—his kinks are in sync with mine. I can do whatever I like, and he'll accept it with a dimpled smile.

I stand behind him and peer at his reflection in the mirror. He is so handsome—he kills me. But it's not just his looks, it's him.

I loop my arms through his and run my fingernails down his chest and across his stomach.

A shiver racks his body.

I dip my hands lower until I reach his cock. I wrap a hand around his shaft and begin stroking him, never taking my eyes off him. He is barely holding on as I watch him shudder with every stroke.

His winded breaths slip past his parted lips as he moves in sync with my rhythm. He's so fucking hot. But he also angers me beyond words, which is why I stop jerking him off.

He slumps forward, a frustrated sigh leaving him. It makes me smile.

It's so frustrating when what you want is within reach, but you can never quite get there, and you don't know why. That's what being with MR. J is like.

MR. J watches me closely with those beautiful eyes.

"I did warn you. I did tell you that you've never met anyone like me before."

"You're amazing. You're the best," he says, and I know he means it. "You're sweet. And sexy."

"Oh, come on, you know this mouth is far from sweet." To prove my point, I stand on tippy-toes and bite the back of his shoulder.

"Can you do that all over, please?" he says, surrendering to me.

I'm no love god. I'm me. But the reason this feels so good is because of the chemistry and the history we share. I wish he would just accept it.

"It just keeps getting better, baby."

I can't allow him to break me again. I know this is what happens when we're together—he gets caught up in the moment, allowing me to believe that it's different this time, and he will finally tell me what I want to hear—that he wants me forever too.

Before he has a chance to rectify the situation, I kneel. He knows what's coming. It's something we talk about often. I know he likes it. I like it too.

I can feel the excitement vibrate through him.

There is something about a man surrendering that just gets me hot. And when that man is MR. J, it drives me wild.

But my heart hurts because I know I should rid myself of this man for good, but I'm a fucking junkie, and MR. J is my next fix.

I do things to him that turn me on.

It turns him on.

MR. J has always been a gentleman in the bedroom. We work because it's an equal playing field.

Yes, he's a kinky, wild lover, but it's always done with respect.

Peering up at him from under my lashes, I relish in the way his eyes roll back into his head and the sexy moans that spill from his parted lips. He's always been vocal and verbal, and now is no exception.

"Oh my god, baby. Fuck!"

His words spur me as I grip onto one thigh, and with the other hand, I hold his hip. He knows what's coming, and the fact he's so open to anything makes me love him all the more. Sex is a freedom of expression. There shouldn't be any shame or inhibition.

And with the right partner, sex can be fucking mind-blowing—like right now.

My dress has ridden up, exposing my lace underwear which shows off just enough ass. I cross my ankles, so MR. J has a perfect view of two of his favorite things in the mirror—my feet and my ass.

He watches in the mirror as I do other unspeakable things to his body. A guttural groan escapes him, and he grips my hair just how I like.

"You're going to make me come."

How I've missed those words.

Just as I'm about to take him deeper into my throat, he lifts me. We make out madly, and MR. J does that thing with his tongue that I like so much. Kissing MR. J is one of my favorite things, but right now, I need to fuck him until I fall into a sated mess.

I plant my hands on his chest and shove him—hard. He falls backward onto the bed, eyes on fire as I crawl on top of him. There's no time to undress. I move my underwear aside and slide onto his cock.

I'm home.

We both gasp because this feels beyond incredible. Peering down at him, I watch MR. J's walls disappear because this is the only time he lets me in. He doesn't close his eyes. He watches me as closely as I watch him.

I lose myself to the man I love. I forget that he doesn't feel the same way because for now, this is enough. I begin to move, our bodies united in a way that always feels right.

I plant my hands on his chest. I love that I can feel how quickly his heart is racing.

I spell coconut with my hips, my secret weapon as MR. J's moans crash into my breathless cries as I feel my release approaching already, which isn't uncommon. MR. J can usually make me come in under a minute. He's not the only one who can't help but come fast.

I get into my favorite position, and he scoops his hands under my ass, encouraging me to move harder, faster, and I almost come when he impales me so deeply it brings tears to my eyes.

I use his chest as an anchor, clawing at his slick skin, and when he thrusts his hips, I almost rocket off the bed because neither of us are being gentle. This is raw and primeval, and it's how I like to fuck. There are no walls between us, and after being surrounded by nothing but just that, it's beautiful to see MR. J let go.

I toss my head back because this is too much. Seeing him this way hurts because I want him like this always. I want him to see what's right in front of him. To realize that it's okay to love. I wish he'd see that what we share is really fucking special and rare.

I wish he would get out of his head and use his heart because he'd see the beautiful connection that continues to grow. But I know that he won't. He won't because he's stubborn AF, and he's been hurt beyond repair.

"I'm going to come, baby. Fuck!" he pants, fucking me hard and fast, never breaking eye contact. "You're so fucking beautiful."

I rock back and forth, and when I wrap my hands around MR. J's throat and milk my orgasm from him, he lifts me and positions me so he can explode in my mouth. He always comes loud and hard and fast, and when he's done, he pulls me toward him so he can slam his mouth over mine.

We kiss avidly with his taste still lingering on my lips.

It's hot. It's possessive. And it leaves me with an even bigger yearning to make this man mine.

When we're spent, we collapse onto the bed, where I cover us with the leopard-print blanket. He pulls me into his side. He always cuddles me. Always. Even if there's no sex involved. Whenever we're lying together, he's always touching me in one way or another.

I really like that.

Our heavy breathing slows, and I rest my hand over his heart. The rhythm is my favorite sound in all the world.

I gently run my fingernails over his skin, watching tiny goose bumps form. I affect him. He affects me. So why isn't this simple?

"I missed you, baby," he says, his voice hoarse, sex ladened with sin.

"I missed you."

He coaxes me closer to his side. God, he smells incredible.

"You fucking rock my world."

I laugh because I didn't do much. "You're just easily pleased."

"I'm not," he states, and I know he means it. He's just as fussy as I am. "I can't see straight."

I burst into more laughter, burying my face into his chest.

"This just keeps getting better and better."

His honesty touches me because it gives me hope that he can finally see what I do; what I *have* since I was eighteen.

He reaches under the blanket and places my leg over him.

Oh, goodbye, heart…

"I didn't even get a chance to get undressed," I say, suddenly realizing I'm still clothed.

"Why waste time?" he replies, his voice lethargic.

I love when he's this way.

His fingers sashay up and down my leg. It feels so good. "So who's the guy who got to worship those beautiful feet of yours?"

The mention of BOSSMAN ruins my high. I don't want to think about him right now.

"Don't worry, you're still the last man to do you-know-what to my feet," I assure him.

"And I better be the one to do you-know-what to them the time after that too. I don't like to share. They're both mine; you know that."

His possession pleases me more than it should.

"This is the best I've felt since the last time we were together," he confesses, which, again, surprises me.

Isn't he sleeping with anyone else? If he is, at least I know I'm not being outranked. The thought turns my stomach. I don't want anyone else touching him. I know he finds sex too personal at times. But he also has needs that I don't always meet because he vanishes.

I don't need a Venn diagram. I know what that means…

This is the time I should be kicking his ass out the door, getting to the inevitable first. But, of course, I don't. Instead, like a lovestruck fool, I kiss under his chin. He moans softly.

I want to kick my own ass.

"Where'd you go? Where do you always go?" I ask, knowing he'll either open up or close down.

I don't expect anything, as I've learned that this is the only way not to be disappointed.

He takes his time to reply, and when he does, I listen closely, almost too afraid to breathe. "I told you about my ex…well, small things lately just remind me of her. I mean, when we were good, we were good. But when we weren't, things were hell.

"When I went into the relationship with her, I thought fuck it, I'm all in. She chose the movies. Where we ate.

"I always tried to make her feel safe and comfortable. I was always the one apologizing, even when I wasn't at fault. But I wanted to make it work. But it was hard with her. She was hard work. But I tried. I really fucking tried."

All I can do is touch him and listen.

"I don't know how to deal with this. You're the first person I've really spoken about this with. I think I'm okay, and then something will remind me of her, and I'll just feel so fucking sad."

I wanted the truth, and here it is.

MR. J opened his heart to someone, something which I know is almost impossible for him to do, and it destroyed him. That explains so much.

Love has hurt him too.

I realize that this may be the reason he can't sleep. During the day, he keeps busy, which silences the voices for a little while. But late at night, when he's all alone, surrounded by nothing but silence, his mind keeps him awake… thinking, thinking about things he might regret.

"I need to go back home. This is the longest I haven't been back since I left. But I never know how I feel going back there. I always am a little anxious."

"Why anxious?"

"Going back home is bittersweet. I moved from New York to Chicago when I was young, and it's funny, the older I get, I now consider Chicago my home and not New York. But when I was younger, I wanted to leave.

"When I was eighteen, I jumped on a Greyhound with a new guitar, new leather jacket, and two hundred dollars I borrowed from an ex, which I promptly paid back, and came to New York. I was clearly out of my mind because now, I would talk myself out of doing something so reckless.

"But no regrets. The plan was executed in less than ten days, but I knew if I was going to do it, I had to do it now."

"I love that story." I snuggle into his side.

I know a part of MR. J is still just as reckless. It's still in him, but he chooses not to go down that path. Age perhaps has taught him? I know he doesn't have any regrets per se, as they're only lessons learned as he once said.

I love that he's opening up to me because getting him to talk about anything personal is not easy for him. But when he does open up, I just love him all the more. I've tried so fucking hard not to love him because I know he'll break my heart—again—but I can't stop something that was fated from the moment we met.

"Would you consider moving back?"

"I've thought about it."

My stomach drops, and I hate when these gut feelings hit me out of the blue. I know I wouldn't even be a factor in his decision, and that fucking hurts.

I need to thank him for a lovely time and hurl his ass out the door. But I don't.

I begin to ponder: if I were to write about this, I wonder who my readers would prefer.

BOSSMAN versus MR. J.

Who would win?

So I decide to level the playing field.

"Can I ask you some questions?"

His eyes are closed. His mouth lax. "Sure," he sleepily replies.

I rack my brain—if I were to write about this moment in time, what would I write? I need readers to understand why I want him.

"How did you find out the secret about Santa?"

Okay, not my best work, but to be fair, his dimples are a distraction.

He smiles, as if mulling over my words. "Wait? What? He's not real?" he teases, the forever joker. "I think I was six or seven. We just figured out on our own that he wasn't real. There was no earth-defying moment."

"Who's your best friend?" He knows mine, so it only seems fair.

"I don't have one," he replies with thought. "I guess if I were to say I did, it would be a guy I went to preschool with. We're still friends now. But he's married and has his own life. I may not speak to him for a month, but we can always pick up where we left off."

This surprises me.

He has a large circle of friends, but it appears MR. J doesn't feel the need to see them often. Or talk to them. But he talks to me every day. I didn't realize this. And I suddenly realize the importance of that fact.

"What's something you're not willing to compromise on?"

It's apparent he's thinking over this question with thought.

"Hmm...that's a good question." His eyes are still closed, and his guard is down. "I suppose not doing things I don't want to do. I'm at the age where I won't compromise on that."

He's here, I remind myself. He wouldn't be if he didn't want to be.

I suddenly am seeing sides to him I didn't even know existed. I often felt he did things just to appease me, but it seems that's not the case.

"If you could hug one person, dead or alive, who would it be?"

"I'd prefer to hug them when they're alive." He laughs, his eyes opening as he turns to look at me.

I kiss the side of his neck on instinct.

His eyes slip shut as he leans into my lips.

"Let me guess."

"Go on then."

I mention his favorite singer and then drop an inappropriate joke, which he of course laughs at. But then he turns serious, and MR. J does something that once again catches me unawares.

"But I guess the obvious answer here is my dad."

For the first time in a long time, I'm at a loss for words.

I knew his father had passed, but it's not something we discussed. He doesn't discuss his family often, so this is really special.

"How old were you when he passed?"

"Seventeen," he replies. "Someone said to me that was a crucial time to lose a father, and I didn't really think much of it. But when I think back, I realize that it was. It's the start of your life. Two weeks after that, I had a car accident where no one should have survived."

I remember he told me about this, and when he goes into detail about what happened and about them ending up in a backyard pool, I am just as horrified now as I was then.

"I remember bits and pieces but not the actual accident itself. I broke the window with the side of my face. It was a mess. In the back of the ambulance, I remember my friend's face as he held his hands to my chest.

"That's when I knew it was serious. The girl I was seeing at the time gave me a necklace with a crucifix for protection, and I remember feeling for it in the back of the ambulance. When I realized it wasn't there, I thought she was going to be so mad."

My heart swells because this is a personal thing to share.

"I asked her to call my mom and start the conversation with everything is all right."

"Did that accident stop you from being so reckless?"

"No," he replies honestly. "I thought I was invincible. I had six more car accidents after that. After Dad died, I thought fuck it."

This explains so much.

I lost my father in my thirties, and that was life-changing for an adult. For someone to lose their dad in their teens at such a vital stage would shape that person in a way they may not have been if the circumstances were different.

"I wouldn't have moved if my dad were still alive."

"Were you close to him?"

"Yes, very."

"Was he a traditional Italian?"

"Not at all. He tried to get rid of his accent. But he was traditional with his family values. None of us worked. He said I'll give you the three dollars you'd earn working at McDonald's."

His father sounded like mine. I instantly feel that pang I always feel when thinking of my dad.

"He moved here when he was twelve. He was an opera singer."

I did not know that.

MR. J sings and is very musical; something which runs in the family, it seems.

"What's your greatest talent?"

Once again, he ponders over my question with thought. "I have yet to find it."

And this is why I adore this man with every breath I take.

He's honest. And so heartfelt. I wish he was this way always.

"You're an amazing guitarist and singer."

"No, I'm not," he says softly. "I'm an okay singer. I get by playing guitar. But I'm no Mozart or Beethoven."

He's not looking for sympathy or compliments. This is him being honest with me and himself, something a lot of people don't have the balls to do.

"Well, I think you're wonderful."

"Thank you, baby." He reaches for my hand.

He continues to speak about his life for hours while I listen, my love only growing and sealing my fate, which I know will end in tears.

Seventeen

"Burning Love"
Elvis

I wake alone, but I didn't expect anything else. MR. J doesn't spend the night—ever.

He's very stringent about his routine; if he doesn't stick to it, a sleepless night will follow. But honestly, I don't mind. I like my space. His not staying the night never bothered me because I always knew he'd leave.

I learned that if you don't have any expectations, then you can't be disappointed, which is why I am not expecting any messages from MR. J. I reach for my cell, and when I see I'm right, I resist the urge to text him and decide to shower instead.

My body has bites and bruises all over it, and I close my eyes, remembering what we did. The water drowns me as I stand under the spray, running a finger over my mouth, remembering when MR. J fucked it without restraint.

"I need help," I mumble, turning off the taps.

Drying off, I dress in a black dress and decide to check my emails. I see BOSSMAN has sent five—persistent asshole.

Opening the first one, I'm a little disappointed when it's all business. We haven't spoken since we had sex like it was the last day on earth, and I don't know, I suppose I thought he'd maybe call. Speaking of…

I check my phone, and against my better judgment, I decide to text MR. J. I never ponder too long on what to say when I text him for fear I'll chicken out. I throw caution to the wind, which sometimes gets me into trouble.

I miss you.

I hit send, and the moment I do, I cringe…for a writer, that was incredibly boring.

However, when I see that the message is read, and he's typing, I yelp and throw the phone across the room. I mean, why is he texting me back so quickly? This is unheard of.

When will I learn that going back to something that makes you cry over and over again is bad for you? But I guess that's the definition of insanity.

Growing a pair, I retrieve the phone, and when I see the awaiting message, I brace for anything.

Thank you for a lovely evening and for listening to me carry on and for putting your toes in my mouth and for rocking my world.

The sign-off is a bunch of kissing emojis and hearts.

But that's it?

No, *let's catch up again soon? I miss you too*? No, *can I come over now?*

My heart sinks, and I don't even know why. This response is so…stagnant. Yes, I did all of those things, but it's so…detached. It's not filled with any promises of doing those things again. No hint of seeing me again.

But FUCK. THIS. SHIT.

When are you coming over to kiss me?

I know better than to expect a response so soon, so I return to my emails, and when I read BOSSMAN's last email, I enlarge the text on my laptop in case I'm seeing things.

LOVE HARD has been nominated for the Golden Book literary award. Ceremony next week. Here are the details.

I don't even read where or when because, what the hell? How can a half-written memoir be nominated for such a prestigious award? This has to be a joke.

BOSSMAN is clearly pissed off I haven't fallen victim to those green eyes and is now just being mean. But when I google the nominations, I see he isn't lying.

This is really happening…and I really need to talk to him.

Groaning, I send him a text.

Just got your email. They must have been desperate for candidates this year. Can we talk?

My phone chimes a few seconds later, and I shake my head, grinning. Has he been waiting by the phone for me to call?

However, when I answer and hear the unmistakable sound of a woman giggling, it seems he hasn't been waiting for anything.

"What's up?"

I clear my throat, not sure how to respond. "Not sure if you've forgotten how to read overnight, but my text was pretty clear to what's up."

Like your dick…I mentally add when I hear the musical giggle once again in the background. Why do I want to throttle the owner of that giggle to death all of a sudden?

"Oh, right. So talk."

"Um, if I've caught you at a bad time, why the fuck did you call?" I say, not interested in being polite.

Silence.

Was he expecting me to fall for his obvious ploy at making me jealous? It's surprisingly worked, but I'd rather cut off my arm and beat myself to death with it than admit that to him. And besides, I did just engage in some perversion last night with MR. J, so I shouldn't be jealous.

But I am because it's apparent I want my cake and I wanna eat it too—but what else am I supposed to do with it? For fuck's sake. Like my life wasn't complicated enough.

"Goodbye, BOSSMAN."

"Meet me in half an hour. I'll send you the address."

And he hangs up.

I would rather do anything but talk to him, but I can't run forever. Been there, done that, and look where that's gotten me.

BOSSMAN is late.

No doubt, it was done on purpose because he is one of those annoying people who arrive early to everything. So I know he's doing this to piss me off. And my annoyance only grows when he coolly walks through the door, dark sunglasses sitting perfectly on his handsome face.

He takes a seat in the booth but doesn't say a word. He flags down the server, giving her a flirty grin as she fills up his coffee cup. When she's gone, he slips off his glasses and sips his coffee. The sun decided to break through the gray clouds, revealing a red hickey on his neck.

I roll my eyes—fucking classy.

"So was I expected to learn Morse code for this meeting? Or are you actually going to speak?"

He smiles. "You're the one who said you wanted to talk."

"Yes, about work. You send me an email like that and then expect me to just sit at home and knit a fucking hat? Of course I want to talk about it."

"Maybe if you read your emails, we could have spoken days ago. But I didn't think it was of any importance to you."

I take a calming breath before I do something I regret, and there are many things I might regret when this annoying ass is involved. "Now you're just being a whiny little crybaby. What's wrong with you?"

"Nothing."

"Don't give me that shit. Why are you behaving like an even bigger dick than usual?"

"I'm playing by your rules."

I recoil in my seat because, what fucking rules? "I didn't even know we were playing a game," I reply, not interested in this pointless conversation if he's going to act this way.

"Of course you didn't because you're the only character in your story. Forget about the supporting cast."

"You need to stop talking in riddles. If you have a problem, spit it out… unlike the girl you were screwing last night."

Oh god, why my mouth filter decided to short-circuit now is beyond me, but I can't take it back now.

A deep laugh rumbles from BOSSMAN. "Girl? You assume only one?"

"Oh, settle the fuck down, Hugh Hefner. You're old, remember."

"For an old man"—he leans forward, totally ignoring personal space—"I was able to make you scream. And beg. I can still hear how loudly too." And he runs his tongue along his bottom lip.

I hate him, and although he is right, I cannot give him the satisfaction of knowing that. "You're still thinking about that?" I say, acting aloof. "I'd forgotten that even happened."

"Too busy fucking your ex?"

Touché.

"Who I fuck is none of your business. You and me"—I gesture my fingers back and forth between us—"it was a mistake."

I regret the words the moment they spill from me like hot lava because I can see they've hurt him, just how I intended. But now, I just feel horrible because no one likes hearing they're a mistake.

"Fair call," he finally says, a wall erecting that makes me feel even worse. I don't like walls. They are impossible to break down.

"BOSSMAN—"

But he shakes his head. "Let's just stick to business."

He explains the details about the awards, which seem pretty chilled, and that the ceremony is to be held in the Hamptons. He said it's for the weekend, so he is willing to drive us, which means I have to spend the entire weekend with him.

I already foretell this weekend to be an utter disaster.

But the truth is, to further my career and to give my memoir the life it deserves, I should go and show face, and I should go with BOSSMAN.

"So I think, hold off on writing anything until the awards night is over."

"Why?"

He pulls back his shoulders, and I burst into laughter. "Oh my god, you're worried I'm going to write about you?"

Truthfully, I hadn't thought about it because the memoir was about me purging and hoping I don't lose my mind in the interim. And I didn't feel like writing about what I did with BOSSMAN because it's not something I need to vent about.

I intend to write about what I did with MR. J because I need my readers to understand why I keep going back to him. Yes, he's difficult, but so am I. He is so incredibly patient with me when I overthink and end up hurling accusations at him that he doesn't deserve.

Something on my face must reveal my thoughts because BOSSMAN clucks his tongue, folding his arms across his broad chest. "So you're back together then?"

"Good God, no," I reply a little too quickly because we were never together. "That's not the way things are between us. They never have been."

"And you're happy with him appearing whenever he needs a quick fuck?"

I don't take it personally because I don't expect BOSSMAN to understand. No one does; not even me. But when I'm with him, him and I, me and him, we make sense. And that's all I care about for now.

"So much for sticking to business."

The silence between us becomes deafening, and I suddenly feel like I'm sitting in front of a jealous boyfriend. I don't like it, but it gives me an idea for my next chapter.

"I'll see you in the office." I go to stand, but BOSSMAN grips my wrist. His touch sets me on fire.

"I just…I just want you to be happy." He surprises me with his honesty.

"It's when I'm fucked up that I write my best stuff. Isn't that the case for all artists? And happy? I don't even know what that is anymore. I have fleeting moments of happiness, and I'm okay with that."

"Okay with being happy sometimes? That's bullshit."

"That's life," I correct, shrugging from his hold. "Don't try to fix me, BOSSMAN."

I leave, suddenly hit with an epiphany. This entire time, I wanted to "fix" MR. J, but maybe he doesn't want to be fixed…because neither do I.

I leave BOSSMAN feeling incredibly shitty, but every action has a consequence, and this is mine for sleeping with my boss.

I make my way through the usual Manhattan cluster of people, needing to get home and write. When I arrive back at my apartment, I check my phone and am surprised to find an awaiting text.

I'll be back soon. REAL SOON. The sign-off is the sunglasses emoji, which is as noncommittal as him.

Eighteen

"Falling in Love"
Cigarettes After Sex

What a cliffhanger I left you on. I would say sorry...but you know that I'm not.

Love is one sadistic bitch.

One day, it gives you everything you want, having you believe in happily ever afters. And the next, it rips out your heart and takes great pleasure in standing back and watching you bleed to death.

Every day, I'm learning something new, and that's because love, for me, is ever-changing. I think I'm done with love, and then BOOM, something extraordinary happens, which shows me that there are no rules when it comes to love.

I've made so many mistakes along the way, and I wish I could say I've learned from them. But I see myself falling into the same patterns because it's hard to kick the habit when you're hooked.

Many scientists have said that your first love is the template for future relationships. You learn what you like so you can chase that high again. But you also know what to avoid.

Falling in love for the first time is unlike anything you've experienced before, and that is why we all have a MR. J.

Many of you have expressed your gratitude to me for writing something so...real. But the truth is, speaking to many of you has helped me too. It's helped me realize that it's okay to make mistakes and not learn from them because we are forever students to this thing called life.

And today, I learned something from someone I've respected since we met. He should have been completely off-limits, but life doesn't work that way. Just because you know better doesn't mean you'll do it.

I knew the love between BO and I was over, but I still stayed.

I knew what would happen the moment I reached out to MR. J, but I still did it.

And now, I know what will happen with BOSSMAN because fighting him is like fighting nature—it's impossible. But I know how this will end, and it's not in a HEA.

But BOSSMAN has taught me a lot—don't tell him that. He's made me realize that I think I've been trying to fix something that isn't broken. Just because I believe MR. J is emotionally inept doesn't mean that he feels that way.

And I realized this when BOSSMAN tried to "fix" me.

Imagine that? Your narrator needing fixing? The horror.

BOSSMAN wants me to be happy, but honestly, I don't know what makes me happy anymore, and that's because, like life, I too am forever changing. Sometimes it can take a minute, a day, or sometimes it can take a lifetime, but I measure happiness in moments in time.

Yes, my love history has been turbulent, but I'm proud of myself for never giving up. I chased MR. J because he was constantly running away. But I wanted him to be running toward me, not away. That's what everyone deserves—a partner who wants them just as much as they want them.

But recently, something happened—MR. J has met me halfway.

I don't know what to make of it other than he provides that happiness I speak of. Yet for how long, I don't know. But being with him makes me happy.

But is it different this time?

I wish I had the answers. But the truth is, I don't know, and in some ways, finding out is half the fun.

MR. J and I have reconnected, and I know you're shaking your heads at me. I want to say it's different this time, but I don't know that it is. All I know is that we can't stay away from one another. We've tried and look where that's gotten us.

So I'm the passenger and the driver; destination unknown.

All I know is that kissing that man is the most potent drug around. All hopeless romantics are rooting for a happily ever after, but this will do for now.

Do I want more? I always want more with him. But like I realized with BOSSMAN, just because someone wants something doesn't mean the other person does. All we can do is set boundaries for ourselves and deem what is right for us.

MR. J has never been "right" for me, but it's those imperfect moments which has me appreciating the times when nothing exists but us. It often feels like we're sucked into a time warp, and when we re-emerge, I don't know how many hours have passed.

And I love that.

There's nothing quite like being lost with the person you choose to get lost with. It's hard to write about because some feelings and experiences can never be put into words. But I love that I can look back on a memory and be hit with the feelings I felt when it happened.

So BOSSMAN, who is he?

Didn't see this coming, did you? Don't worry; neither did I.

He is an enormous pain in my ass. But he doesn't make apologies for it, and I kinda like that. I like that he doesn't put up with my shit. Although I want to strangle him most days, I like that he doesn't try to spare my feelings.

He is real, and in this world, that's rare.

You may find a handful of people who do that, who love you, flaws and all, and as you've seen, I have a lot of them. If circumstances were different, BOSSMAN and I might work, but honestly, I think we're both too stubborn to compromise.

However, he has taught me some things about myself that allowed me to see that I'm still a work in progress. I thought I had it figured out when I got married because that's the thing to do, right?

It may be for some, but it wasn't for me.

If anything, it made me even more confused because instead of growing old and happy, I craved the youth that was dwindling away before my eyes. I suppose that's why MR. J has a permanent place in my heart.

When I look at him, I still see the young man who stole my heart with that fucking dimpled smile. Yes, we're both older—definitely not wiser—but he represents a time in my life I can never get back to, which is why I fight so hard.

This can't be for nothing. Surely, life cannot be this cruel.

And if matters weren't complicated enough, enter BOSSMAN with his arrogant smirk and ridiculous good looks. Top that off with smarts and wit, and I am so fucking screwed.

I never saw this coming. BOSSMAN blindsided me. I suddenly feel so exposed because I know if BOSSMAN digs, he'll unearth the real me. And the scary thing about that is that I think he'll like what he sees.

He doesn't expect perfect, and frankly, the messier I am, the more intrigued he becomes. Maybe he's just as fucked up as me. Or maybe he's trying to fix me, just as I'm trying to fix MR. J.

Just one big happy family we are.

Today's chapter is a little different, I guess, as it isn't really me detailing past relationships as such. It's me using past relationships as a blueprint for the future. I once thought MR. J was the future I wanted, but now, I'm not so sure.

I see changes in him, but is it enough? Time will tell, but time has always been the enemy for us. And each second that passes is a second I can never get back.

Is this revelation all because of BOSSMAN? Could it be that I actually can see some sort of future with him that I can't with MR. J?

But the thought of not seeing this through with MR. J feels like a defeat, and I don't like to lose. The thought of not waking up to his messages or feeling those bothersome butterflies every time I see him makes me...sad.

So it seems my woeful love life has just become even more complicated, if that's even possible. I don't share, and I know MR. J doesn't play well with others. How I know is because when he was on his knees before me, he mentioned a threesome in passing.

It's hot watching someone else worship something that's yours; I get it. I used to feel that way when I watched MR. J onstage. He'd have women throwing themselves at him, and he only had eyes for me. It still makes my heart race to this day.

One day, I was speaking to a friend about what MR. J had said, and they offered to be tribute. So I mentioned to MR. J I could make it happen if he wanted, and his reply was just perfect.

He said, I do want that, but I want you all to myself too. So in other words, hell to the fuck no. I said why not? He said the thought of it gets him hot jealous, and I'd be unleashing a feral animal, and if it happened, he would destroy me...in all the best ways.

So it's probably a good thing MR. J doesn't know about what my feet and I have been up to over the years, especially of late.

Are you looking at me with judgy eyes? You have every right to because, yes, BOSSMAN and my feet have become acquainted. I don't even know how or why. I could plead insanity, but madness has never felt this good.

Is this about to become a threesome? Not in the traditional sense, but nothing about me ever is.

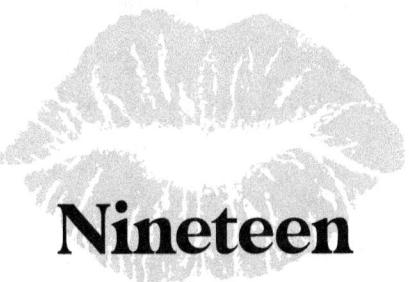

Nineteen

"I Believe in a Thing Called Love"
The Darkness

I couldn't sleep, which is why I'm standing in the fucking snow in the middle of Times Square at 11:30 p.m. looking at a green neon hand. For ten whole dollars, I can get my palm read.

I am so fucking sold.

You can't make this shit up—the ground level is a pizza place with the best damn pizza in New York. I can vouch for this because I just shoved the non-gluten-free slice into my face two seconds ago.

I open the glass door and walk up the carpeted stairs.

The second floor is a tattoo studio. The buzzing of the tattoo guns has my skin itching. But not today, because today, I'm about to get my palm read for ten bucks in a stranger's house who is on the third level.

This is a wonderful idea…said no one ever as I reach the third floor and am greeted by a clear seat and small round table with astrology printed all over it.

This is *not* how every horror movie starts, I assure myself…

This is so like me. I act without thought and then at the last minute, question if maybe I shouldn't have acted in such haste.

But no turning back now as I knock softly on the gray door.

A moment later, I can see an eye in the peephole before hearing a chain unlock. The door opens a millimeter, and I see a woman peering at me through the crack.

"What you want?" she asks, and I wonder if I have the wrong door.

"Oh, hi, um, I saw the sign downstairs for a ten-dollar palm reading. I—"

I don't get a chance to finish before she yanks open the door and shakes her head. "No, you don't need one of those. You need a soulmate reading."

Hot damn. Yes, I do.

Before I can high-five her, she produces a can of Lysol. I don't know what to do, so I smile politely. Maybe she's a germaphobe?

"Show me your feet."

Oh, sweet Jesus, here we go.

"Your soles," she clarifies when she sees my confusion.

I do as the nice psychic lady asks, and she then proceeds to disinfect each sole with Lysol.

"Give me your palms."

Again, I trust this psychic stranger at 11:30 p.m. and do as she orders.

She sprays my palms—once, twice, three times for good measure—before letting me in.

I see a Siamese cat and instantly go to pat him, but she shoves me into a large red armchair in the corner of the room.

"I—"

"Shh, no talking," she demands, shaking her head and sitting across from me.

I place my bag on the floor, and when I place my phone on the table near her, she recoils and points at my bag. "I read energies, and your phone will only interfere."

Gotcha.

Once my phone is stowed away, PSYCHIC looks at me. No, correction, she stares through me. Or more specifically, over my left shoulder. Her eyes are the most intense blue I have ever seen.

"Who's the J you love?"

And it seems the psychic cosmos is on fire today.

"He's an old boy—"

"Shh, no talking," she orders once again. "You and him are twin flames. Soulmates."

My mouth falls open because what in the ever-living psychic fuck?

"You have been in and out of one another's lives for many years. But you just can't be together. Why?"

"I don't know. You're the psychic, you tell me."

She hmphs. No wonder she doesn't want me talking.

"I see you together, but not together. I don't mean sex. I mean, the physical side is not the issue. It's the commitment. Have you told him you love him?"

Vomit rises, and I grip the arms of the chair like it's my life raft.

"Why haven't you told him?" Her eyes look through me once again, but she nods as if someone spoke to her even though I don't see anyone behind her. "He has a lot of regrets in his life. He cares a lot about you…but I don't see you ending up together."

Well, I didn't need to pay this stranger ten bucks to know that.

"Do you love him?"

"What?" I squeak, wondering if maybe she's read my memoir. Is this how she knows?

"Do you love him?" she repeats blankly.

"I don't know."

"Yes, you do. Do you love him?"

I suddenly get hot and itchy.

She reads my discomfort and eases up. "Show me your palms."

Okay, good, this is better. A little palm reading never hurt anyone…

"You were married too young."

Oh, for the love of God...

"He wasn't your soulmate...J is. You always thought about him. Even when you were married. Your ex-husband was a selfish man." She turns up her lip like she's eaten something rotten. "You stayed two years too long."

Okay, now this is getting way too spooky. I always say I stayed two years too long.

"You were supposed to have two children, but your body didn't allow it."

I listen intently, tears instantly stinging my eyes.

"I don't see kids in your future. I'm sorry."

So far, I'm winning at life with this reading. Just as I'm about to stand and pay her ten dollars, she says something which throws me on my ass.

"Your father has BW. He said not to worry. He is looking after your dogs."

This time, the tears fall.

"He died too young."

I nod, holding back my guttural sobs.

"J helped you with his death." It's not a question but rather a statement.

"He did."

"Do you love him?" she asks a third time.

When I hesitate, she sighs as if annoyed by my indecision. *Join the club, lady.* "Why can't you say it?"

"Because...we throw that word around so freely, but what does it really mean?"

It's now my turn to toss her world upside down as she ponders my question. But what she says next reveals I am just a baby grasshopper to this thing called life.

"Love doesn't have a meaning...it just is. You know what love is because it's everywhere. Do you love him?"

Pushing aside the weight pressing against my chest, I nod. "Yes."

She smiles for the first time since I sat down. "Do you want to be with him?"

"Yes." The emotional constipation is suddenly relieved, and I can see clearly.

"Good. I can help. I don't do love spells. That's not how love works. But sometimes the universe needs a little push."

Or, in our case, a fucking shove by ten thousand quarterbacks.

"Close your eyes, put your head back, and open my hands."

Okay, not gonna lie, the first thought I have is that she's gonna slit my throat and rob me, but I forget all those crime documentaries I've binged and do as she says.

"Now manifest him in your mind. I don't want you to manifest a situation. I just want you to manifest the man you love…MR. J."

What in the ever-living psychic fuck?

I do as she says, and silence follows for minutes.

I don't feel anything. But I don't think I'm supposed to.

"Okay, open your eyes."

I slowly open one eye, afraid she may be standing before me in a clown suit, but alas, it's just PSYCHIC, smiling.

"Now it's up to you…and him."

I have so many questions, and I ask her every single one for about an hour.

She goes into detail about my writing and about how my crystal can talk to hers for an extra hundred bucks if I wanted more. Most would scoff and say she is a fraud, but she is the real deal.

She answers everything and shares that her abilities stem from generations.

"Why didn't you allow me to speak?" I ask as I stand.

"Because I don't need you to. Your energy speaks for you."

Okay, this woman is my forever psychic guru.

Someone else knocks on the door, and I can't believe people are seeking psychic guidance at such an hour of the night. But perhaps, another hopeless romantic insomniac is looking for answers at midnight too.

I've been here for far longer than expected, so I offer her a hundred dollars, but she shakes her head. "Only ten dollars."

"No, but that was for the palm reading, and you did a lot more than read my palm."

I mean, she cleared whatever emotional caca I have clogged in my psyche. She simply smiles.

And that's how I know PSYCHIC is the real deal. She wasn't here to rip me off or give me false promises. She told me what she saw and then I am to do with that as I wish.

I pay her ten dollars and am finally able to pat her cat.

I leave her home, nodding at the woman in the plastic chair.

She's in good hands.

After my late-night revelation, I slept about two minutes before packing frantically as BOSSMAN will be here soon to drive me to the fucking Hamptons. I didn't want him to meet me at my place because it was too risky, so I said we should meet at the local diner.

MR. J has surprised me and texted me this morning. I want to believe it's a sign, but I need to calm the fuck down. It seems we just continue to fall back into this pattern over and over again. I wonder how long it'll last this time.

I've not submitted my latest chapter, but that has nothing to do with what BOSSMAN said. I don't have the guts to, which, again, isn't like me. I usually do what I want, when I want.

Having millions of strangers read your most personal thoughts is easy. But the thought of BOSSMAN reading it makes me want to hurl.

I raise my hand, alerting the server at the small diner I'm hiding in that I need another coffee. Or maybe ten.

My cell chimes, and I see that it's a text from ANGEL. She's sent a YouTube link so I click on it. ANGEL is renowned for finding anything online. We often joke she missed her calling for the Secret Service. And when I see what she sent, I don't know if I should curse or cry because on my screen is a video of MR. J—back in the day.

I don't know how she found it, but she's clearly been thinking about why I can't let MR. J go. She's been with me since the very beginning of our "relationship." She's seen it all. And the next text message she sends surprises me because she's never been his biggest fan.

I get it...I remember the way he looked at you. I remember how it felt like it was only you and him. I get it now...but if he hurts you—again—I'll rip off his dick.

And her sign-off is an eggplant followed by the scissors emoji.

I view the video with a smile because watching MR. J sing and play guitar onstage is a happy memory for me. God, he was so hot in his tight leathers and that black guitar. But the thing is, I still find him as sexy and composed as I did the former MR. J.

I actually find him hotter now. Maybe it's because I've matured. I don't know what it is. All I know is that I want him. Now. And always.

I send him the link and ask, **If you could say one thing to your former self, what would it be? And yes, I'm going to write about it.**

He replies moments later.

I'd say, "You're gonna be around longer than you expect...so take care of yourself now."

A second later, another text comes through.

...But where's the fun in that?

Such a wise response, which just confirms he's grown. But of course he had to add that cheekiness I love.

It does have me wondering how he envisioned his life turning out. Was it what he expected it to be? PSYCHIC did say he has a lot of regrets.

My cell lights up again, and when I see what Mr. J texts, I actually swoon—I want to kick my own ass for being so ridiculous.

I can't write those same, "fuck me, suck me," lyrics anymore. That was okay in my 20s... now I just send those thoughts to you here!

Well, that makes me happier than it should, because does that mean when he has the urge to talk dirty, he only comes to me—in every sense of the word? But then my brain has to overthink as usual and rain on my parade.

That doesn't mean he isn't fucking anyone else. He's not getting it from you regularly, so he's getting it elsewhere.

Yeah, fuck you too.

I'm about to reply, but when I hear an English accent, I know trouble is about to be had.

"You're texting your boyfriend," J-DOG singsongs while I laugh.

"Hello to you too."

J-DOG has no mouth filter—like, none—which is why I like him so much. He did some handiwork on my apartment, and we bonded over terracotta tiles.

He takes a seat and looks at me closely. Another thing I like about him is that he doesn't just listen because he is eagerly waiting for his turn to talk. He actually gives a fuck about the people he likes. I consider myself lucky to be one of those people.

"What's the matter? Trouble with the fella?"

"Am I that obvious? You men, you make us crazy," I share, waiting for his sarcasm.

"No, us men, we're just stupid," he deadpans.

"You said it."

He leans back in his chair, and I know he's about to reveal some pearls of wisdom which I'm going to soak up. "You know the fire triangle?"

I nod.

"There are three components needed to ignite and sustain a fire. Heat, fuel, and oxygen. I like to apply this principle to men, but instead of a triangle, we're squares."

I listen closely, unable to hide my smile.

"Men have four basic needs, and for argument's sake, let's say those needs are food, beer, sports, and sex. Take one of those things away…and we have a meltdown. We can't cope. We need to have all four of those things to function.

"What's your fella's four basic needs?"

I think hard about it. "Wrestling, music, sex…and his freedom."

J-DOG nods cleverly. "And what happens when you chase him and his freedom is at risk?"

"He has a meltdown," I reply, mouth agape.

"See, we're basic creatures. To keep the fire going, so to speak, like the fire triangle, your fella has to have his four needs in order. That's the secret." And he taps his nose.

"He turns me into a psycho," I reveal, shaking my head at my idiocy.

"He wouldn't stick around if he didn't like you. And he's an idiot if he doesn't. Besides, us men, we think we can get any woman we want."

I burst into laughter because this is so typical of J-DOG. He doesn't discriminate—he hates everyone.

"And when we see that is not true, we will come back, tail between our legs because we are the inferior race."

I applaud him because that's some analogy.

"So the moral of the story is to stop overthinking. If he doesn't text, he's probably busy. Or he forgot because we're stupid, remember?"

Harsh words, but I take them in because they have helped. Talking to the opposite sex always does because I've given up trying to work out how men think.

"You know what I heard the other day?"

I'm almost afraid to ask.

"That women have two sets of lips—one for making war. The other for making peace. I love you women."

I shake my head. "And I heard that men were born with two heads, and they're both dicks."

He bursts into laughter. "Thatta girl. Now, go get serviced by your fella."

If only it was that simple.

J-DOG's breakfast bagel is ready to go, so he bids me farewell, leaving me with quite the analogy.

Although life confuses me most days, I do find it most fascinating. Are people, experiences, and events thrown at us by the universe as a challenge? A lesson? I mean, what are the odds that I saw J-DOG at that particular time, in this particular place?

And I don't even want to touch on my fateful meeting with PSYCHIC…

Does the universe have a grand plan for us? Or maybe she's just a sadistic whore, throwing grenades and taking great pleasure in witnessing the chaos she created just because?

I decide to text MR. J two questions because I suddenly have an idea for my next piece.

How many girlfriends have you had? (Ballpark is okay)

Are you the heartbreaker? Or the brokenhearted?

I still find it hard to believe that being in this shit show that I'm in seems to be the remedy to write. The sadder I am or the more fucked up my life is, the easier the words flow.

My cell lights up. It's BOSSMAN.

I'm outside your door.

Nice to see he listens.

Settling my bill, I run the ten blocks to my apartment, and when I see BOSSMAN leaning against the wall, sunglasses perched on his head, I decide to ask him the same questions I asked MR. J. I want to make it an equal playing field.

"You're late," he says without looking up from his screen.

"How many girlfriends have you had?" I ask, out of breath.

When he meets my eyes, I hate that he affects me this way. I wish sleeping with him had gotten him out of my system. But I just want him all the more.

"Eight," he replies without missing a beat.

"Wow. You know that by heart?"

He nods, placing his phone in his back pocket. "Of course I do."

He doesn't offer me anything else, but he doesn't have to. I know that when someone like BOSSMAN commits, it's with someone who has touched him in some way. That has me wondering about his ex-wife, who, on most days, would be off-limits.

But not today.

"Are you the heartbreaker? Or the brokenhearted?"

I open my door, thankful I packed my luggage last night. But I still want to do a last sweep of my apartment in case I missed something.

"Depends."

"On?"

"On the situation."

I turn over my shoulder, pursing my lips. "You're so the heartbreaker."

He simply shrugs. "What I'd give to be inside your head."

"Trust me, it's a place you don't want to be."

BOSSMAN takes my luggage and doesn't hide his appraisal of my appearance. He clears his throat, and I know he likes what he sees. I do too because that white shirt clings to him like a second skin—skin I want to lick.

No. Bad, Z—no licking BOSSMAN again.

We ride the elevator downstairs, and I follow BOSSMAN to where he parked his car. There is an uneasy silence—this is new. This is going to be a long-ass drive.

We get into his black Mercedes, and before I have a chance to put on my seat belt, he's zipping into traffic, ignoring the blaring horns of angry New Yorkers. I like the way he handles the car with confidence and control.

Reminds me of when he had me on my stomach…

Needing to get that image out of my head, I say the first thing that pops in my head. "Do you still speak to your ex-wife?"

His fingers clench the steering wheel.

Probably not the best lead-in, but I roll with it.

"No."

I wait for him to elaborate, but he doesn't. But that doesn't stop me.

"Why not?"

"Because I would rather give myself a lobotomy." He slams down the horn, screaming obscenities to a driver who didn't go through a red light.

"Why?"

BOSSMAN turns over his shoulder, glaring at me with those beautiful eyes. "What is this? Twenty questions?"

"Just making conversation."

"I'd rather make conversation about anything other than my ex-wife."

"You still love her." It's not a question but, rather, a statement.

He scoffs, but it's apparent he does.

"I do not love her." I expect his bottom lip to puff out like the spoiled little brat he sounds like.

"It's fine if you do. I mean, I'm not one to judge. I just thought it would help."

"Help with what?"

"Help with your assholeness."

This time, the car behind us is the one to beep, interrupting this very pleasant conversation.

My text chimes, and when I see it's MR. J, I can't help but smile.

I think the heartbreak duties get shared around. There's enough heartbreak for everybody. Now I can hear Oprah yelling, "You get a broken heart! You get a broken heart!"

His response to the girlfriend comment throws me, as I expected more.

Probably 5 or 6 long-term. Longest would have been 4 or 5 years.

His answers just feed my need to write.

I tell him I'm away for a book thing but don't give him the details. I put my cell into my backpack, totally forgetting about BOSSMAN.

"Is he coming?"

"Who?"

"MR. J," he replies while I burst into laughter.

"No way. I've given up asking him to anything."

BOSSMAN looks relieved, but I know a lecture looms. "For someone who is the bossiest, most stubborn woman I've ever met, you sure as hell back down with him. I don't understand it."

"That makes the two of us."

"I often think it would be easier if we could erase those memories of the people who are bad for us. If only we could forget them, we could move on."

I know we're not just talking about me.

"Where's the fun in that?"

BOSSMAN smirks. "When fun dithers with insanity, I think I would prefer boring any day."

"But would you really? I mean, I think after a while, you'd be chasing the high that comes with the drama."

"Is that what you do?"

This isn't the first time he's called me dramatic.

"I don't want drama. No. It just seems the things I want or the situations I find myself in are rather eventful. I'm just desensitized to it all now."

And I am.

I know when it happened too. It was when BO broke my heart.

He was the only man I ever surrendered to completely, and in return, he proved he was just like the rest.

At least MR. J doesn't pretend to be someone he isn't. He doesn't want what I do—end of story. I'm the masochist who keeps going back for more.

"You can't be that way forever."

"Wanna bet?"

"Z," BOSSMAN says, shaking his head. "I wish you could see how bad he is for you."

"Oh, I have twenty-twenty vision when it comes to that. But it doesn't make a difference. I know what happens when I drink the Kool-Aid."

"So how does *Love Hard* end?"

"That's a good question. I don't know. I guess as long as I'm still breathing, there is no ending. Only possibilities to find my happily ever after."

"And what if your happily ever after is right in front of your eyes?"

"Then it seems I may be blind."

We ride the rest of the way in silence since it seems being a Debbie Downer is contagious. I should be overjoyed I'm here. And I am.

But it's hard to get my hopes up for anything these days in fear of being knocked down.

And speaking of fear, the poor assistant behind the counter cowers as BOSSMAN glares at him like he is the antichrist reincarnate.

"I am so sorry, sir. There is only one reservation under your name."

"Check again," BOSSMAN says through clenched teeth.

"Don't worry." I interrupt, swiping the key card from the counter. "One room is fine."

The assistant looks at BOSSMAN, who finally nods.

"Chill out, will you. Your virtue is safe."

He sighs, running his fingers through his hair. "It's not my virtue I'm worried about."

I'm left with a mouthful of nothing as the concierge takes our bags to our room.

The hotel is beautiful, and I like that the venue where the awards ceremony is being held is within walking distance. I also like the way BOSSMAN's ass looks in those pants.

He turns over his shoulder, and I smile, so busted. But I don't care.

However, the moment we enter the room, I do care because it's very… romantic. With an oceanfront view and that king-size bed draped in velvet and silk, I suddenly feel hot. BOSSMAN appears to have the same thoughts.

"I can sleep on the couch."

"Why? I won't bite."

He walks over to where I stand, and I'm hit with his delectable scent. "I will."

I appear unmoved, but my body responds to him in ways it shouldn't. "Please, you'll be asleep by seven o'clock."

A laugh rumbles from him, and I'm glad the air cools—for now.

His cell rings, and he walks out onto the balcony to take the call.

I decide to take a much-needed bathroom break because the moment I step inside, I fold in half and take three calming breaths. I don't feel better. Only lightheaded.

Why is he being so forward? I don't not like it, but I can't go there with him. Not again. I think I'll go crazy this time—like for real crazy. But goddammit, I can't deny I like everything he's throwing down.

If this were a movie, I'd turn on the taps and splash water on my face, pondering the woes of life. But anyone with eyelash extensions knows better than to get them wet, kind of like Gizmo.

I burst into laughter at the thought of a little Gizmo with eyelashes.

"Oh my god. I'm losing my mind," I mumble, placing the back of my hand on my forehead. I'm burning up.

This was a very bad idea.

"Everything okay in there?" BOSSMAN asks from outside the door.

"Yes, just peachy."

"Good, 'cause we're having drinks with ROW. She's one of the judges. So quit talking to yourself and meet me downstairs."

I salute him with the middle finger when I hear the door close.

Looking into the mirror, I tell myself to get over this bout of insanity because this is important. My words speak for themselves, and I can't change them now, but meeting the judges allows them to see I'm not always unhinged.

Just on every second day.

Once I've reapplied my lipstick, I take the elevator downstairs and see some blonde woman all over BOSSMAN. I want to rip out her eyeballs, but I smile sweetly when they see me because I guess this is ROW.

"The infamous Z," she says, managing to detangle herself from BOSSMAN to give me a double air-kiss on the cheeks.

I hate these pretentious affairs. They aren't me. It's not why I write. But I suck it up and smile.

"Oh please, don't stop."

I end up regretting those words three hours later because ROW doesn't stop…talking about herself, that is.

The only way to deal with this is to get drunk—like I can't remember my name drunk. Sounds fun, but when you're trying to make a good impression, it's a bad idea. I can't see straight and end up missing my mouth, spilling gin all down the front of my dress.

BOSSMAN subtly removes the gin from my hand and replaces it with a glass of water. "How 'bout some water?"

"I can't sit here sober, listening to her talk about alpacas a second longer. I'll give you ten thousand dollars if you stab me with that knife."

I peer at the knife between us.

BOSSMAN covers his snort with an elusive cough.

ROW is oblivious that no one is listening to her, or maybe she is, and she just doesn't care. This world is full of pretentious assholes, and although BOSSMAN can be one too, he actually listens when others talk. I turn to look at him, and fuck me dead, why does he have to look so hot?

I don't even think twice about it and poke him in the cheek with my pointer finger. "You're adorable."

The table goes quiet.

"Says you," he replies, gently gripping my wrist to stop me from poking him in the face.

"She's right," says ROW, deciding to stray from her alpaca talk to talk about BOSSMAN.

I suddenly prefer her boring me to death.

"You should see how adorable his but—"

"Okay, let's get you upstairs," BOSSMAN says, cutting me off.

I don't argue and am thankful when he helps me stand because my legs are suddenly jelly being pressed up to BOSSMAN this way.

"Put her to bed and come back down," ROW says, not keeping the contempt from her voice.

She's just dug herself a very big hole…one I intend to bury her and her alpacas in.

"The thing he will be going down on is—"

BOSSMAN slams his hand over my mouth. Of course I bite his fingers, which he removes from my mouth with a pained hiss.

"And by the way, alpacas are fucking ugly-looking palm trees."

ROW's mouth falls open, horrified I insulted her spirit animal, while BOSSMAN carries me out of the room. Laughter erupts from me because it looks like the Hamptons is super fun after all.

"Z?"

I see BLUE, and my high instantly fades because I know how this will end.

"You don't call? You don't write? My feelings are hurt."

BOSSMAN's grip around me tightens because he doesn't need a map. He knows that I was approached by Incognito and failed to mention the fact. He doesn't put me down, which is such an alpha move, and I suddenly want to lick his face.

"I can see you're…indisposed right now. But have lunch with us tomorrow? My boss would love to talk to you."

I don't have a chance to get a word in edgewise because BOSSMAN carries me away, his heavy footsteps echoing the anger he feels. I am in so much trouble. The moment he marches me into the room, I expect him to put me down, but he doesn't.

He walks me out to the balcony, and only then does he set me down. But he doesn't let me go. His broad back holds me prisoner as he presses me into the railing. His hard body against mine only stokes this internal fire.

"Why didn't you tell me you got scouted by Incognito?"

"It slipped my mind."

"Z!"

"BOSSMAN!"

An irritated groan gets caught in his throat. "Why didn't you accept? That's fucking huge."

"I didn't not accept…I just didn't call them back."

Silence.

The waves of the ocean could stop wars because if you stop and listen to the sound, really listen, you'd soon realize how insignificant we are in the greater scheme of things. Merely a drop in the ocean.

"Tell me why you didn't."

I focus on the starless sky because if the universe can do a complex thing like turning and giving us life, then I can tell BOSSMAN I didn't accept because of him. The thought of not seeing him every day, of not annoying him until he curses my name fucking hurts. It hurts because somehow, love has crept up and yelled FUCK YOU VERY MUCH, and has made me feel…this.

Vomit rises, like literal vomit.

I push back, and thankfully, BOSSMAN lets me go.

I run to the bathroom and throw up the entire bottle of gin I consumed into the toilet. But I wish I could purge this darkness, this sadness eating away at my insides because I'm so fucking messed up in the head.

"Oh, Z."

"Go away." It comes out muffled as my head is still buried in the toilet bowl.

Of course he doesn't listen, and when I hear the tap running, I wonder why his wife would cheat on him. Yes, he's an asshole, but he's kind and attentive to the people he likes. And I know that he likes me. And I…like him.

"Why are you being so nice to me?" I ask when I hear him sit beside me, only to place a wet towel on the back of my neck.

"I'm doing what every person should do in a situation like this."

"Not everyone would."

MR. J has never done anything for me like this. Or BO.

"Why are you so damaged, Z?" BOSSMAN asks with a sigh.

I shrug. "Glutton for punishment?"

"You need to stop it. You need to see that other people love you very much."

"And there's that word I have a love-hate relationship with. I wish it would leave me alone because love has done nothing for me but break my fucking heart."

A sob suddenly echoes in the bowl, and I can't stop. A torrent of emotion pours out of me with no end in sight. And BOSSMAN is here for it.

He rubs my back. "Everything will be okay. You just need to believe."

Finding the courage to lift my head, I look at him, unable to mask my pain. "Believe in what?"

He places his hand on my cheek, washing away my tears with his thumb. "In yourself."

He gathers me into his arms, and I cry a lifetime of tears because I don't even know who I am anymore. The person I once was is fading away, day by day, until eventually, all that'll be left are my words…my legacy to the world that I once was.

Twenty

"Not About Love"
Fiona Apple

Lesson number...I don't know. I've lost count. But always remember, gin makes you cry.

A dickhead ex once told me this, and it stuck. Or maybe he ruined gin for me? I don't know. What I do know is that I got very drunk last night, insulted ROW and her alpacas, and cried like a baby in BOSSMAN's arms until I passed out.

All in all, just an average night for me.

Groaning, I throw a pillow over my face in hopes I suffocate myself instead of facing the mess I've made.

"Good morning, sunshine."

"Is it?" I muffle from under the pillow.

The bed dips, and I fight with BOSSMAN as he tries to remove the pillow from my face. He wins.

When I open my eyes, I curse the gods because does he really have to look this hot in the morning? I look like a hot mess, no doubt.

He offers me a cup of coffee. I accept.

Settling against the headboard, I'm lost for words—ironic for the sarcastic writer. BOSSMAN doesn't speak either.

Well, this is going well.

"So how's them alpacas?" I finally say, which has BOSSMAN's lips twitching.

"Are you okay?"

"No," I reply honestly. "I don't even know what that entails anymore."

"Maybe you need to write?"

"That's the last thing I need." I can only imagine the content that would spew from me like hot lava if I had to write right now. "On a scale of one to ten, how badly did I fuck up?"

"It's fine."

I scoff, not believing a word. "It is not fine. Let's just leave. I don't want this stupid award anyway."

"We can't," BOSSMAN says, lifting his glasses and massaging the bridge of his nose. "I have lunch with ROW. She asked, and after last night…"

I wave him off, not wanting to hear any more. "I'm so sorry, BOSSMAN. I don't know what's wrong with me. I want to fix MR. J, but I'm the one who needs fixing. I'm so messed up."

BOSSMAN sighs, his lips turning into a frown. "Who isn't? Stop being so hard on yourself."

Why is he being so nice to me?

Something is rotten in Denmark…

When I see my open laptop on the nearby chair, all the answers smack me in the face. "Oh my fucking god! You read it, didn't you?"

"It's not my fault your password is written on a Post-it note on the front of your laptop."

I want to die.

"You have no idea about boundaries, do you?"

BOSSMAN shrugs, totally unapologetic, and it's hot. "When you write, it's the only time I understand you. And I was worried about you."

"When did you read it?" I ask, wondering if that's the reason he was so nice to me when I was howling into his chest.

"After I put you to bed," he replies, and for that, I'm thankful because I know his kindness was from a genuine place and not because he read my chapter and felt sorry for me for being a pathetic loser.

I don't know what to say other than FUCK!

He knows I like him more than I should. I'm beyond embarrassed, which is why I never wanted him to read it.

"So…" He clears his throat.

"I was drunk when I wrote it," I blurt out as a last-ditch attempt.

BOSSMAN laughs. "They do say the truth comes out when you're drunk. And there was a lot of truths in that chapter."

I don't even have the energy to deny it because that's the thing about my writing—it's brutally honest. And I was brutally honest when I spewed my emotions all over the page.

"I liked it," he says, and I don't know if he's referring to my writing or my feelings. "Do you want to publish it?"

I stare at him like my madness has rubbed off on him. "No, I do not want to publish it. I mean, do you want me to?"

"When have you ever listened to me?"

"True, but everyone will know it's you."

He looks at me like I'm stating the obvious.

"And you're okay with that?"

BOSSMAN mulls over my question. "I think that I am."

Oh, well…plot twist. I did *not* see that coming.

I'm so accustomed to hiding men that I've forgotten what it feels like to have one who actually wants to be seen with me in public.

"Well…let me read over it and make sure it's not total dog shit."

"Nothing you ever write is dog shit, Z. Except for the cats." And he shudders.

"I have to get ready for lunch."

I clench my coffee cup but nod. He's doing this because of the circus I created last night.

He grabs some clothes and showers while I get my ass up and decide to sit on the balcony and attempt to be somewhat productive. I'm checking emails when I get a text from MR. J.

When are you there till? I was going to pop down and say hi. Is that ok?

Fuck. Shit. *Fuck.*

He wants to come *here?*

In what universe does he come to my book things? And what if someone spills the tea on what I wrote?

Those words were never meant for him to read. Yes, they're about him. But that doesn't mean I wanted him to read them. No one knows it's him. I know he may feel like I've betrayed him in some ways, but he was always going to remain anonymous.

And I needed to detail him and his past for readers to understand our history. For them to understand him and for them to understand *me*. But I know he may feel exposed in some ways.

This is so fucking personal, but it's a memoir, so for it to be authentic, I had to pull back the layers, and like an onion, all it's done is make me cry.

I'm away for a few days. Talk when I get back x

It's a shitty response, but I can't have him here.

I smell BOSSMAN before I see him. His cologne catches the cool breeze, and when I turn to see him in a tight black shirt and pants, I want to claw out ROW's eyeballs all the more. I try to smile, but I'm sure I resemble a deranged clown.

"Have fun."

He rolls his eyes, and I appreciate him cleaning up my mess.

"Please try to stay out of trouble."

"Only because you said please," I reply, throwing him a sickly sweet smile.

He shakes his head and surprises me by kissing me on the forehead. "I won't be long."

I don't know why he's telling me this. He doesn't owe me a thing. Something in my stomach churns, and I know it's not the gin because I threw that up last night.

BOSSMAN leaves while I question what the fuck is wrong. *That was nice*, I tell myself. He has been nothing *but* nice. So what's the issue here?

I call the only person who can explain what's going on.

"Because you always self-sabotage any happiness you have," BUNNY says, and I can hear her camera click. She's in the middle of work but always has time for me and my drama—bless.

"Am I that fucked up?"

"Yes," she replies without pause.

"MR. J messaged. He wants to come."

"That's a good thing."

But my silence states otherwise.

"You two are both so emotionally inept. He needs to accept he loves you and get over his fear of commitment. Or, you know, you could tell him that you love him."

I suddenly get hot.

"So have you fucked your boss yet?"

"BUNNY!" I admonish, which just reveals my guilt.

"No, but you're gonna. Or you're at least thinking about it."

"I don't know what's going on, but him being nice is…weird."

"No, it's what normal human beings do."

I sigh because she's right. "Why do we always want what's bad for us? Food? Expensive shit we can't afford? Men?"

"Because we're always searching for more. MR. J is finally giving you more, and you're running away? Tell him to get his ass down there right now and be with the man you want. Whichever one that may be."

It seems we always want the opposite of what we have, and why? Because most of us are curious creatures, and we can't help but wonder if the grass is greener on the other side.

I hang up and think about what BUNNY said.

I've been asked how *LOVE HARD* ends, and honestly, I don't know because life is forever changing. But the memoir needs an ending. And I think I've just worked out what it is.

I'm lost in so many words, I can't type fast enough. It's like my fingers are possessed.

This is why I write. This is what I was born to do.

I've penned endless works before, but this one, this piece, is my baby. Every writer gets asked which piece of writing is their favorite. And for me, it changes with my mood. But *Love Hard* will be that for me because nothing has been more raw, more emotional for me than writing about my life and sharing it with the world.

I know I'll be judged, and that's okay. That's not why I wrote this memoir. I didn't even know I needed to write it until the words spilled from me freely. But I've learned…from myself. Ironic, right? I just hope my readers can take at least one thing from the memoir to cherish in their heart of hearts and think of me because we're not alone in this game of love.

"Drinking alone today?"

Peering up from my laptop, I see BLUE standing by my table.

Reaching for the tall glass of juice, I raise it in a salute. "No drinking for me for a very long time. I vaguely remember seeing you last night, but I'm sorry for whatever I said."

A smile lights up his handsome face. "Can I sit?"

I nod.

Kids are building sandcastles while their parents drink their margaritas. The vibe is chill. This is why I love writing outdoors. Anything can happen, just like running into BLUE.

"Z, I haven't been honest with you."

I wait for him to continue.

"Incognito does want you to write for them. I know this because the boss… that's me."

Well, holy shit. I did *not* see that coming.

"Everything I said to you still stands. You're uncouth and unpredictable, but that's why we want you. Everyone is going nuts over the memoir because you've shown the world that you fuck up…a lot," he adds while I purse my lips and nod because he's right.

"We all put our idols up on a pedestal, thinking they can do no wrong, but you've torn down that notion and allowed them to see that at the end of the day, we're all human. We make mistakes. We make fucking horrible decisions. And we're all still learning, regardless of our age.

"I know your loyalties are with BOSSMAN, but he will agree that this is bigger than him. I know he wants what's best for you. Whether you win this stupid award or not means nothing to me. I want to work with you because you have talent and you have heart.

"It's not something we see often. Everyone gets so caught up in the notoriety of being an author that they soon forget what being an author is actually about; writing a good fucking story. And *Love Hard* is just that."

His compliments make me uncomfortable, but BLUE is genuine. He isn't trying to sweet-talk me, so I say yes. He's pleading his case so whatever decision I make, he can say to himself that at least he tried his best.

"You know where to find me if you want to talk."

He leaves me with a thousand questions because I can't deny I like what he said. He is a straight shooter, and I sort of respect him for lying to me about who he actually is. But the thought of writing for someone else makes me feel sick to my stomach.

Yes, I'm loyal to BOSSMAN because he helped my career, but I'm loyal to him for another reason too.

And speak of the devil himself...

He and ROW are walking along the beach, and I can't deny that wave of jealousy that overcomes me once again. I hate that she's touching his arm. I hate that he's making her laugh. I hate that I can't just be honest with myself that BOSSMAN is the man who could make me happy—if only I tried.

With a sigh, I look at my laptop, and it only cements that my "ending" is the only ending I could ever write.

It's dark by the time BOSSMAN returns. I'm proud of myself for not drowning my sorrows in the minibar and that's because I've written all day.

My back, fingers, and eyes ache, but that comes with the job of being a writer. It's far from glamorous. So when BOSSMAN enters the room, I have no doubt I look like utter crap.

"Have you eaten?" he asks, tossing his key card onto the coffee table.

I'm perched on the sofa and crack my neck from side to side, cringing because ouch.

"Move over."

I don't have time to ask him what for before he arranges himself behind me and rubs my shoulders. I want to push him away, but it feels too good.

"Have you written all day?"

I hum in response, my eyes dropping to half-mast.

"What are you writing?"

"The end," I reply lazily.

"Oh? So you know how your story ends, then?"

"No."

"No? Then how can it be the end?"

"You'll just have to wait and see. I can't give away the ending. How was lunch?" I hope it was awful.

"It was okay. I met with some people in the industry and talked a bunch of bullshit. The usual at these sort of events."

"Glad I wasn't there." BOSSMAN's fingers are like magic, and I feel myself falling into a bubble of bliss.

"You wrote outside, didn't you?" Before I have a chance to ask why, his warm breath skates along the slope of my neck. "I can smell the ocean on your skin."

His lips are a hair's breadth away, and all I want is to feel them on me.

"I was thinking about what you wrote…what you wrote about me," he clarifies. "I don't want to fix you, Z. Don't you see? I want *you*…in whatever way you can give."

I slowly open my eyes.

"Give me a chance. That's all I ask. Let me show you a different kind of love."

"And what kind of love is that?" I whisper as his fingers caress between my shoulder blades.

"A love that is mutual. A love that doesn't want anything in return. A love that loves you how you deserve."

Tears roll down my cheeks. What is it about BOSSMAN that always makes me cry?

"I'm scared," I confess. "What if that love is not enough?"

"Love is always enough."

Turning around to face him, I see nothing but love reflected in those poignant eyes. "No, I mean, what if my love isn't enough."

BOSSMAN shakes his head sadly. "You are enough. You're too much for some. Let him go, Z. If he cared, he'd be there every day and every night, loving you how you've loved him."

"I wish I could. If it were that easy, you don't think I would have done so already?"

"What does he give you? Tell me. Help me understand."

I don't want to have this conversation, but BOSSMAN grips my cheeks, begging me to explain why I allow myself to be treated this way.

"He gives me butterflies every time he speaks. He makes my heart race the moment I see his texts. And he makes me believe in love every time we touch. I can't let that go because no one makes me feel that way," I confess, not wishing to hurt BOSSMAN, but he wanted the truth.

"But what about all the other times? When he doesn't reply to your texts? When he's okay with seeing you once every few months? When he leaves you questioning everything because you've given him your all, and it's still not enough? Is that love then?"

More tears fall because he's right; I know that he is. But it's the good that outweighs the bad when I know that it shouldn't.

"You know who you need to love the most?"

I shake my head slowly.

"Yourself. And everyone else can fall into place around you."

"Why do you want me? I am so fucked up."

"Who isn't?" he states, gripping my cheeks harder. "We smile and act how we're expected to, but on the inside, we're all just wishing to claw off our faces and be free.

"Try. That's all I'm asking. Try to be with me and only me."

It takes a lot to shock me, but it seems to be a common occurrence with BOSSMAN.

"I don't know that I can. I don't think being loved or being in love is destined for me."

"Try," he repeats, pressing his lips to mine.

His taste is mixed with my salty tears, and it's something I could become addicted to.

"I don't want to lose you. I try to, but we fail? What happens then?"

"Try," he says one final time before kissing me deeply.

I want to argue, to push him away, but I can't. Kissing BOSSMAN appeases the noise and embraces the silence where only he and I exist.

But my mind does nothing but overthink, and although kissing BOSSMAN is becoming my new favorite drug, he isn't who I want. And I love him enough to know that. I love him enough to push him away.

"BOSSMAN, no," I say, regrettably ending our kiss.

He doesn't argue. But I can see his sadness as he knows his love isn't enough.

He stands and silently leaves the room.

I have a man who wants me, flaws and all, but I don't want him because I love someone else.

My cell chimes, and it's from MR. J.

Once upon a time, I asked him a hundred questions because I hoped he'd open up. He answered some, but others, personal ones, he didn't. But now, text after text comes raining in as he answers every single question I asked.

He would have had to scroll through our thousands of messages to find them, and I don't know why, but the fact makes me burst into tears.

The questions are the most random questions—ever. Ranging from what were you like in high school to what superpower would you have. MR. J answers every single one. He answers them with honesty and with wit, which I love about him. He can make me laugh and swoon in the same breath.

The messages don't stop, and neither does my heart as it beats profoundly for this man.

It seems that when MR. J senses me pulling away, he gives me so much. But is this like every other time? I don't think I can handle any more heartache.

But what he replies next has my heart lifting her tired head.

What makes you feel most loved? That was my question.

And his one-word response has me falling in love with him all over again.

You x

Twenty-One

"*Lovely*"
Billie Eilish

In just a few hours, it'll be revealed who the winner of this award is. I don't care either way, but BOSSMAN does.

He's already downstairs like a good BOSSMAN, being social while I decide what shoes to wear. I'm wearing a red halter-style mermaid gown. It cinches the waist in just the right way to accent the high slit in the long skirt.

The split is rather revealing, which is why I decide to complement the dress with my red glitter heels. Someone once said they're like Dorothy's ruby slippers if she visited a porn set.

Seems appropriate seeing as the publishers tonight are the pimps, and we are merely their whores. We're here to make them money and bring them notoriety. Not BOSSMAN, though. He is the exception to the rule.

My makeup is pinup style—cat eyes, red lips, and just enough highlighter to reflect the lights in just the right way. My hair is curled.

I have no idea what the dress code is, but I don't care because I don't follow the rules. Come to think of it, I don't know much because I trust BOSSMAN.

He said it was a casual affair. Nothing too fancy.

After spraying myself with my favorite perfume, I grab my bag and am out the door with no time to spare because I'm late—as usual. When I catch the elevator to the lobby, I see fellow writers and their colleagues mingling outside the ballroom doors.

BLUE looks rather dashing in his suit and raises his glass of champagne when we lock eyes. I haven't told BOSSMAN about our encounter because I still haven't decided what I want to do.

BOSSMAN stands in front of me wearing a tux. I almost forget to breathe.

"You look beautiful," he says, offering me a glass of red wine.

"What about the shoes, though?"

Regardless of what happened or didn't happen last night, our chemistry is forever present.

I notice everyone staring and wonder if I forgot to put on underwear as this split is extremely indecent if I shift my leg in the wrong or, rather, the right way.

"They're jealous," BOSSMAN whispers into my ear, reading my thoughts. "You've won this."

I pull back, stunned. "Who'd you bribe? Oh god, do I want to know?" I add, thinking about ROW and how cozy they looked together on the beach.

"I didn't bribe anyone," he says, grinning. "Your talent speaks for itself."

"How can they award me when it's not even finished? What if the ending is a huge disappointment?"

BOSSMAN bends low and kisses my cheek. "You can never be a disappointment. Let's go."

My head resembles a bobble toy because he could ask me to follow him into hell, and I would say yes.

He leads me into the lavish ballroom with his hand against my lower back, and I like that he doesn't shy away from public affection. It's foreign.

We take our seats and then let the boring commence. I hate these kind of things, and usually, I would need to get utterly drunk to sit through it, but I steer clear of anything alcoholic as I don't want a repeat of the other night.

Speakers from all over the country are invited to share their stories and experiences, and an hour later, I'm looking at the exit like it's my saving grace. BOSSMAN places his hand on my bare thigh, sending a volt of electricity straight through me.

"Don't hate me."

"Too late," I reply, not even sure what we're talking about because his touch distracts me from coherent thoughts.

But when I hear my name being called, I know nothing can distract me from wanting to slap BOSSMAN in the face.

"It's time for our contenders to read from their nominated works, and then the winner will be announced," the MC says, waving for us to join him on the stage.

I turn to look at BOSSMAN, who smirks sweetly.

"You said all I had to do was sit here," I say between clenched teeth, trying my best not to cause a scene.

"If I told you, you wouldn't have come." He gently coaxes me to stand while I not so gently throw a bread roll at his head.

All eyes are on me as I make my way to the stage. At least I look semi-decent. But this is a disaster. I don't want to read in front of people. I'm a writer. I don't liaise with real people. I talk to the ones in my head.

Now I have to read my most personal inner thoughts to a room filled with strangers. Since when is that a good idea?

I climb the three stairs onto the stage and try to hide behind the curtain, but to no avail as some asshole shoves me to stand with the other four writers to take a picture. This is fucking ridiculous. I wrote some words. I didn't cure cancer.

But I smile nonetheless.

Each candidate reads their work, but I'm barely listening because I don't like this. Writing is art, and I don't think judging someone for their creativity is fair because art is subjective. I don't like the term "bigger author." I think it's just an insult to every writer out there.

I started writing to escape the norms and stereotypes of society. I was always a misfit. A freak. A weirdo—terms I still wear with pride. But this bogus affair just celebrates everything I hate. I can't believe I agreed to be a slave to the grind.

So with that thought in mind, I discreetly make my way down from the stage and leave the room.

"Z!" BOSSMAN calls out as I press the elevator call button. "What are you doing?"

"That isn't why I started writing." I hook my thumb toward the ballroom. "That is fucking bullshit. I'm sorry, but I won't be paraded like a prized pig. What makes those judges an expert on who the winner is? We're all fucking winners for having the guts to write, exposing ourselves to criticism and bad reviews.

"But we do it because, for most of us, it's an escape…away from bullshit like tonight. You should have told me it was going to be a gala for utter fuckheads. You said it was casual. You lied to me."

BOSSMAN frowns, and I can see he's hurt, but I don't care. "If I told you the details, would you have come?"

"No, and that's because I don't need a piece of paper or a title to tell me what a good writer I am. I know I am. And that's all I need. I want to connect to people, not with a fucking title, but with my words. And if winning this bullshit thing is so important to you, then you don't know me at all."

BOSSMAN sighs, tonguing his top lip in frustration. "Why do you have to fight me over every fucking thing?" He slams his fist against the wall, angered.

"Because that's who I am! You've read my writing! I hardly follow the rules of society. You knew what you were getting yourself into the moment we started this! And just because we did what we did that one time doesn't mean I'm going to forget who I am!

"It doesn't mean I'm going to do something against what I believe in. I'm not a sellout. I honestly don't care if no one likes what I write because I write for myself! I curse. I like my own company more than I do others. And I make stupid decisions…every single day, like fucking you!"

"Baby?"

Fuck you, universe, and your sick sense of humor.

With a sigh, I turn and see MR. J standing feet away. He's heard it all because I'm pretty sure I've yelled it loud enough for everyone to hear.

"Hey," I say, unable to contain my happiness that he's here.

"Are you okay?"

I laugh in response because I haven't been okay for a very long time. "At least I have on pretty shoes."

MR. J smiles.

And just like that, the noise settles, and he provides me with a happy place that I want to get lost in. BOSSMAN decides to shit all over the serenity.

"We've not met. I'm her boss." He walks over to MR. J and shakes his hand. "And I'm guessing you're the notorious MR. J."

"BOSSMAN, enough." I shake my head because I don't want trouble.

MR. J shakes his hand cautiously, looking at me for any cues. I simply inhale deeply, wishing I could click my heels three times and go home.

ROW comes running into the foyer, stopping dead in her tracks when witnessing the sight before. "You won," she says, eyes wide. "You've got to go back in there."

I look at BOSSMAN. This is his chance to show me what's more important—me or this stupid fucking award.

His hesitation is all I need.

MR. J reaches for my hand, and the moment our fingers entwine, I know this is the reason I choose him. Why I think I will always choose him.

He is so far from perfect, but he doesn't push. He is patient with me. He tells me when I overthink, putting my mind at ease. I'm a fucking handful, but he keeps coming back to me, and that's got to mean something.

I don't know what, and I probably never will. But for now, this is enough.

BOSSMAN turns and follows ROW into the ballroom to accept the award for his company, while MR. J and I ride the elevator upstairs to my room. We don't speak. He just wraps his arm around me and holds me close.

He's taller than I remember. Even in heels, he's taller than I am. I like that. I like a lot about him.

We enter the room, and I gather my things because I want to leave. He waits for me patiently. I'm about to take off my shoes, but I glance at MR. J and know he would like to do it instead. So I sit on the edge of the bed and smile.

"Come here."

He does as he's told.

"On your knees. Take off my shoes, please."

Again, he submits, but he leaves my heels on as I know he likes looking at them as much as I do.

He's instantly hard, so I rub my foot over the front of his black jeans. "Why did you come?"

"Because I wanted to see you," he replies, those chocolate-brown eyes melting me to the core. "This is incredible. Congratulations, baby. You've worked so hard. You deserve this."

"You're not mad that I'm writing about us?"

"No, I'm not mad," he says with a dimpled smile. "I'm just…overwhelmed. But in a good way, though."

My overthinking kicks in as if on cue and decides to shit on my happiness as it puts the doubt in my mind that he only seems to care when it involves sex.

But something suddenly happens—I fight against myself for once, forcing myself to remember all the times he's assured me that that's not the case.

That's you overthinking. In a world filled with so much negativity that I switch off from, you're my sunshine.

Memory after memory smashes into me because the signs were always there—I was just too broken to see them.

Sure, MR. J and I are probably fated for yet another collision course, but this time is different, and that's because our path is paved with love.

"What's the best gift anyone has ever given you?" I ask, thinking about all the questions he answered for me. I could ask him a thousand and still have a thousand more.

He grins, winding me with those dimples. "The best gift is still your mouth…and your left foot and your right foot…in no particular order. But also, the best gift is when your tongue is in my—"

"Okay, enough." I chuckle because he's so silly. "I meant a gift, as in something other than my mouth or feet from another person."

He ponders my question, and I know that I could ask him anything, do anything to him, and he would allow it. "I guess Randy was a beautiful gift from my sister. He changed my life."

You see, sometimes, I just have to push MR. J to feel. But it's clear I make him feel a little too much when he adds, "Another beautiful gift is when you are licking my—"

I press my mouth over his to silence him. And I pull away when he slips in his tongue just to frustrate him.

"What is your favorite childhood memory?"

He smiles as if reliving the memory itself. "Maybe Saturday mornings after sitting through about six hours of morning cartoons feeling like I had an abundance of time to do and go wherever I wanted, which was usually in my imagination."

My heart swells at the thought of a little MR. J doing that.

I remember he once told me that when in high school, he was always getting into something other than schoolwork because he wanted to be anywhere but there. He was a daydreamer. He was also the class clown, which was easy to see.

He hasn't changed much, and that's because I guess when MR. J loves, he loves hard.

He is an enigma to me, and I just want to know more. "How have you changed in the past several years?"

He thinks on this. "I feel like I've detached myself from my ego, although some may disagree, but maybe that's just age?"

"What surprises you most about where you are now?"

He laughs. "I'm surprised I'm still alive. I didn't have a death wish, but I was pretty reckless. Friends used to tell me I wouldn't make it out of my twenties. I showed them."

His answers reveal how he's matured with age, but I wonder why that doesn't apply to matters of the heart. Perhaps it's with age that he's realized that this…situationship is what he desires?

Maybe one day he will open up and share more, but I know I could ask him anything, and he would answer truthfully. This is the epitome of trust.

So I decide to share something with him.

Here goes nothing…

"I've…been in love with you since I was eighteen years old," I confess, swallowing past my fear of rejection.

If this is to work, really work, then something needs to be different, and what's the most earth-shattering thing that can change the course of everything?

…Love.

MR. J doesn't say a word.

"I don't know how you feel about me and that's because I've never asked. I've always been too afraid to ask because of your answer…whatever it might be."

MR. J lowers his chin.

"I know you've been hurt, but I need you to see the things that I do every time we kiss. Every time we touch. Every time we gravitate back to one another when something good or bad happens. I need you to see that this can't have been for nothing."

His silence has tears falling down my cheeks. But I don't wipe them away.

"But if you can't, then you're nothing but a coward," I whisper, standing because I need space. "I don't want to be an option…because you're never one for me."

He stays on his knees while I peer out the window, those same feelings I experienced when this shit show first started are drowning me whole.

"It's been so long since I needed to think about anyone but myself. I've forgotten what it feels like," he finally says.

I keep my back turned because I can't face him if this is really it this time.

"But you're all I think about. How do you keep destroying me?"

He's the only man who makes me cry this way.

"What we had years ago, it was beautiful. Every moment spent with you is."

I'm waiting for the inevitable, but…

I hear his boots on the carpet as he walks toward me and stands beside me, peering out into the vastness.

"But now, everything is so much…more."

My heart demands I put an end to this once and for all because no heart deserves to be broken this way—over and over again.

"Not seeing you all the time isn't necessarily what I want, but I just don't know how to do this."

I squeeze my eyes shut.

"Those walls you mentioned me having, they're just reinforced even more so than before."

"Then leave me alone. What you're doing is mean, and it confuses me."

"You don't think I would if I could?" he asks, coaxing me to look at him.

His sadness and pain are evident because MR. J isn't a bad guy. He's just wounded by…love, the asshole which seems to destroy everything it touches.

"What do you want from me?"

He sighs heavily. "I don't know."

I shake my head, tonguing my upper lip because I have no words.

"Then let me make it really easy for you. Please leave me alone. Forget my number. Forget me."

He flinches as if my words slapped both cheeks.

"I can't. But if you want to walk, then walk. It's not my intention to mess you around."

Now I am fucking pissed.

"So you want me, but on your terms? Is that it? There are two of us in this. If you don't want this, then don't reply to my texts. Don't turn up at something like this and expect me to understand why you're here if you don't want me!"

"I do fucking want you," he says with as much passion as me. "If I didn't, this would be so much easier."

"Nothing about us has ever been easy, so why start now? Get out, and go for good this time. Loving you hurts, it hurts so much. But I have to love myself more."

"Baby—"

He reaches for me, but I recoil. "You're my once in a lifetime, but thanks for the highlights…because we're done. So done."

He grips my wrist and drags me into his arms. I fight him, but he presses me against his chest. "You feel that?" he asks, eyes locked with mine. "That's the sound of our love song."

I know he speaks from his heart.

"Don't say things to me you can't take back," I whisper, tears spilling into my lips. "I'll always want you but can't have you because you won't let me."

"Why do you want me?"

The fight in me soon dies because he is just as scared as I am. This thing between us has never made sense. We can't seem to stay away from one another, but when together, we both want to run away.

"I can't not," I confess in a whisper. "I've tried, I've really fucking tried. But I can't stop. No matter who I'm with, it's you I always want. This between us is so rare. After almost two decades, for this chemistry to still burn as strong…it means something.

"I don't know what. But I do know that it continues to grow. And I know you feel it too. Maybe you're afraid? Maybe I'm just a hopeless romantic? I don't know. What I do know is that I love you, but I need to love myself more.

"Which is why this is your choice. You decide because I can't do this anymore. I love you. I want you. You and only you. Just give this a chance."

MR. J holds me closely, saying nothing but taking it all in as he always does.

He isn't unfeeling. I can see and feel his pain. Is he afraid? Has love broken him too?

The door suddenly opens, and BOSSMAN enters, glass award in hand. I don't know what's about to happen. But I never do. He places the award on the table before taking off his jacket and draping it over the back of the chair.

He slowly walks to where we are and grips my hand.

MR. J holds the other, and I am led to the couch.

BOSSMAN gently coaxes me to sit, and when I do, both men leave me speechless as they drop to their knees before me.

The sight is beautiful and empowering because two men wish to love me. No words are spoken as MR. J unfastens the buckle on my shoe. He's done this countless times before, so he has home ground advantage.

But BOSSMAN follows suit soon after.

I look from man to man, appreciating the differences between them. If I had to choose, who would it be?

Both shoes are removed, and I can see MR. J grit his teeth.

"Does this make you jealous?" I ask him.

"Extremely."

"Why?"

BOSSMAN caresses my bare leg, revealing he knows my body like a lover does.

"Because I want you all to myself. I want to watch, but it's hard. I don't like someone touching what's mine."

"She's not yours," BOSSMAN says angrily. "You've had years. Let her go. I can treat her how she deserves."

This shade of green suits MR. J. "Fuck off."

BOSSMAN does nothing of the sort and instead licks up my leg. MR. J watches, his jealousy almost suffocating.

I run my fingers through BOSSMAN's hair. "You should be groveling for the shit you pulled."

"Oh, baby, I can grovel all you want."

MR. J isn't blind. He can read the chemistry between BOSSMAN and me. But BOSSMAN knows the history I share with MR. J.

Two men on their knees before me; what's a girl to do? Both men are as toxic as the other, and if I had any sense, I would kick both out the door.

But I can't.

Gripping MR. J by the front of his T-shirt, I slam my mouth to his, making out with him slowly. I don't want to rush this. I want to savor every second with him because I don't know what tomorrow holds.

Against my better judgment, I know who I choose—but does he choose me in return?

"I wish you could see what I do," I whisper against MR. J's lips.

Nothing makes any sense, but I know I need space.

Without a word, I stand and leave both men behind as I leave the room. I can't think straight with them in my life. I get into the elevator with no real sense of where I'm going. I need air. But instead, what I get is the wind ripped from my lungs because as I exit the elevator, I bump straight into three people who throw me onto my ass.

They hold on to me to stop me from falling, which is ironic, considering the role they're about to play in my life.

One has kind chocolate-colored eyes and a scar in his left eyebrow which gives him an edge I like. I soon like it too much because that edge will leave me an inconsolable mess.

The younger one is trouble with his tattoo sleeve, a mouth to die for, and nose ring, but his heart, it's so kind. He will frustrate me beyond words, but he will also prove to be unbelievably patient.

The other boy has the most beautiful smile I've ever seen. But that goddamn face…he has a cluster of freckles under his left eye in the shape of a triangle.

A Superman curl, a nose ring, and black nails are man number one. Nothing but honey will tumble from those sinful lips, but they're swathed in poison, which I soon happily drink. He is someone who changes my life…I just don't know it yet. His name…his name is GHOST.

Man number two intrigues me because although young, his confidence makes him wiser than his years. His teeth are twisted in the way I like, and his eyes are the most unusual color. He holds my gaze, and I soon will learn that he doesn't back down. I see something in him that perhaps he doesn't see in himself. When he smiles, I die a little inside because fuck me dead, he has dimples. And that's what he will be called—DIMPLES.

And that leaves us with man number three. He's tall and so damn cute I forget my own name. He has a sleeve full of color, and both hands inked. On one, a clock, which is ironic because we would always be a race against time. The other, a tiger. Those hands will heal me in every possible way.

He is calm.

I instantly feel safe.

He will soon become my boy…and me?

I'm soon to become his girl.

And his name…his name is SWITZERLAND.

I know I can't keep him, but I can't stay away.

He will show me kindness.

But he will also prove to be the most stubborn, bossiest man I've ever met, which makes him, him. I don't stand a chance.

He will teach me things about myself.

He will challenge me.

He will make me laugh.

He will make me cry.

He will kiss the back of my shoulder as he holds me tight.

He will ensure I'm touching him any time we're lying side by side.

He will fill the void…for a little while, anyway.

He will be everything I want…

But, in the end…he will break me.

And I know it from the first moment we kiss.

But that doesn't stop me.

GHOST, DIMPLES, and SWITZERLAND.

SWITZERLAND, DIMPLES, and GHOST.

Their smiles promise me the world…but how does this end?

Twenty-Two

So here we find ourselves—at the end.

Congratulations, dear reader, you made it. I know there were many casualties lost along the way. But all's fair in love and war.

So how does it end? The truth is, there is no end while my heart continues to beat. I've learned many things as a writer, but the one thing that most writers agree on is that you can never please everyone with the ending you choose.

Therefore, I'm going to try something a little different.

You've stuck with me throughout this crazy ride, so you choose. You choose which ending you want; choose your own adventure.

Are you ready?

"I Fell in Love with the Devil"
Avril Lavigne

Every human relationship evolves over time, but MR. J wouldn't let me in. Our relationship was stagnant—stuck in time with no progression. I wish he taught me how to switch off my emotions like he did. I would give anything not to feel this pain.

This chapter is therapy in a sense because this is for MR. J. They're words he never let me speak because when it got tough, he ran away. He showed me that love wasn't worth it to him in the end.

And now, all I can do is heal.

These are the words I wanted to say to him, if only he gave me a chance. If only he had allowed me to explain instead of shutting me out like he always did.

So, faithful reader, welcome to the breakup, the makeup, the closure, to the whatever the fuck this is. But this is what I wanted to say to him...if only he let me in.

I can't crack you. And it frustrates me. I see glimmers of you letting go. Then your walls are re-erected. Are you afraid? It saddens me that you won't open yourself up to love because I know you can love hard. I've seen it, and it's so beautiful.

We've always been so in sync in the bedroom, but we speak different languages when I try to work you out. I wish you'd let me in. I won't hurt you. I am in this for whatever is thrown our way. But you just won't try.

And I wish that you would.

I wish you'd let me love you. But most of all, I wish you loved me.

But I have to let you go because I've caught feelings and that doesn't get me anywhere but heartbreak with you.

I'm waiting for you to see what I do. But maybe it's wishful thinking. Or maybe I'm just fucking blind.

When something makes you vomit, you don't want to eat it again, so I can only hope this principle applies to you because I can't, I won't do this again.

I'm the one in control of this destructive behavior, no one else but me. You never promised me anything. I knew what this was.

But I just couldn't stop.

I shouldn't expect what you can't give. But this hurts, and I need it to stop. This has always been my problem with you—I always want more. But I need to accept that you don't.

For endless years, you've been in my heart, and now, I have to learn how to live without that piece of my heart.

Will I survive?

Yes, and that's because love is not about survival, it's about living, and I need to live without you.

The simple fact is I want someone who wants me as much as I want them.

I know the truth—we just don't work. It's always the wrong time for us. We keep missing one another. Missed chances. And we seem to continue to fall in and out of sync with one another, and I don't know why.

Yet I still had hope...

I did everything for you because I...I can't even write it because I know you will never say it back.

But I persevered, forever the optimist, waiting for the day for you to let me in.

But look where that got me.

Wasted time.

Wasted opportunities...waiting...waiting for this.

It would be so much easier to hate you and not want you the way I do. But I yearn for you because you'll always be a part of me. You were my first everything.

My first boyfriend.

My first sexual experience.

And...my first love.

And you never forget your firsts.

When I look at you, I still see the boy who singled me out in a crowd and started something you just finished.

You took my breath away, and I forgot how to breathe without you. Forever drowning in a merciless current that just swept me farther out to sea. And now, I'm trying to find my way back to land.

I need to save myself and to do that...I need to say goodbye.

I need to accept that you were never man enough to keep up with a woman like me.

This is me, signing off, wanting to say thanks for the memories, but that would be clichéd.

So, MR. J, if you ever read this, I want you to know that you will always be my biggest regret—in so many ways.

I regret not walking away sooner.

I regret rekindling when I knew it would end in tears.

I regret not being honest with you.

But most of all, I regret not being honest with myself.

So if these are my parting words to you, then I want you to know that I love you. I always have...I'm just sorry that love wasn't enough.

"Lover You Should've Come Over"
Jeff Buckley

It doesn't matter if you have one hundred partners or just one—there is always one who stays with you, and that's MR. J for me.

This entire experience taught me that love doesn't get easier; it gets harder. But love is worth fighting for, and I couldn't give up on MR. J. He was worth it to me. He always has been.

It was slow, frustrating, and I wanted to give up—so many times. But I didn't...and for once, neither did MR. J.

There's nothing quite like enjoying the silence with the person you love.

This story was always destined to end this way because love hits you when you least expect it, and all you can do is try to keep up.

We're still recovering from what love did, but we're doing it together, and I know without a doubt, that MR. J will do so holding my hand.

He is beautifully broken, but so am I. But together, our pieces seem to fit.

As for BOSSMAN, we're still friends. But I hurt him when I chose MR. J, when we all know I shouldn't have. BOSSMAN on paper is the better fit, but life doesn't work that way.

The love I feel for both men is different, and I believe you can love more than one person at a time. But for me, my love for MR. J never faded, and I had to go with my gut. I wish BOSSMAN nothing but the best, and I'll never forget the times we shared.

They mean something to me because every person we meet makes an impression on us in one way or another, and BOSSMAN has made an impression that will stay with me until the day I die.

MR. J and I live separately because I don't want to marry again. Or live with someone else. I did that once, and it wasn't for me. I like my own space, my own time. It makes seeing MR. J all the more special.

Our relationship isn't conventional. It never has been. But the constant is that we can never stay away from the other. Our chemistry just grows, and it's hard to ignore a rampant inferno.

He understands me.

And I understand him—most times.

But the language we speak when together is the only language I need.

He is still a terrible texter. And can't seem to do more than one thing at once. But I'm still a right royal demanding stubborn pain in the ass, so we balance one another out.

He is the calm I need.

He calms my mind.

My heart.

I learned that love isn't forced—it just exists, even when you don't want it to. Things just grow, as do I.

MR. J has helped me heal when I didn't even know I was broken.

He's my sounding board.

My voice of reason.

He's my lover.

He's my friend.

He kisses me with a fiery passion.

He hugs me with sleepy love.

He looks at me with nothing but utter devotion, and those dimples…

He's my real.

Being with him isn't just being comfortable, it's innate. He calms me with merely a touch.

Love for us isn't easy, and he's still the most frustrating man I've ever met, but I can't stop falling in love with him all over again the moment he walks through my door.

No matter my mood, he makes life better…and that's what love should do because, in the end, love was enough…and that's how every story should end.

Love ♡ Hard

"Back to Black"
Amy Winehouse

Life has taught me so much.

Some lessons hurt a lot more than others, but they helped me become who I am today.

Thinking back, I see that love played a big role in my past. Some decisions I wish I had never made. Others, I wish I did differently.

But that's the thing about hindsight. It's useless. You can only accept your choices and choose to grow.

S was my first crush.

MR. J was my first love.

R was my rebound love.

BO was my "true" love.

And BOSSMAN…BOSSMAN is just love in every sense of the word.

And the other men I've seen are everything in between.

When I told S I was writing this book, he joked that I make him lovable. But that was easy. I am glad he was my first crush.

I've not spoken to R since we broke up. I don't know where he is, and I choose to leave it that way.

BO seems happy with someone other than me. He is an integral part of my story. He taught me that love could be kind even though it came with an expiration date. It doesn't have to be passionate. But it's love nonetheless. I will always love him. It's just too bad my love wasn't enough for him.

BOSSMAN showed me that love hits you when you least expect it, and it is exciting. He also showed me what it's like to be loved in return.

As for MR. J, he taught me that love is forgiving. Because no matter what happened in my life, my affection for him never stopped. And it never will.

Loving MR. J showed me that when I love...I love hard. I have a selective taste. I always have, which is why walking away was never easy. I wasn't raised a quitter, but sometimes, you have to choose your battles...and MR. J was a battle I was always destined to lose.

I believe MR. J is my soulmate, twin flame if you believe in that, but that doesn't mean we will ever live happily ever after...together. With him, I think this entire time, I was falling in love with falling in love.

But he just never felt the same way.

I know what you're thinking.

Did BOSSMAN and I end up together? No.

Do I still talk to MR. J? Sometimes.

Did I ever see either of them again? Perhaps.

To burn out, you've got to be on fire...and MR. J and I will always be on fire.

So the ending to this story is that it's still ongoing. As long as I have air in my lungs, I'll never stop writing my story because my story continues to write itself every day. GHOST, DIMPLES, and SWITZERLAND, those men need a book of their own because not all love stories end in a happily ever after. But that doesn't mean it's the end because they have made a huge impact on me. They showed me that I fought for love, and love prevailed...just not with the man I fought so hard for.

I'm still learning what love is. But I've experienced all kinds of love. Does this make me an expert? Hell no.

But what I can say is...

Love messy.

Love long.

Love spontaneously.

Love without regret.

But most of all, love hard.

Because most things come and go, but love, love stays. And that's why we love. It may hurt, but it's memorable, and it's something I like to believe remains with us until the day we die.

We live.

We love.

We die.

This story is one in a million, but it's mine, and if you take anything away from this tale, it would be to never be afraid to love. And live. Life teaches you that love is beautiful. And rare. And when you find it, never let it go.

But, most of all, remember it's okay to be in love with yourself because that, my friends...that is the greatest love story of all.

Love,

Z xoxo

Subscribe to my Newsletter: https://tinyurl.com/k3b76tw7
LOVE HARD TRACKLIST: https://tinyurl.com/yn36vy3c
LOVE HARD PLAYLIST: https://tinyurl.com/3s9pt8du

Postface

Congratulations, you made it to the end. You're far braver than some. So, I know what you're thinking…*Is the madness that I just read based on real life?*
And the answer is…abso-fucking-lutely.

The story continues. LOVE HARDER coming soon!

About the Author

Monica James spent her youth devouring the works of Anne Rice, William Shakespeare, and Emily Dickinson.

When she is not writing, Monica is busy running her own business, but she always finds a balance between the two. She enjoys writing honest, heartfelt, and turbulent stories, hoping to leave an imprint on her readers. She draws her inspiration from life.

She is a bestselling author in the U.S.A., Australia, Canada, France, Germany, Israel, and The U.K.

Monica James resides in Melbourne, Australia, with her wonderful family, and menagerie of animals. She is slightly obsessed with cats, chucks, and lip gloss, and secretly wishes she was a ninja on the weekends.

Connect with
MONICA JAMES

Facebook: facebook.com/authormonicajames
Twitter: twitter.com/monicajames81
Goodreads: goodreads.com/MonicaJames
Instagram: instagram.com/authormonicajames
Website: authormonicajames.com
TikTok: @authormonicajames
BookBub: bookbub.com/authors/monica-james
Amazon: https://amzn.to/2EWZSyS
Join my Reader Group: http://bit.ly/2nUaRyi
Newsletter: https://tinyurl.com/k3b76tw7

www.ingramcontent.com/pod-product-compliance
Lightning Source LLC
Chambersburg PA
CBHW071900290426
44110CB00013B/1218